Walking in This World

ALSO BY JULIA CAMERON

NONFICTION

The Artist's Way
The Artist's Way Morning Pages Journal
The Artist's Date Book
    (illustrated by Elizabeth Cameron)
The Vein of Gold
The Right to Write
God Is No Laughing Matter
Supplies *(illustrated by Elizabeth Cameron)*
God Is Dog Spelled Backwards
    (illustrated by Elizabeth Cameron)
Heartsteps
Blessings
Transitions
Inspirations: Meditations from *The Artist's Way*
The Writer's Life: Insights from *The Right to Write*
The Artist's Way at Work
    (with Mark Bryan and Catherine Allen)
Money Drunk, Money Sober *(with Mark Bryan)*

FICTION

Popcorn: Hollywood Stories
The Dark Room

POETRY

Prayers for the Little Ones
Prayers for the Nature Spirits
The Quiet Animal
This Earth *(also an album with Tim Wheater)*

PLAYS

Public Lives
The Animal in the Trees
Four Roses
Love in the DMZ
Bloodlines
Avalon *(a musical)*
The Medium at Large *(a musical)*
Tinseltown *(a musical)*
Normal, Nebraska *(a musical)*

FEATURE FILM

(as writer-director) God's Will

Walking in This World

Practical Strategies for Creativity

Julia Cameron

RIDER

LONDON · SYDNEY · AUCKLAND · JOHANNESBURG

While the author has made every effort to provide accurate telephone numbers and Internet addresses at the time of publication, neither the publisher nor the author assumes any responsibility for errors, or for changes that occur after publication.

Most Rider books are available at special quantity discounts for bulk purchase for sales promotions, premiums, fund-raising, and educational needs. Special books or book excerpts also can be created to fit specific needs. For details, write to Rider Special Sales, Random House, 20 Vauxhall Bridge Road, London SW1V 2SA.

1 3 5 7 9 10 8 6 4 2

First published in 2002 by Jeremy P. Tarcher,
an imprint of Penguin Putnam Inc., USA.
This edition published in 2002 by Rider,
an imprint of Ebury Press, Random House,
20 Vauxhall Bridge Road, London SW1V 2SA
www.randomhouse.co.uk

Random House Australia (Pty) Limited
20 Alfred Street, Milsons Point, Sydney,
New South Wales 2061, Australia

Random House New Zealand Limited
18 Poland Road, Glenfield,
Auckland 10, New Zealand

Random House South Africa (Pty) Limited
Endulini, 5A Jubilee Road,
Parktown 2193, South Africa

The Random House Group Limited Reg No. 954009

Book design by Marysarah Quinn

Papers used by Rider are natural, recyclable products made from wood grown in sustainable forests.

Printed and bound by Biddles Ltd, Guildford and Kings Lynn

A CIP catalogue record for this book is available from the British Library

ISBN 0-7126-6053-4

This book is dedicated to Jeremy P. Tarcher,
editor, publisher, and visionary.
With gratitude for his clarity, wisdom, and wit.
Above all, with gratitude for his friendship.

ACKNOWLEDGMENTS

Sara Carder, for her meticulous care
Carolina Casperson, for her believing eyes
Sonia Choquette, for her visionary optimism
Joel Fotinos, for his faith and vision
Kelly Groves, for his clarity and enthusiasm
Linda Kahn, for her clear-eyed perception
Bill Lavallee, for his optimism and strength
Emma Lively, for her stubborn faith
Larry Lonergan, for his humor and guidance
Julianna McCarthy, for her artful heart
Robert McDonald, for his inspiration and artistry
Bruce Pomahac, for being a believing mirror
Domenica Cameron-Scorsese, for her love and discernment
Jeremy Tarcher, for his friendship and guidance
Edmund Towle, for his good-humored wisdom
Claire Vaccaro, for her sense of beauty

Jerusalem Is Walking in This World

This is a great happiness.
The air is silk.
There is milk in the looks
That come from strangers.
I could not be happier
If I were bread and you could eat me.
Joy is dangerous.
It fills me with secrets.
"Yes" hisses in my veins.
The pains I take to hide myself
Are sheer as glass.
Surely this will pass,
The wind like kisses,
The music in the soup,
The group of trees,
Laughing as I say their names.

It is all hosannah.
It is all prayer.
Jerusalem is walking in the world.
Jerusalem is walking in the world.

CONTENTS

INTRODUCTION

IT IS A DIM DECEMBER DAY. Outside my window, down in Riverside Park, an old woman strolls in the weak sunlight, leaning on the arm of her companion. Slowly and carefully they move along the cobbled path. Every so often they pause to take in the antics of a squirrel scampering along a tree branch or a bold blue jay swooping noisily down in front of them to claim a crumb.

One of my favorite ways to talk with friends is to walk with them. I love being engaged with the larger world and with each other. I love having my thought interrupted by the raven sailing in to land on a stone wall. I love the slow drift of autumn leaves, of snowflakes, of apple blossoms—each in season. Walking and talking humanize my life, draw it to an ancient and comforting scale. We live as we move, a step at a time, and there is something in gentle walking that reminds me of how I must live if I am to savor this life that I have been given.

Savoring this life becomes an automatic and appropriate response the minute I dispense with velocity and pressure. This earth is beautiful and so are we—if I just take the time to notice. At this time I split my life between New Mexico and New York, between walks in Riverside Park and walks on a dirt road through sagebrush, where we need to be alert for rattlers, to whom the road is an inconvenience, an interruption of their fields of rolling sage and fragrant piñon.

It is on these walks that my best ideas come to me. It is while walking that difficult clarity emerges. It is while walking that I experience a sense of well-being and connection, and it is in walking that I live most prayerfully. In New York I am a cave dweller, walking in the late afternoons, dazzled by the gold

I try to catch every sentence, every word you and I say . . .
ANTON CHEKHOV

beribboned sunsets that bedizen the city skyline. When I can, I walk with friends, noting always how companionable our silences become, how effortlessly deep and true our conversations. It is my hope that the careful, slow structure of this book will allow it to approximate such walks for you. By going slowly, we move quickly through our many layers of defense and denial until we touch the living pulse of creativity within us all. The Great Creator made this world to dazzle and move us. When we slow our tempo to match the natural world's, we do find ourselves dazzled and moved.

Ten years ago I wrote a book called *The Artist's Way,* suggesting that our creative unfolding was a spiritual unfolding and that we could work—and walk—hand in hand with the Great Creator. A decade has passed and the teachings of that book still ring true to me. The two pivotal tools, three pages of longhand morning writing called Morning Pages and a weekly solo adventure called an Artist's Date still serve me—and now a million plus readers—very well. In ten years nothing has changed. The drill remains exactly the same. In addition, another powerful tool, the Weekly Walk, has emerged as pivotal.

Time is not a line, but a series of now-points.

TAISEN DESHIMARU

Nothing brings home the beauty and power of the world that we live in like walking. Moving into our bodies, we embody the truth that as artists we are out to make a "body of work," which means we must encompass more than each day's march. A Weekly Walk helps us to acquire such an overview. It allows us to find both perspective and comfort. As we stretch our legs, we stretch our minds and our souls. St. Augustine, himself a great walker, remarked, "Solvitur ambulando"—"it is solved by walking." The "it" that we solve may be as particular as a bruising romance or as lofty as the conception of a new symphony. Ideas come to us as we walk. We also invite their quieter friend, insight. Walking often moves us past the "what" of our life into the more elusive "why."

Perhaps it would be helpful to give you a sense of what my

creative practice is like. It is daily and portable. Its only requirements are paper, pen, and shoes.

I wake up in the morning, reach for a pen and a Morning Pages journal, and I dip my soul into my current life, noting what makes me agitated, what makes me irritable, what finds me excited, what feels like drudgery. I dip my pen to the page with the same methodical devotion that a woman in the high mountains of Tibet scrubs clothes in the stream, scouring them against a rock. It is a ritual, a way to start the day and a way to come clean before myself and God. There's no pretending in Morning Pages. I really am that petty, that fearful, that blind to the miracles all around me. As I write, the light dawns—just as the sun comes up over the mountains—and more is revealed. I see why I am frightened, whom I should call to make amends to, what I need to do in this particular day's march to inch ahead a little. Just as the women washing clothes may pause long enough for that one moment of connection as the sun dazzles the flank of a towering peak, so, too, I get my moments of insight, my glimpses into the why behind the what that I am living. But for the most part, the pages are routine. I do them because I do them. I do them, because they "work." They keep my consciousness scrubbed clean.

Once a week I take some small adventure, an Artist's Date. And I do mean small. I go to the fabric store. I visit the button shop. I sneeze as I enter a dusty secondhand bookstore. I take myself to a pet shop and go to the bird section, where zebra finches, lovebirds, and cockatiels vie for attention under the doleful watching glance of a slow-moving African Gray. If I am lucky, I might visit a rug store and sense a swath of eternity tied down a knot at a time. I might visit a large clock store and hear the rhythmic ticking, steady as a mother's heart.

When I am on an Artist's Date, I stand a little outside the flow of hurried time. I declare an hour off limits from hurried production and I have the chance to marvel at my own "being"

The best thoughts most often come in the morning after waking, while still in bed or while walking.

LEO TOLSTOY

produced. I am just one soul amid so many souls, one life led amid a bouquet of lives. When I step aside from pushing time, from racing the clock, even for just one hour, I feel myself drawn to merciful scale. "We are all in this together," I learn. That and, "It is beautiful."

As driven and stressed as anyone I have ever taught, I had to learn to stop running. Walking did not come naturally to me—and it did not come a moment too soon. I was in my mid-forties before I discovered the power of this essential tool. Now, if I can daily but at least once weekly, I take an extended, soul-refreshing walk.

In our busy lives these walks may be sandwiched in by getting off the subway one stop early, leaving the house a few minutes earlier to walk instead of cab short distances. Lunch hours may become walk times, or a walk may be fit into the very late afternoon. How you walk matters less than *that* you walk. Walking allows the insights of your own inner teacher to enter a dialogue with the teacher you encounter in these pages.

Since I wrote *The Artist's Way,* I have heard many stories of the miraculous. Sometimes in a restaurant or on a crowded street someone will stop me and say the sentence, "Your book changed my life." I am glad to have been a conduit, but that is what it is that I have been. I simply wrote down the precepts of divine intervention in our lives the moment we engage our creativity and, through that, engage our Great Creator. What I taught, essentially, is that we are all connected and that as we notice that and surrender to that, we join a long and safe lineage: The Great Creator loves artists and is waiting as a lover waits to respond to our love when we offer it.

What we call God does not matter. That we call on God does. There is an interactive, benevolent, well-wishing something that buoys the sails of our dreams, softens our landings when our parachutes billow closed after a creative flight. This creative something, the Great Creator, takes interest in our cre-

Ideas come from everywhere.

ALFRED HITCHCOCK

ativity, moves naturally and inevitably to support our creativity, recognizing our creative ideas as children of its own making.

Walking in this world, we do not go unpartnered. We do not speak our prayers unheard. There is someone or a something listening with the most tender of hearts. As we open to our inner life, our outer life also shifts. Lives are transformed by a gentle form of listening that is like walking with a cherished friend who listens and then says, "You might want to try X. Oh, look at that great squirrel. . . ."

As artists in tune with the Great Creator, we are coaxed along, cajoled along, coached along. I am not saying that God is Burgess Meredith turning each of us into a Rocky, but that image might not be so far off. God is the Great Artist, and every artist encounters God in the precise form or forms most helpful and necessary to his own creative unfolding. Kindness begins to occur and it occurs as we need it, where we need it, and how we need it. One woman finds a voice teacher. Another finds a source of wonderful yarn. One man gets free editing time on an AVID bank. Another man discovers an art supply store that carries the most beautiful German pencil sharpeners to use on his composing pencils.

Nothing is too small. Nothing is too large. As we practice walking, writing our Morning Pages daily, and venturing into our Artist's Dates weekly, we begin to get a notion of the scope and scale of God—one eye on the sparrow and the other on the vast and starry universe. We are a part of all that, and, by the simple act of reaching out our hand to connect, we become a partnered part of life.

As we go within, we discover that we are not alone there. The loneliness we fear finding in art is actually the loneliness of disconnecting ourselves from our creativity and our creator. As we try our hand literally at the making of something, we do meet our maker. As we try to make more and more, more and more is made of us and through us. "Not I, but the Father doeth the work."

Our aspirations are our possibilities.

SAMUEL JOHNSON

Artists throughout the centuries have talked about inspiration. They have reported the whispers of the divine that came to them when they inclined their ear to listen. Aligning their own creativity with that of their creator, composers exclaimed, "Straight away the ideas flew in on me!" Such ideas can—and do—fly in on all of us. They are the squirrel scampering along the branch. They are the stray pink blossom lighting on a cheekbone. They are the light but definite touch of the unseen world touching our own whenever we are willing to be touched.

Walking in This World is intended as a gentle pilgrimage. We will move issue to issue, walking and talking about the deeper concerns of our souls. I say "souls" because creativity is a spiritual rather than an intellectual endeavor. Creativity is a daily spiritual practice and, like all spiritual paths, it is both mysterious and trackable.

Walking in This World is intended to demystify the obstacles commonly found on the creative path. It addresses issues common not only to creative beginners but to those much further down the creative road. If *The Artist's Way* can safely be said to have launched many travelers on the creative seas, this book is intended to bring to those travelers needed supplies in the form of clarity and encouragement. The creative life is rewarding but difficult. Much of that difficulty is eased by a sense of shared faith and companionship.

Walking in this world a footfall at a time, we walk accompanied by angels, by and large unseen but not unfelt. As we open ourselves to divine guidance—in the form of our own listening creativity—we are brought to the divine in this world and in our all-too-worldly hearts.

It is your work in life that is the ultimate seduction.

PABLO PICASSO

Basic Tools

MANY PEOPLE who have worked with my earlier books *The Artist's Way* and *The Vein of Gold* will have a familiarity with the basic tools of my creative practice. Newcomers will need such a familiarity. Therefore, all readers should take the time to review or learn the three simple tools: Morning Pages, the Artist's Date, and the Weekly Walk. You will be asked to practice them for the duration of this course.

TOOL 1: Morning Pages

Morning Pages are the primary tool of a creative recovery. From my perspective they are the bedrock of a creative life. Three pages stream-of-consciousness writing done before the day "begins," Morning Pages serve to prioritize, clarify, and ground the day's activities. Frequently fragmented, petty, even whining, Morning Pages were once called "brain drain" because they so clearly siphoned off negativity. Anything and everything is fuel for Morning Pages. They hold worries about a lover's tone of voice, the car's peculiar knocking, the source of this month's rent money. They hold reservations about a friendship, speculation about a job possibility, a reminder to buy Kitty Litter. They mention, sometimes repeatedly, overeating, undersleeping, overdrinking, and overthinking, that favorite procrastinator's poison artists are fond of.

I have been writing Morning Pages for twenty years now. They have witnessed my life in Chicago, New Mexico, New York, and Los Angeles. They have guided me through book writing, music writing, the death of my father, a divorce, the

. . . we all need the reassuring and healing messages that treasured rituals provide.

SARAH BAN BREATHNACH

purchase of a house and a horse. They have directed me to piano lessons, to exercise, to an energetic correspondence with a significant man, to pie baking, to rereading and refurbishing old manuscripts. There is no corner of my life or consciousness that the pages have not swept. They are the daily broom that clears my consciousness and readies it for the day's inflow of fresh thought.

I write my Morning Pages in *The Artist's Way Morning Pages Journal* that I designed for just such use. You might write your Morning Pages in a shiny spiral-bound notebook. Some people write their pages by computer, although I strongly recommend writing them by hand. Even the shape of my writing tells me the shape and clarity of my thoughts. Of course, at times Morning Pages are difficult to write. They feel stilted, boring, hackneyed, repetitive, or just plain depressing. I have learned to write through such resistant patches and to believe that Morning Pages are a part of their cure. I know people who are "too busy" to write Morning Pages. I sympathize, but I doubt their lives will ever become less busy without Morning Pages.

It is a paradox of my experience that Morning Pages both take time and give time. It is as though by setting our inner movie onto the page, we are freed up to act in our lives. Suddenly, a day is filled with small choice points, tiny windows of time available for our conscious use. It may be as simple as the fact that we wrote down "I should call Elberta" that cues us into calling Elberta when a moment looms free. As we write Morning Pages, we tend to get things "right." Our days become our own. Other people's agendas and priorities no longer run our lives. We care for others, but we now care for ourselves as well.

I like to think of Morning Pages as a withdrawal process but not in the usual sense, where we withdraw from a substance taken away from us. No, instead, we *do* the withdrawing in Morning Pages. We pull ourselves inward to the core of our true values, perceptions, and agendas. This process takes approximately a half hour—about the same time normally set aside for meditation. I have come to think of Morning Pages as a form of

We must be willing to get rid of the life we've planned, so as to have the life that is waiting for us.

JOSEPH CAMPBELL

meditation, a particularly potent and freeing form for most hyperactive Westerners. Our worries, fantasies, anxieties, hopes, dreams, concerns, and convictions all float freely across the page. The page becomes the screen of our consciousness. Our thoughts are like clouds crossing before the mountain of our observing eye.

When I first began writing Morning Pages, I lived at the foot of Taos Mountain in New Mexico. I was stymied in my life, my art, and my career. One morning I simply got the idea to write Morning Pages, and I have been doing them ever since. A day at a time, a page at a time, my daily three pages have unknotted career, life, and love. They have shown me a path where there was no path, and I follow it now, trusting that if I do, the path will continue. For the duration of work with this book, and, I hope, far longer, I would ask you to write daily Morning Pages. They will lead you to an inner teacher whose profundity will amaze you. Only you can swing open the gate for your teacher to enter. It is my hope you will do so now.

TOOL 2: The Artist's Date

Pivotal to a creative recovery is a second essential tool: the Artist's Date. Grounded in a sense of adventure and autonomy, the Artist's Date is a once-weekly, hour-long solo expedition to explore something festive or interesting to your creative consciousness. If Morning Pages are assigned work, the Artist's Date is assigned play. But do not be misled into skipping it as "less important." The phrase "the play of imagination" has well-earned currency because art *is* made by an imagination at play. The artist who forgets how to play soon enough forgets how to work. The flier into the unknown, the leap of faith onto page, stage, or easel, becomes ever more difficult to take without practice.

At bottom, art is an image-using process. We dip into the well of our consciousness to find images and events for our imagination to employ. Unless we are careful, it is easy to over-

It's a great relief to me to know that I can actually be creative and be happy at the same time.

JAMES W. HALL

fish our inner well, to deplete our reservoir of images. Fishing for something to say, do, or draw, we find new ideas more and more elusive. Nothing "hooks" us.

The conscious use of a weekly Artist's Date, and double that, if we are working flat out, replenishes the inner well and creates a sense of well-being. Synchronicity—that uncanny knack of being in the right place at the right time—picks up markedly as we practice Artist's Dates. Just as cabin fever and a sense of personal restless claustrophobia overtakes an invalid who is sick and too long housebound, so, too, an artist without Artist's Dates suffers a sense of constriction. I know this from personal experience, as I have suffered long periods of ill health. Always, when I return to the practice of Artist's Dates, my sense of well-being increases and my work deepens and enlarges.

For the duration of this course, and longer I would hope, you are asked to take your inner artist on a weekly outing. Expect resistance and self-sabotage—as you plan something adventurous and enjoyable, only to catch yourself sabotaging your date. Our inner artist is a volatile and vulnerable creature, needy as the child of divorce. It wants your undivided time and attention at least once a week so that it can tell you its dreams and difficulties. Painful as these may be, is it any wonder we sometimes avoid such contact? Be alert to resisting your resistance.

A hunch is creativity trying to tell you something.

FRANK CAPRA

TOOL 3: Weekly Walks

Most of us spend life on the run, too busy and too hurried to walk anywhere. Beset by problems and difficulties, we feel walking is a frivolous waste of time—our valuable time. "When will I do it?" becomes one more problem, one more question for our busy mind. The truth is that walking holds our solutions.

It was during a time in which my life felt directionless both personally and creatively that I discovered the solace and direction to be found in walking. At the time I owned a 1965 Chevy pickup named Louise. Every afternoon I would load Louise with a half-dozen dogs and point the truck down a dirt road into the sagebrush. A mile into "nowhere," I would park the truck on the roadside and signal to the dogs that they were free to roam—as long as they stayed within hailing distance. Then I would set off walking. I would walk a forty-five-minute loop, south and east toward the foothills, then north and west directly toward Taos Mountain. As I walked, emotions would wash through me. I was grieving a lost marriage and the death of my father, for many years a close creative companion. I would walk and ask for guidance. Clouds would pass in front of the mountain. I would notice the cloud and then notice that I did have a sense of guidance. I knew what to write, how to write it, and that write it I should. A day at a time, a walk at a time, even a simple step at a time, my sad and tangled life began to sort itself. I say sort itself because all I did was "walk through it." I have been walking ever since.

"Walk on it" is good advice, whether the problem is a persnickety plotline or a persistent personality clash. Native Americans pursue vision quests, Aborigines do walkabout. Both of these cultures know that walking clears the head. Too often in our modern culture we mistake the head for the source of all wisdom rather than the manufacturer of malcontent. For the duration of this course, you are asked to take at least one twenty-minute walk a week. You will find that these walks focus your thinking and instigate your breakthroughs. You will contact the "imagic-nation"—that realm of larger thoughts and ideas well known to shamans and spiritual seekers. It is my hope that the habit of walking and the habit of talking to those you love as you walk will both be awakened by this course.

What we have to learn to do, we learn by doing.

ARISTOTLE

HOW TO Use the Basic Tools

1. **Set your alarm clock to ring one half hour earlier than usual; get up and do three pages of longhand, stream-of-consciousness writing.** Do not reread these pages or allow anyone else to read them. Ideally, stick these pages in a large manila envelope or set them aside and hide them somewhere. Welcome to Morning Pages. They will change you.

2. **Take yourself on an Artist's Date.** You will do this every week for the duration of this course. A sample Artist's Date: Take yourself to your local children's toy store. In the front of the store, near the cash register, you will find "impulse buys" like stick-'em stars, funny pencils and pens, bubbles, and stickers. Let your artist have a treat or two. You may want gold stars for every day you do get your Morning Pages written—that's seven stars for seven days, we hope. The point of your Artist's Date is more mystery than mastery. Do something that enchants and entices your artist.

3. **Take a Weekly Walk.** Outfit yourself in your most comfortable socks and shoes. Set out for a good twenty-minute ramble. You may choose a park, a country road, or an urban route. Where you walk matters less than that you walk. Go far enough and long enough that you feel both your body and your mind "unkink." You may discover that you like walking very much and that you enjoy doing it more than once weekly. Walks definitely help you to metabolize the content of this course.

CREATIVITY CONTRACT

I, _Clare Cathcart_ commit myself to the regular use of the three basic tools. For the duration of this course, I will write Morning Pages daily and will take an Artist Date's and Weekly Walk once a week. Additionally, I commit myself to excellent self-care, adequate sleep, good food, and gentle companionship.

Clare Cathcart (signature)

_7/5/03_ (date)

Discovering a Sense of Origin

This week initiates your creative pilgrimage.
You are the point of origin. You begin where you
are, with who you are, at this time, at this place. You
may find yourself hopeful, skeptical, excited, resistant,
or all of the above. The readings and tasks in week one
all aim at pinpointing the "you" you have been evading.
When we avoid our creativity, we avoid ourselves.
When we meet our creativity, we meet ourselves,
and that encounter happens in the moment.
The willingness to be ourselves gives us
the origin in originality.

Setting Out

You say you want to make art. You want to begin or you want
to continue. This is good. We need a more artful world, and that
means we need you and the specific contribution that you and
you alone can make. But to make it you must start somewhere,
and that is often the sticking point.

"It's too late."

"I'm not good enough."

"I'll never be able to pull this off."

We all have our fears, and they feel as real as the chair you are
sitting in. Like that chair, they can be slouched into or left behind. Sometimes we need to sit up and ignore the cricks in our

back and shoulders and just begin. That's how it is with art. We just need to begin.

Begin where you are, with *who* you are. In order to go where you want to go creatively, you have to start somewhere. And the best place to start is precisely where you are. This is true whether you are a beginning artist or someone with long miles down the track. In fact, seasoned artists can waste time and energy mulling the dignity of their acquired position in the field when the truth is, they still need to just start again.

Writing doesn't really care about where you do it. It cares *that* you do it. The same is true for drawing. I watched a friend of mine waste a solid year because he "couldn't work without a studio." When he did get a studio and went back to work, what he made were a few largish paintings but a great many beautiful miniature charcoal and pencil drawings that he could have done on a TV table had he been so inclined. No, he didn't work—not because he didn't have a studio but because he didn't work. There is room for art in any life we have—any life, no matter how crowded or overstuffed, no matter how arid or empty. We are the "block" we perceive.

If you are a beginning musician and want to learn piano, sit down at the piano and touch the keys. Great. Tomorrow you can sit down at the piano and touch the keys again. Five minutes a day is better than no minutes a day. Five minutes might lead to ten, just as a tentative embrace leads to something more passionate. Making art is making love with life. We open ourselves to art as to love.

Instead of thinking about conquering an art form, think instead of kissing it hello, wooing it, exploring it in small, enticing steps. How many of us have burned through promising relationships by moving too swiftly? How many of us have burned out in new creative ventures by setting goals too high? Most of us.

Doing any large creative work is like driving coast to coast, New York to Los Angeles. First you must get into the car. You

All serious daring starts from within.

EUDORA WELTY

must begin the trip, or you will never get there. Even a night in New Jersey is a night across the Hudson and on your way. A small beginning is exactly that: a beginning. Rather than focus on large jumps—which may strike us as terrifying and un-jumpable—we do better to focus on the first small step, and then the next small step after that. "Oh, dear," you might be sniffing, "where's the drama in such baby steps?" Think about that for a minute. When a baby takes its first step, it is *very* dramatic.

Today my mail contained a manila envelope from a friend, a born storyteller who spent years wanting to write and not writing. Last June, on a perfectly ordinary day, Larry did an extraordinary thing for him: He picked up a pen and started writing. I now have a fat sheaf of stories in my hand. All he needed to do was begin. And then begin again the next day.

Often, when we yearn for a more creative life, we cue up the sound track for high drama. With great dissonant chords crashing in our heads, we play out the scenario of leaving those we love and going somewhere lonely and perhaps exotic, where we will be Artists with a capital A. When I hear this plan, I think, *Okay. You do it.* Experience has taught me that my artist performs best when the stakes are lower. When I keep the drama on the page, pages accumulate.

I hate to say this, but making art is a little like dieting. One day you just have to start and what you do that day is the beginning of success or failure. I cannot write an entire book today, but I can write one page. I cannot become an accomplished pianist, but I can put in fifteen minutes of piano time. Today you may not get a one-woman show in SoHo, but you can sketch the battered leather chair with your cocker spaniel sprawled in splendid comfort or you can sketch the curve of your lover's arm. You *can* begin.

Creativity is inspiration coupled with initiative. It is an act of faith and, in that phrase, the word "act" looms as large as the "faith" that it requires.

The realization of the self is only possible if one is productive, if one can give birth to one's own potentialities.

JOHANN WOLFGANG
VON GOETHE

In dreams begins responsibility.

WILLIAM BUTLER YEATS

When we do not act in the direction of our dreams, we are only "dreaming." Dreams have a will-o'-the-wisp quality. Dreams coupled with the firm intention to manifest them take on a steely reality. Our dreams come true when we are true to them. Reality contains the word "real." We begin to "reel" in our dreams when we toss out the baited hook of intention. When we shift our inner statement from "I'd love to" to "I'm going to," we shift out of victim and into adventurer. When we know that we "will," then we couple the power of our will with the power of future events. In this sense, what we "will do" becomes what "will happen." To prove this to ourselves, we need to couple the largeness of our dream with the small, concrete, and do-able "next right thing." As we take the next small step, the bigger steps move a notch closer to us, downsizing as they move. If we keep on taking small enough next steps and therefore keep chipping away and miniaturizing what we like to call "huge" risks, by the time the risk actually gets to our door, it, too, is simply the next right thing, small and do-able and significant but nondramatic. Many of us falter, thinking that in order to begin a creative work we must know precisely how to finish it and, beyond that, to insure its reception in the world. We are, in effect, asking for a guarantee of our success before we have taken the single most important step necessary to insure it. That step is commitment.

When we realize that we want to make something—a book, a play, a sketch, a poem, a painting—we are yearning for the completion of that desire. We hunger to make art the same way we may hunger to make love. It begins as desire, and desire requires that we act upon it if we are to conceive things.

Despite our culture's well-earned reputation for encouraging instant gratification, we are *not* encouraged to act decisively upon our creative desires. We are trained to think about them, doubt them, second-guess them. We are trained, in short, to talk ourselves out of committing art or committing *to* art.

When movie director Martin Ritt told me "Cerebration is

the enemy of art," he was urging that as artists we follow that Nike slogan, "Just do it." He wasn't saying that brains were counter to the creative process, but he was urging us to use our brains to actually make art, not think about making art. Thinking is not the enemy, but overthinking is.

If you *conceptualize* launching a project, you begin to understand the issue of overthinking. Think of your project as "the arrow of desire." Imagine yourself eyeing the bull's-eye, pulling back the bow—and then thinking about it. Worrying about it. Considering whether you are aiming exactly right or whether you should be a smidgen higher or lower. Your arm begins to get tired. Then your aim begins to get shaky. If you manage to finally shoot the arrow, it does not sail with confidence and strength. You have that in your vacillation about exactly *how* you should shoot. In short, you have mistaken beginning something with ending something. You have wanted a finality that is earned over time and not won ahead of time as a guarantee. You have denied the process of making art because you are so focused on the product: Will this be a bull's-eye? We forget that intention is what creates direction. If we aim with the eye of our heart—"*That* I desire to do"—then we aim truly and well. "Desire," that much-maligned word, is actually the best guide for our creative compass. Horseback riders who jump the Grand Prix fences of terrifying heights talk of "throwing their heart" over the fence so their horse jumps after it. We must do the same.

We have attached so much rigamarole to the notion of being an artist that we fail to ask the simplest and most obvious question: Do I want to make this? If the answer is yes, then begin. Fire the arrow.

We take no step unpartnered. We may feel like the fool from the Tarot deck, stepping heedlessly into blank space, but that is not reality. The Great Creator is an artist and he/she/it is an artist in partnership with other artists. The moment we open ourselves to making art, we simultaneously open ourselves to our maker. We are automatically partnered. Joseph Campbell

Action is eloquence.

WILLIAM SHAKESPEARE

speaks of encountering "a thousand unseen helping hands." I think of these hands as an invisible web ungirding any creative endeavor. It is like throwing a switch or toppling the first domino—there is a spiritual chain reaction that occurs the moment we act on faith. Something or somebody acts back.

It is when we fire the arrow of desire, when we actually start a project, that we trigger the support for our dream. *We* are what sets things in motion—people and events resonate toward our fiery resolve. Energy attracts energy. Our arrow is the speeding pickup truck that attracts summer dogs to chase it down the road. We generate the energy and excitement. Then others will give chase. "Build it and they will come."

Creative energy is energy. When we are worrying *about* creating instead of actually creating, we are wasting our creative energy. When we are vacillating, we are letting air out of our tires. Our pickup is not speeding down the road and may never even get out of the driveway. Our project goes flat.

Does this mean we should race off wildly? No, but it does mean that once we have a heart's desire we should act on it. It is that action, that moving out on faith, that moves mountains—and careers.

The book you are holding now is a book that I am writing on Riverside Drive in Manhattan and in my upstairs bedroom in northern New Mexico—also, in the car and in truck stops as I drive cross-country between the two. None of this behavior matches my drama about being a real writer. In that drama, either I have gone to Australia, where I walk the beaches and beg for inspiration, or else I am freezing in a cabin near Yosemite with nothing to do all winter but shiver and write. When we approach creativity that way, it smacks of the creativity firewalk or the creativity bungee jump—definitely terrifying and not something I'd want to try in the next few minutes or without my will made out. It is one of the ironies of the creative life that while drama is a part of what we make, it has almost no place in how we make it. Even those famous artists who suffered fa-

Nothing great was ever achieved without enthusiasm.

RALPH WALDO EMERSON

mously dramatic lives were remarkably undramatic in their actual work habits. Hemingway wrote five hundred words a day, wife in and wife out. Composer Richard Rodgers wrote a composition every morning, nine to nine-thirty. His colleague, Oscar Hammerstein, rose at six and put in banker's hours on his farm in Doylestown, Pennsylvania. Unseduced by glamour or by drama, their output was both steady and prodigious. This argues that we get a lot further creatively by staying put and doing something small and do-able daily in the life we already have.

So much of the difficulty with beginning lies in our perception that we have "so far to go." We have separated art from process into product—"So far to go until it's finished"—when we think like that and we have also separated ourselves from God. When we are afraid to begin, it is always because we are afraid we are alone—tiny, like little Davids facing giant Goliaths. But we are not alone.

God is present everywhere. The act of making art is a direct path to contact with God, and we do not need to travel any geographic or psychic distance to experience the grace of creation in the grace of our own creating.

Goethe told us, "Whatever you think you can do, or believe you can do, begin it, because action has magic, grace and power in it." This was no mere bromide. It was a report on spiritual experience—an experience that each of us can have whenever we surrender to being a beginner, whenever we dismantle our adult's aloof avoidance and actively seek the Great Creator's hand by reaching out our own to start anew.

If we stop watching the movies in our head with the scary sound tracks and start listening to things like "Whistle While You Work" or "Zippity Doo-Dah," we may begin to make a little headway. We need to get into reality. Art is about making art, nothing more dramatic than that. Puccini may have written *Madame Butterfly,* but he still hummed as he walked on a sunny street. He still ate pasta and he still spent enough time with his friends to concoct a plot the village gossip might handily have

I expect the gift of good and industrious hours.

RAINER MARIA RILKE

provided. High art is made by people who have friends and the need to dine on more than inspiration soup.

TASK:

What the Hell, You Might As Well

Often we experience a sense of powerlessness because we do not see any direct action that we can take to concretely alter our sense of being stuck, in a particular way. At times like this we'd do well not to be so linear. Sometimes, we need to exercise just a little elbow grease in any creative direction that we can find. If nothing else, taking a small creative action moves us out of the victim position. Suddenly, we realize that we do have choices and options and that our passivity may boil down to a stubborn laziness, a sort of tantrum that says "If I can't make X better right now, then I am not going to do anything." Instead of a tantrum, try doing this instead:

In Heaven an angel is nobody in particular.

GEORGE BERNARD SHAW

Take pen in hand and number down from 1 to 20. List 20 small, creative actions you *could* take. For example:

1. Paint the kitchen windowsill.
2. Hang lace on my bedroom door.
3. Put the primrose into a good pot.
4. Change the downstairs shower curtain.
5. Buy photo albums and put my dog pictures in one.
6. Send my sister the fudge recipe she asked for.
7. Send my sister fudge.
8. Buy red socks.
9. Wear them to church.
10. Make a computer file of poems I love.
11. Send a great poem to each of my friends.
12. Photograph my current life and send the pictures to my grandmother.

13. Designate something a "God Jar," a special incubator for my dreams and hopes.

14. Designate something else a "what the hell!" basket for my resentment, annoyances, and fears.

15. Throw a slumber party and request that each guest bring a good ghost story to tell.

16. Make a pot of soup.

17. Give away every outfit I even mildly dislike.

18. Get a CD player for my car and stock it.

19. Go to a great perfume store and get one great perfume.

20. Take an elderly friend to a good aquarium.

Commitment

Very often, calling it professionalism, we become too busy to make art for art's sake. We are committed to a certain careerist, professional agenda and we tell ourselves that is all we have energy or time for. This is false. When we make the art we love, it *makes* time and energy available to us for our professional pursuits. Why? Because we feel more vital, and that vitality is assertive energy that makes room for its own desires.

Follow your bliss.

JOSEPH CAMPBELL

When we say "I will articulate my true values, I will express my essence," that word "will" throws a switch. When we "will," then we "will." In this sense we are predicting our future and shaping it simultaneously. Everything is energy. Ideas are simply organized energy, a sort of mold into which more solidified energy can be poured. A book begins as an idea. So does a social movement. So does a building. We cast our dreams and desires ahead of us, and as we move toward them, their content takes on solidity. We cocreate our lives. This is both our responsibility and our privilege. A symphony moves both through and ahead of a composer. As he moves toward it, it moves toward him. In a sense, as artists, we both pitch a ball of creative energy and catch it.

Commit to make something you love and you will find that the needed supplies come to hand. You must "catch" them when they do. A free studio for recording. Use of an editing bank. A windfall of costumes from your aunt's attic. A church space newly renovated and looking for a worthy cause, like your embryonic theater company. Our creative energy triggers a creative response.

Commit to playing the music you love, and the music of life becomes more lovely. Just as making love can quite literally make love, so, too, making art—a form of the verb "to be"—can quite literally make art out of being. The art of creative living, like the actor's art, is a moment-to-moment receptivity, a harmonious leaning into the unfolding melodic structure of existence such as great string ensemble players use in cocreating chamber music. Those who create for love—like the devotees who practice their spiritual tradition with ardor—give off a certain undefinable something that is attractive, and it attracts to them their good.

When we make art for the sake of making art, we tend eventually to make money. Money is energy, and it follows the path we lay down for it. When we commit that we will do something, the finances that allow us to do it follow. Our committed intention attracts supply. This is spiritual law, if not what we are taught to believe. Money is really a codified form of power. Often we think we need X amount of money to attain Y space, but what we really need is the space itself. Intention creates power, often as money, sometimes as access. Art triggers abundance, but it triggers it in diverse forms. Our cash flow may not immediately increase, but our opportunity flow *will* increase. So will many benevolent coincidences or synchronicities that will enrich our lives and our art if we let them. Receptivity is key, and that key unlocks the treasure chest.

Faith moves mountains, and when we see art as an act of faith, then we begin to see that when we commit to our art, mountains may indeed be moved as a path becomes clear. Committed to the "what," we trigger the "how"—needed money

Change everything,
except your loves.

VOLTAIRE

may appear in the form of an unexpected bonus, a timely and lucrative freelance job, a surprise inheritance, matching funds, or even a corporate scholarship. When we invest energy in our dreams, others often invest cash. A gifted young pianist receives an unexpected year's financial backing from an older couple from his hometown who are "betting" on him and his talent. A young actor, similarly marooned in a backwater, is given travel funds to audition for the conservatory that chooses him and gives him a scholarship. As we commit to our dreams, something benevolent commits back. Supportive coincidence can be counted upon. Artist to artist, we can safely have faith in the Great Creator's interest in our creative pursuits.

Art is a matter of commitment. Commitment is of interest to the Great Creator. When we display the faith necessary to make our art, the Great Creator displays an interest and an active hand in supporting what it is we are doing. We receive supply in all forms.

A composer who works most often on commission for others recorded for himself a small personal work that he thought of as a musical prayer. It is a simple piece of music and a simple, short recording. So simple and so short that the composer looped it four times and considers the resulting twenty-minute version something a person might meditate to—"just something I made for myself, for my own spiritual use."

Staying a few days as a houseguest at another composer's house, he played the brief recording for his friend. It happened to be running when the doorbell rang and a prominent record company executive came to visit. "What's that?" he immediately wanted to know.

"Just a little personal something I laid down to express myself."

"You mean a prayer?"

"Something like that."

"I've just been made the head of a new division on contemporary spiritual music. Do you think you could build an album around that?"

How often things occur by mere chance which we dare not even hope for.

TERENCE

"Yes, I suppose I could."

Out of the tiny recording, a large and beautiful album was born. Out of the album, a new direction for the composer's career was born. He began to work with larger choral groups and to write more music for voice. This new direction was profoundly satisfying.

"I had always loved chorales, and the idea of a modern oratorio expressing our spiritual values was like an answered prayer for me—a prayer I had barely voiced before it was answered."

It may well be that the "self" in self-expression is not only the voice of our finite, individual self but also the voice of the Self, that larger and higher force of which we are both subject and substance. When we express our creativity, we are a conduit for the Great Creator to explore, express, and expand its divine nature and our own. We are like songbirds. When one of us gives voice to our true nature, it is contagious and others soon give tongue as well. There is an infallibility to the law that as we each seek to express what we are longing to say, there is always someone or something that is longing to hear precisely what we have expressed. We do not live or create in isolation. Each of us is part of a greater whole and, as we agree to express ourselves, we agree to express the larger Self that moves through us all.

To be what we are, and to become what we are capable of becoming, is the only end of life.

ROBERT LOUIS STEVENSON

TASK:

Express Yourself

Take pen in hand and number from 1 to 10. List 10 positive adjectives used to describe you, for example:

1. Inventive
2. Original
3. Zany
4. Hard-driving
5. Humorous

6. Articulate
7. Innovative
8. Generous
9. Enthusiastic
10. Active

Take pen in hand again and write yourself a personal ad using the terms you listed to create a positive and provocative picture of your uniqueness, for example:

Experience the laser insights of an inventive, humorous, and innovative creative guide.

It is worth noting here that the point of this tool is not self-transformation but self-acceptance. If you are intense, so be it. There are those who love intense. If your irreverent humor offends the hyperserious crowd, it *will* be appreciated elsewhere. When we affirm rather than deny the characteristics often singled out, we begin to have a much more accurate idea of by whom, and where, our traits will be appreciated.

Snow

There is a soft and beautiful snow falling outside my window. The ink-black trees in Riverside Park look like a line drawing of trees. The sky is gray and luminous. It's a day for soup and knitting, if we did that anymore. It is certainly a day for knitting up the soul.

We go pell-mell, most of us, and a day like this, when the snow muffles the drumbeat of that insistent sound track that urges us to achieve, achieve, achieve, can come as a relief—the way a bad cold can force us to bed and to getting current with ourselves.

The snowflakes are more than flurries, less than a storm.

The most beautiful thing we can experience is the mysterious.

ALBERT EINSTEIN

They fall each with a particular velocity, feathers from a pillow given a firm celestial shake. Higher realms feel very close in a snowstorm.

As a little girl, my bedroom window overlooked our driveway. The peak of our garage had a floodlight, and when it snowed, I would lie in bed and watch the dancing flakes falling in swirls, sometimes rising in a whirl like a great petticoat. I grew up in Libertyville, Illinois, in a house in the country, yellow wood and fieldstone, a kind of overgrown cottage filled with small rooms and odd corners, places for the imagination to play, to stare out the window at the snow.

We all need a window for the imagination. We need a time and a place to stare out the window at the snow. On a day like today, with a great black crow flapping through the dark limbs, it is easy to see how Poe could write his *Raven,* mere blocks from here, staring at the same snow and some dark bird, a century ago. Artists have stared out of windows and into their souls for a very long time. It is something in the staring-out that enables us to do the looking-in. We forget that.

So often we try to gird ourselves to face a harsh and difficult world when we might instead gentle both ourselves and our world just by slowing down.

We worry rather than ruminate. We fret rather than speculate. Even football teams take time-outs, but it is so hard for us, as artists, to do the same. So often we feel there is so much we yearn to do and so little time to do it in. We could take a cue from music here: "Rest" is a musical term for a pause between flurries of notes. Without that tiny pause, the torrent of notes can be overwhelming. Without a rest in our lives, the torrent of our lives can be the same.

Even God rested. Even waves rest. Even business titans close their office doors and play with the secret toys on their desks. Our language of creativity knows this. We talk about "the play of ideas," but we still overwork and underplay and wonder why we feel so drained.

Genius, in truth, means little more than the faculty of perceiving in an un-habitual way.

WILLIAM JAMES

A friend of mine, a glorious musician, works on two music faculties and tours internationally. Sometimes his great voice, an instrument of beauty as large and soaring as a pipe organ, reaches my ear haggard with fatigue. His great strength becomes his great weakness. He forgets to rest.

As artists living with the drone of commerce, we have forgotten that "rest" is a musical term, and that to hear the music of our lives as something other than a propulsive drumbeat, driving us forward as the war drums drove men into bloody battle, we may *need* to rest.

The ego hates to rest. The ego doesn't want to let God, or sleep, mend up the raveled sleeve of care. The ego would like to handle all that itself, thank you. As artists, we must serve our souls, not our egos. Our souls need rest. This is something my artist-mother knew well.

As artists, it serves us to consciously find windows to the world of wonder—we must locate places that open the trapdoor in our imagination and allow the breath of greater worlds to enter our too-claustrophobic lives. You may find the window for your imagination in the upper cranny of your neighborhood library. There, tucked amid the rafters, amid the high and dusty tomes, you may look out an upper window and sense a world of other writers staring over your shoulder with you. Or you might find your imagination climbing aboard a Persian carpet in an Oriental-rug store, where the leaf-by-leaf turning of intricate patterns, like woven stained-glass windows, might transport you to bygone centuries. A clock store might paradoxically help you step beyond time as you stand amid a small forest of chiming and ticking grandfathers and magical cuckoos.

For Allison, it was always a visit to a grand plant store that gave her imagination room to breathe. Something in the steamy jungle air, the brightly flaming colors, spoke to her of special worlds. Carolina loved antique-clothing stores. She would handle a vintage frock and feel herself transported to a gentler world. For David, the world of vintage model cars lit up the boy

We are the children of our landscape; it dictates behavior and even thought in the measure to which we are responsive to it.

LAWRENCE DURRELL

The most visible joy can only reveal itself to us when we've transformed it, within.

RAINER MARIA RILKE

explorer that is his inner artist. He loves the sleek lacquered shells resembling beautiful oversized bugs. Just whizzing a model along a showcase lid gives him a thrill. For Edward, model trains and great toy stores—more for himself than his "excuses," his young nephews—light up his imagination.

The imagination is not linear. It needs to step beyond ordinary time and space. This is why the world of vintage movie posters gives Michael a thrill. This is why Lorraine loves to visit the large, multifloored fabric stores downtown in Chicago's Loop and the bigger ones over near Greek Town. "I can make anything I want," she often thrills, and although she may choose a dark navy gabardine for a sensible office dress, she has still fingered a rustling taffeta that she would have worn to a turn-of-the-century tea dance.

For each of us, safety and rest come in myriad and very personal forms. My childhood friend Carolina just sent me a long white antique nightgown that makes me feel cherished. Baking pies makes me feel safe—pie making is a tradition among the women in my family. Making vegetable soup, another family tradition, also soothes and calms my hectic citified, careerified soul. My mother, Dorothy, when overwrought, would retreat to the piano and play the Blue Danube waltz until her soul settled back into three-quarter time.

Jean, in the throes of an unexpected and overwhelming divorce, found herself agitated and adrenalized, afraid of "going under" financially. She needed more hours in a day to frantically do all that she felt should be done. A wise older friend familiar with Jean's abandoned hobby, doing needlepoint, and familiar, too, with the fact that such a meditative activity would help Jean to quietly tap her deeply creative sources, suggested that Jean return to needlepoint. When she did, she returned also to a sense of optimism and perspective. A stitch at a time, she began to mend her heart and her life—slowing down, she speeded herself toward recovery and creativity.

I am typing on a manual typewriter, looking at the snow from a window I have curtained in white lace. The white lace reminds me of my mother's love of snow. Maybe because she grew up in a strict wooden farmhouse surrounded by strictly planted fields and level ground, my mother loved a snowy day. Snow brought magic to such landscape, you couldn't see ten miles to the next red barn and silo. You were back to the enchanted land that must have existed before we cleared the great broad-leaf forests of maple and oak. Before you could see too far and not enough. In the winters my mother sat us down at the dining table and taught us to cut snowflakes from folded paper, stiff and white. We would tape them to the windows to have the delight of snow on winter days that were simply dark and short. Reminding me to rest, the snow reminds me of my mother, resting now, in peace.

Sometimes on Sundays in Manhattan, my musical colleague, Emma Lively, and I attend a tiny church where the music consists of nineteenth-century Protestant hymns with uplifting and reassuring literary images. "God is a rock, a harbor, a haven, a sanctuary, a fortress." Above all, God is a place of rest and safety.

The proper use of imagination is to give beauty to the world . . . the gift of imagination is used to cast over the commonplace workaday world a veil of beauty and make it throb with our esthetic enjoyment.

LIN YÜ-T'ANG

TASK:
Do Nothing

This task asks that you do nothing—and that you do it thoroughly for fifteen minutes. Here is how to set your "nothing" up. First of all, cue up a piece of music that is both calming and expansive. Secondly, lie down. Stretch out on your back, fold your arms comfortably, and let your imagination speak to you. Close your eyes and follow your train of thought wherever it leads you—into your past, into your future, into some part of your present that you have not been able, due to busyness, to fully enough inhabit. Listen to the music and to your thoughts gently unspooling and repeat to yourself gently this simple phrase, "I am enough . . . I am enough . . ." Stop striving to be more and appreciate what it is you already are.

CHECK-IN

1. **How many days this week did you do your Morning Pages?** If you skipped a day, why did you skip it? How was the experience of writing them for you? Are you experiencing more clarity? A wider range of emotions? A greater sense of detachment, purpose, and calm? Did anything surprise you? Is there a "repeating" issue asking to be dealt with?

2. **Did you do your Artist's Date this week?** Did you note an improved sense of well-being? What did you do and how did it feel? Remember, Artist's Dates can be difficult and you may need to coax yourself into taking them.

3. **Did you get out on your Weekly Walk?** How did that feel? What emotions or insights surfaced for you? Were you able to walk more than once? What did your walk do for your optimism and sense of perspective?

4. **Were there any other issues this week that felt significant to you in your self-discovery?** Describe them.

Discovering a Sense of Proportion

This week inaugurates an ongoing process of self-definition. As you redraw the boundaries and limits within which you have lived, you draw yourself to a fuller size. Coming into ourselves, we sometimes encounter resistance from those in our immediate environment. The readings and tasks of this week aim at bolstering the sense of a realistic self in the face of difficulty and even discounting.

Identity

All of us are creative. Some of us get the mirroring to know we are creative, but few of us get the mirroring to know *how* creative. What most of us get is the worried advice that if we are thinking about a life in the arts, we'd better plan to have "something to fall back on." Would they tell us that if we expressed an interest in banking?

It could be argued that as people and as artists, we are what we are—however, we also become ourselves, *all* of ourselves, by having our largeness mirrored back to us. I think of a scene from the Disney version of *Cinderella,* when the heroine sees herself in the dress for the first time and realizes she is a beauty. It's like the scene when the young hero first puts on his military uniform and becomes who he is. There is a magical "click" of recognition when the looking glass says back, "Yes, we are what we dream."

Too often we lack such mirrors and such transforming moments. No magic wand taps our life to make us into what we dream.

Like Rumpelstiltskin, the artist most frequently has to name himself. "I am an artist"—a filmmaker, a composer, a painter, a sculptor, an actor, a something—something the outer world has yet to acknowledge. Often braced by scanty support, an artist's identity is tied to a stubborn seed of inner knowing, a persistent "unrealistic" certainty in the face of sometimes daunting and difficult odds, sometimes doubting and difficult friends, sometimes dismaying and even arid creative circumstances. The fledgling composer composes, the fledgling writer writes, the fledgling painter paints from an inner imperative.

As artists, we are often in the ugly-duckling position. We have been born into families that regard us as "odd"—and we come to regard ourselves that way. (Sometimes our families are supportive, but our culture, as a whole, is not.) Our desire to make things and to make something of ourselves in the arts is often reflected back to us as "Who do you think you are?" I call this "growing up in the fun house," where our soul's aspirations are mirrored back to us in a distorted and distorting fashion that makes them appear egotistical and unrealistic: "Don't get too big for your britches," "Who do you think you are?" We often don't really know the answer to that. We know something along the lines of "I think I might be . . ." When we are surrounded by people who either cannot see us or cannot acknowledge what they see, our image blurs. We begin to feel both a certain self-doubt *and* a certain stubborn inner knowing that we may then dismiss as crazy. Part of us knows we're more than they see; part of us fears we're less than we hope. This inner friction is painful.

As artists, when a shoe doesn't fit us, we may try to walk in it anyway. If we are told that it fits, we may start to use our ex-

It is Nature who makes our artists for us, though it may be Art who taught them their right mode of expression.

OSCAR WILDE

cellent creative imaginations to imagine that it fits. We may further tell ourselves that our own discomfort at the pinching and the pain of a wrong shoe—and a wrong personal and creative identity—is just our "ego." And, we might add, just our "grandiosity." For many of us, declaring ourselves an artist is a "coming-out" process. "I think I am, I think I might be, I really identify with . . . oh, dear God, I think I am." Like any coming-out process, this is turbulent.

If we have been raised to be "officially talented" in one arena and not in another, we can be deaf and blind to the guidance that tries to nudge us toward an expanded role. "You are so musical," Julius was frequently told—but he couldn't hear it. In Julius's world, his concert pianist brother was musical and so was his operatic younger sister. "I'm just the appreciator," Julius would say. "Everybody needs an audience." A full two decades' worth of musical compliments fell on Julius's deaf ears. He wrote lyrics to "help out" his songwriter friends. When they said "You've really got an ear," he ignored them—despite the mounting evidence that he had something musical that kept slipping into expression. Oddly, it took a trip to foreign soil—to a locale where no one knew his famous family and his musical limitations—for Julius to begin writing music. A summer's European vacation became a musical odyssey.

An ounce of action is worth a ton of theory.

FRIEDRICH ENGELS

"I swear there was music in the air. It was everywhere," Julius reported back. Away from his family role and definition, Julius began jotting down his "tunes," humming them into a tape recorder, putting them down in rudimentary fashion on children's notation paper. He didn't call himself a composer, a songwriter, or even a musician, but he did call himself happy. "Maybe I am a little musical," he finally conceded. He has been writing music and slowly learning to make music ever since. At this writing he's just started piano lessons, and when his teacher says "With your gifts you could go far," he no longer argues or turns a deaf ear. He just says thank-you and continues his exploration of unwrapping his newly acknowledged musical gift.

I was born at the age of twelve
on a Metro-Goldwyn-Mayer lot.

JUDY GARLAND

It could be argued that as artists we are less made than born, and often into circumstances that mask our identity. The realization often comes like something from a fairy tale—a glimpse in a cracked mirror of a creature they did not know they were. It is here the phrase "takes one to know one" comes into play. It is often an older artist who says "This is what you are, or what you might be."

All of us need and require accurate Believing Mirrors. Believing Mirrors reflect us as large and competent creatively. They mirror possibility, *not* improbability. They ignore "the odds" against us. These mirrors are held by people large enough and expansive enough spiritually not to be threatened by the size and grandeur of another artist shaking out his sizable wings. When I was twenty-two and a fledgling artist, veteran literary agent Sterling Lord took me on. The same year, William McPherson, who later won a Pulitzer of his own, hired me to write for him at *The Washington Post*. These men saw something, and all artists tell stories like mine of older artists who "mysteriously" gambled on them.

As artists, we are often grateful and indebted to those who help us know the things we know. An unhappy violist encounters an older composer who suggests a possible affinity for arranging. An arranging career sprouts wings. A singing teacher tells a young pianist, "Don't sing, play!" A photo-shop owner tells a farmer's wife, "You've got quite an eye. I wonder what you could do with a real camera." The answer is "Be a photographer," and that answer, like the film itself, develops over time when exposed to the right encouragement.

Sometimes our encouragement bubbles up unexpectedly in the passing interest of a neighbor, an art-supply clerk, an elderly aunt. Sometimes we come across a magazine article or book, catch a half hour of talk radio in our area of interest, run across a video or an Internet site specializing in our interest. We also experience a phenomenon that I call "inner support." This is an insistent and private inner knowing that tells us we are meant to be, do, or try something—even when there appears to be no outer support.

Richard Rodgers grew up with a doctor father and a brother who also entered medicine. When his own interests ran straight to the Broadway footlights, his family was supportive but un-schooled in how to lend that support. Rodgers remembers going to see Saturday matinees of Jerome Kern musicals and knowing he had to grow up to be a composer—but just how to do that was uncharted territory. He tried "regular" high school, and when that failed to compel his interest, he went to the fore-runner of Juilliard, where he was the only declared Broadway-bound composer on the premises.

"Everyone was very kind," he remembers—his classically oriented classmates regarded him with fondness as well as cu-riosity. They shared his love of music, but after that and beyond that he was on his own, making his way as best he could through friends of his brothers and schoolmates and a certain lucky break involving a family friend. There was no map and, in later years, he would remark that he found his way by "just doing it." That inner itch to "just do it" is the artist's compass.

Although as artists we make maps, we seldom find them. An artistic career does not resemble the linear step-by-step climb of a banker's career trajectory. Art is not linear, and neither is the artist's life. There are no certain routes. You do not become a novelist by moving from A to B to C. Novelists are made from schoolteachers, journalists, and grandmothers. You do not be-come a composer by attending music school. That might make you a splendid theoretician, an avid structuralist, a discerning critic, but a composer? That is something made by music itself.

Sometimes, in the throes of an identity shift, we say in de-spair, "Sometimes I don't know who I am," and we are ab-solutely right. We are correctly sensing that some part or parts of our self are not yet spoken for—or perhaps not yet listened to.

No bird soars too high, if he soars with his own wings.

William Blake

We are far more multiple and rich than most of us assume. We are far larger and more colorful, far more powerful and intricate, far more deep and far more high than we often concede.

This is the way it is with artists. The painter becomes a potter in a fit of pique and boredom, only to discover an unsuspected passion. Like Joshua Logan, the actor becomes a director, the writer steps forward to act. None of it is expected, none of it is predicted, and yet, in cozy retrospect, the tracery of what might be called destiny is often clear. "This is what I am. This is what I am meant to do."

It is one of the mysterious happinesses of the creative life that when we become willing to listen, the "still, small voice" seems to grow louder. The web of life is interconnected and an artist's prayer in Omaha is as clearly heard as the same prayer uttered in Manhattan. "Help me become what I am," we pray—and we do.

Cole Porter was from Indiana, not a hotbed of composers, not a musical Mecca, although it now features a marvelous music school. In his day it featured only his mother's gentrified encouragement. From birth Porter was a citizen of the world— and a worldly citizen at that. He knew because he listened to what he "knew." Art begins in the heart. By listening to our heart's desires and listening to them closely, we are not only led into making the art we dream of making but also into the dream of that art being realized on a meaningful scale. Like the farmer in *Field of Dreams,* we must trust enough to build it—whatever "it" is—and trust that "they" will come.

For each of us the "they" will be different. For one it will be the loving recognition from a spouse or admiring neighbor. For another the scholarship to study abroad. For another the photo published locally. For yet another the chance to perform the Christmas solo. It is a spiritual law that no art blooms without an artist also blossoming. Like the wild rose, we may be spotted by the wayside in Nebraska or drifting with a gracious tendril on the weathered wallpaper of a country home. All art calls forth

Curiosity is one of the permanent and certain characteristics of a vigorous intellect.

SAMUEL JOHNSON

art. When we say "I am," those around us speak up. Some will say "I always knew you were." Some will say "I am too."

Mystics hear voices. The question "Do you hear voices?" is used to sort the sane from the insane. And yet, as artists, we do hear voices and most insistently when we seek the guidance for our art. We are led. We are prompted. We are urged. We are *called*.

We do experience synchronicity—the fortuitous intermeshing of an inner need with an unexpected and grace-filled outer circumstance. We are forced—and reinforced—to know our path, and the more willing we are to ask what our true creative identity is, the clearer and more unmistakable our guidance becomes.

As a young, inexperienced writer, I was working at my babysitting job, when my phone rang and a high school colleague inquired whether I would like to take a job at *The Washington Post*, opening letters. I went for the interview. "I hope you don't think you're a writer," the man who hired me dolefully warned. I responded, "Oh, I am a writer. I hope you don't think I'm a journalist." He hired me and in the end we were both right—I became a first-rate journalist, writing for him and covering arts for *The Post*.

This is not to say that we will always believe our guidance or trust it. It is simply to say that the guidance is there. We are made by the Great Creator and we are intended to be creative ourselves. As we seek to cooperate with that intention, the still, small voice that all spiritual paths speak of becomes an ever more present reality. When we "go within," there is someone or something there to meet us and it is *not* mute as to our identity.

"I don't know where I got the strength of character to believe in myself," an artist will say. "It was just blind faith." And yet, faith is not blind. It is farseeing and, even as we claim to stumble in believing darkness, we are led inch by inch and hunch by hunch into what we are becoming—and so is our art.

As artists, we often speak of our creations as our "brainchil-

Guided by my heritage of a love of beauty and respect for strength—in search of my mother's garden, I found my own.

ALICE WALKER

dren," but we forget that our ideas and dreams impregnate us. We are inhabited by a larger life than we know. As we doubt our own identity, that identity is still guiding us, still nudging us to our rightful path. We may doubt our creative viability but, like children who *will* be born, our dreams and desires nudge us forward. Something larger and finer than we know calls us to be larger and finer than we dare. So we act on faith, descend into doubt, and watch in amazement as our dreams carry us forward with a knowing of their own. Sometimes our dreams feel born despite us.

As we dare to make our brainchildren reality, our dreams take on flesh and sinew. Not all dreams will come "true," but there will be truth present in all our dreaming. The Great Creator made us. We are ourselves works of art, and as we work to bring forward the art within us, we express our inner divinity. Perhaps this is why so many artists' stories abound with miraculous coincidence and "inspired" hunches. Art may be the finest form of prayer. Making art is quite literally a path "to our Maker." In the act of creation, the creator reveals himself or itself to us and we, too, are revealed to ourselves as something of the divine spark from which we ourselves are made. It is this primal fact of connection, artist to artist, Great Creator to us as creator, that the truest sense of our own identity is born. We make art not merely to make our way in the world but also to make something of ourselves, and often the something that we make is a person with an inviolable sense of inner dignity. We have answered yes when our true name was called.

Pure logic is the ruin of the spirit.

ANTOINE DE SAINT-EXUPÉRY

TASK:
Identify Your Identity

Take pen in hand and answer the following questions by filling in the blanks as rapidly as you can:

1. When I was a small child, I dreamed of growing up to be _____.

2. In my childhood, my interest in what art was encouraged? _____.

3. In my childhood, my interest in what art was discouraged? _____.

4. If I had had more encouragement, I would have probably tried _____.

5. The teacher who helped me see my gifts was _____.

6. The childhood friend who helped me see my gifts was _____.

7. If I had another life, the art form I would start exploring early is _____.

8. The reason it is too late for me in this lifetime is _____.

9. One action I can take in the direction of my childhood love is _____.

10. I now commit to this dream by _____.

For many of us, questions such as these bring up sadness. Schedule an hour's undivided time and take your adult self on some small walking adventure. Do not be surprised if many feelings and intuitions and insights bubble to the surface during this Artist's Date. For many of us, our artists have been waiting to speak with us for years.

Becoming Larger

One of the pivotal problems in creative growth is the question of accurate self-assessment. How do we know how large we can be if we don't know how large we are? Frightened of being big-headed and egotistical, we seldom ask "Am I being too limited,

Genius is mainly an affair of energy.

MATTHEW ARNOLD

too small for who I really am?" Expansion can be frightening. Growth can feel foreign, even "wrong."

Most of us know the story of the three blind men who are asked to describe an elephant. One feels the trunk and says, "Ah. It is long and thin and wriggly like a snake."

Another feels the leg and says, "Ah. It is round and sturdy and a great deal like a tree."

The third blind man feels the elephant's side. He says, "Ah. An elephant is very like a wall. . . ."

The joke, of course, is that the elephant was very like all of these things and that its sum is something larger than any of its parts.

As artists, we are often in that elephant's position—a large and complicated creature poorly known to itself and others. Like Alice after she ate the mushroom, we experience shifts in size as hallucinogenic events. One day we will feel very large and competent. The next day we will feel that yesterday's grander size was just grandiosity and that we are really much smaller and more wobbly than we knew. Changing sizes, we go through growing pains, and many of those pains are the pangs of an identity crisis. We may pray about it only to discover prayer is no help: God himself seems to be forging our new identity. The more we pray for it to go away, the stronger it actually becomes.

At age forty-five, after twenty-five years as a writer of words, I suddenly began to hear melody. Music piped through my system like a small chapel flooded with sound by an outsized organ. I found this scary. After all, I "knew" I was a writer, but a musician? This was "too much" to even dream.

When we change sizes creatively, we begin to wonder, *Oh, dear.* Now *what kind of animal am I?* And usually we begin to ask people to help us to know. This is where we often get in trouble. Many times our friends will know only the trunk part of us, or maybe even just the tail. In other words, what is mirrored back to us may be only the part of our artist a friend is comfortable with or can easily see.

It is better to ask some questions than to know all the answers.

JAMES THURBER

In this way, quite inadvertently we often get miniaturized. We often get fragmented. We often feel "shattered" as we go through change because we need people who can help us to hold a larger and clearer picture of the whole creative animal we are. And, yes, that animal just might be an elephant. Oh, dear!

Understandably, friends can tend to reinforce the you that they see. They can want to hold on to a you that doesn't threaten them and that gives them a comfortable sense of their own size and importance. It is not that they are competitive precisely, it is just that they are used to thinking of you in a certain way—as a screenwriter, say, not a director—and used to thinking of themselves in relationship to you in a certain way. When you start to get bigger, it can scare both you and your friends. They worry about being abandoned. You worry about being grandiose. It is very hard to say to yourself and to others "Actually, I think I might be an elephant. I think I might be much bigger and grander than I thought. But don't worry, elephants are loyal." More often, we are disloyal to our newly emerging parts. We can allow ourselves to be talked out of our possible creative flights. Like *Dumbo,* we can be made to feel ashamed of our newly discovered, magnificent ears.

Some of our friends might tend to want to downsize us again to what we were. They have our second, third, and fourth thoughts for us. Other times, we deliberately call those friends who we know will downsize us to who we were before. "You're a perfectly good playwright. *Why* would you want to try writing a movie?" We want to be grounded by their negativity back into our formerly comfortable size and shape. The problem is, we aren't that size, and we aren't that shape. Not any longer.

The tricky part about changing sizes creatively is that we want to keep our old friends but not our old identity. We can keep those who are willing to see more of the elephant. But some of our old friends may need—at least temporarily—to be declared off limits, those who see only the elephant's tail. Their doubts of our new size are a poison for our emerging elephant.

The beginnings of all things are weak and tender. We must therefore be clear-sighted in beginnings.

MICHEL DE MONTAIGNE

An alternative is to find new friends who can see, recognize, and support what it is we are becoming. "Ah, yes, you're an elephant, come over here."

When I suddenly began writing music, I thought I might be crazy, and so did a lot of my friends. I wasn't any longer the Julia any of us knew. Following the muse was one thing—following music, quite another.

"You write *books,*" one friend actually wailed.

"You have such a gift for melody," a new friend, a composer himself, told me—and thank God he did. It can be difficult to hold our belief in the emerging parts of our creative identity. We even more than our friends may fear that we are acting crazily. A new gift can seem too good to be true. We can have a debilitating attack of modesty, asking, "Who do I think I am?" Our behavior may feel crazy, especially if the new talent was unsuspected for many years.

It's part of our cultural tradition to believe and act as if artists are crazy. Is it any wonder we sometimes feel that way ourselves? At our craziest-looking, we are sometimes our most sane. Michelangelo looked pretty strange, flat on his back, near the ceiling. With sweat, plaster, and paint stinging his eyes, not even he may always have enjoyed the comfortable certitude that he was painting a masterpiece. Strapped to a plank, with an arm tired from painting at a contortionist's angle, he, too, may have wondered, *What am I doing?*

What the hell *are* we doing? Who the hell *are* we, really? That is what we are trying to find out, and asking people is one way to do it. Often, older or more experienced artists can say, "Of course you're an actor!" or "Of course you are a writer." They can smell out our identity because it resonates with their own. They've seen baby elephants in the pupa stage before. We may not know what we are, but they do.

My friends now number many musicians who routinely think of me as "just a musician." One, who worked with me on two

If a plant cannot live according to its nature, it dies; and so a man.

HENRY DAVID THOREAU

musicals, knew me two years before he realized I "also" wrote books. So, when a new gift puts in a sudden appearance, remember: If elephants have long memories, they also have long lives. And in a single life you may inhabit many different arts.

Nelson Mandela has remarked that we do no one any favors "hiding our light" and pretending to be "smaller than we are." And yet, calling it modesty, we often try to play small and even stay small. When the creative power moving through us asks us to expand, we would rather contract, calling it more comfortable—it isn't really. We are spiritual beings, and when our spirit grows larger, so must we. There will be no comfortable resting in yesterday's definition of ourselves. It is spiritual law that as the Great Creator is always exploring, experiencing, and expanding through its creations, we must cooperate or feel the pitch of spiritual dis-ease. We can try to play small, but if the universe has big plans for us, we are better off cooperating than resisting. Creativity is God's true nature and our own. As we surrender to becoming as large as we are meant to be, great events can come to pass for us and countless others. In a sense, the size the Great Creator makes of us is none of our business. We work on art and we are the Great Creator's work of art. Perhaps we shouldn't meddle.

All aglow in the work.

Virgil

TASK:
Size Shifting

Although many of us have accomplished estimable things, although we may hold demanding jobs and have extensive professional résumés, when it comes time to look at our own dreams, we are suddenly struck by a debilitating modesty. Our dreams seem too big and too good to be true. We doubt our ability to accomplish them. Use the following quiz to miniaturize your doubts instead of yourself.

Take pen in hand and finish these phrases as rapidly as you can:

1. If I let myself admit it, I think I have a secret gift for _____.

2. If I weren't afraid, I'd tell myself to try _____.

3. As my own best friend, I would really cheer if I saw myself try _____.

4. The compliment I received that seemed too good to be true was _____.

5. If I acted on that compliment, I would let myself try _____.

6. The best person to cheer me on in my secret identity is _____.

7. The person I should carefully *not* tell my dream is _____.

8. The tiniest realistic step I could take in my dreamed direction is _____.

9. The hugest step I could take in my dreamed-of direction is _____.

10. The step I am able to take that feels about right to me is _____.

Many small maken a great.

GEOFFREY CHAUCER

Sometimes, we are so overwhelmed by our life events, so swamped by the needs and expectations of others and our own feelings of (over)responsibility, we can feel completely lost, wandering in the dark woods of our own life, as hapless and at risk as Hansel and Gretel. *Where am I?* and *Who am I?* we wonder, anguished and often angry. Creating a wish list helps us remember who we are—and take small, concrete, creative actions to reinforce that identity.

Number a blank sheet of paper from 1 to 20. Writing very quickly, finish the phrase "I wish" twenty times. Your wishes will range from large to small, from simple comforts you yourself can provide to large life desires you can begin to outline for later action. This tool *never fails* to point out some small, do-able steps and, even more important, to locate our position in the compass of our own true desires. A wish list might read:

1. I wish my health were more solid.
2. I wish I had a perfume I actually liked.
3. I wish I could see my daughter.
4. I wish workmen would arrive on time or at least call if they're going to be late.
5. I wish I had a pair of nice slacks for walking.

Very often, each "wish" will suggest some small action. For example:

1. Health more solid—step up walking regime and schedule a doctor's visit. Check results of bone density test.
2. Perfume—get to a good department store and "try" a few.
3. See my daughter—schedule a visit from her formally. Call and "really" invite her. Don't just "miss" her.
4. Workmen—call and say, "Where are you? When are you coming?"
5. Slacks—go looking even if you hate shopping. See if you can find a local seamstress if shops and catalogues yield nothing.

A wish list often reveals that we need to take a concrete action for optimism to return. When we are active on our own behalf, we tend to feel less overwhelmed by the needs and wants of others.

Sometimes to "embody" knowledge we must literally get into our bodies. Take the information you have just gleaned from the above task and one more time walk on it. Allow yourself to walk into a new and larger identity in your imagination. It is often there that we first learn to comfortably inhabit a larger self.

The eyes upturned to Heaven are an act of creation.

Victor Hugo

Transformation

Art is not linear. Neither is the artist's life, but we forget that. We try to "plan" our life and "plan" our career—as if we could. We also try to plan our growth. This means transformation catches us by surprise. The notion that we can control our path is pushed on us by advertisements and by books and by experts who promise us we can learn to control the uncontrollable. "Empower yourself," magazine headlines trumpet. Seminars and whole expos promise the same illusory goal. And yet, experience teaches that life, and especially life in the arts, is as much about mystery as it is about mastery. To be successful we must learn to follow not the leader but our own inner leadings, the "inspiration" artists have acknowledged through the centuries. "Something" is telling us to make art. We must trust that something.

But not only medicine, engineering, and painting are arts; living itself is an art.

ERICH FROMM

Because we cannot see where we are really going, because we do not believe that the universe has any plan for us, any worthy plan we might like, our imagination begins to fly frantically around the cage of our circumstances like a cooped-up bird. We want freedom—and we will get it—but we need to get it gently and with grounding.

"I am already successful," we may tell ourselves—and rightly. We may have spent years and considerable energy getting to the top of our profession, only to be struck by a bout of inner restlessness and the unshakable, unpalatable, and unwelcome conviction that our life no longer fits us and we must try to find a new one. Tempted to "ditch everything," we may fantasize running off to the South of France or the north of Africa. We may say to ourselves, "It would be wonderful never to have to do X again," naming something for which we are well paid and well respected. Our professional niche may be so perfect, so carefully chiseled, and so "right," we do not see how we can make any change at all without totally shattering the life we have so carefully built up.

It is a spiritual law that when we are ready to transform, transformation will come to us. We are all conduits for a great creative energy that seeks expression in us and through us. When we yearn to be different, it is not just our restless ego. It is our accurate response to the creative energy within us that is seeking a new venue for expression. We are all creative and we are, in turn, creations. Just as we get restless to make something new, so, too, our creator may be restless to make something new from us. We are not experiencing a bout of hubris, we are actually experiencing a bout of humility. As we let go of our ego's demands to be totally in charge, we slip gently and quietly into a series of changes that we may set in motion through our own hand but experience as the hand of the Great Creator working through us. As we do as inwardly directed, a direction emerges.

Nature never did betray the heart that loved her.

WILLIAM WORDSWORTH

Think of taking yoga and receive a yoga flyer in your mail. Develop an interest in France and spot the ad for a bicycle vacation just after you've said, "Oh, but France would be fattening." Clarify any wish or dream or goal and experience the uncanny feeling that you have somehow magnetized information, people, and opportunities to flow toward you. The spiritual shorthand for this is the phrase "Take one step toward God and discover that God has taken a thousand steps toward you."

Call it "open-mindedness" or "the willingness to be always a beginner," but receptivity and openness characterize the temperament of all great artists, and as we consciously foster these qualities in ourselves, we are given the chance to grow and transform—not perhaps by large and immediate strokes but by small. And each tiny shift can be accompanied by inner quaking. "What's going on? Who am I? What am I doing?" we may inwardly howl as our known identity shifts.

When we begin to see that we can actually change our life, we often panic. Of course we do—prisoners often panic when they realize they can open the door of their cell and walk out "free." "Free" is terrifying after confinement. That's why we panic. "I have no idea who I am!" we gasp.

It is only by risking from one hour to another that we live at all.

WILLIAM JAMES

Often we are surprised to discover that there even *are* new parts to our identity. If we have surrounded ourselves with only one set of mirrors—academics, for example, or corporate types, they may see and reflect back only the parts of ourselves that they can understand. They may not show us anything like our full nature. It's a little like bird-watching. Many specimens look a lot alike until they start to fly, then you see a flash of scarlet and say, "Oh, my, that wasn't a . . . It was a . . ."

When Michael first entered creativity work, he was a lonely and alienated man. Of course he was. A man of quicksilver intelligence and rapier wit, he was ill matched to the tightly laced academic circles he traveled in. His humor was viewed with suspicion; his levity was not welcome. Self-importance was the order of the day, and self-important people liked to make Michael feel like nothing. Once Michael realized he was something, just not the something they were buying, he began to seek colleagues and pastimes where his personal traits were appreciated. Eventually, he navigated out of an academic career and into a creative one. The author now of three books, he is in demand for his lively and good-humored lecture style.

When we are changing sizes, we feel large, clear, and powerful one day, tiny and defenseless the next. We feel euphoric and then we feel enraged. This is good. This is healthy. It just doesn't feel that way. Our identified self seems false. It is not "false," just incomplete. We have the reverse of the phantom-limb syndrome, where an amputated arm or leg still itches or pinches where there is no arm or leg. Our itching and pinching may presage the sudden appearance of a new creative limb—an arm or leg of a creative career we hadn't anticipated. No wonder we panic! What are these weird sensations? Why are we suddenly interested by performance poetry, Puccini, oil paints?

We may try several sets of creative hats and shoes looking for those that fit. This is normal, natural, and to be encouraged. It is also very threatening to those who want an artistic career to progress in neat linear increments like an academic or professional career. Would that it could. More often we experience awkward growing pains as we grope toward a new identity role.

DO NOT INSIST ON BEING LINEAR.

To avoid panic, it helps to think of change as experimental and to treat ourselves a little like a science project. You will need to try small doses of new identity and see how it wears. Your best gift to yourself in this time will be humor. You do not need to "make yourself over" wholesale. You just need to give the newly discovered and varied parts of yourself some gentle play. And the key word is gentle. Your panic does not mean you *are* crazy, just that you feel it.

DON'T PANIC ABOUT PANIC.

If you are panicked, tell yourself, "Ah! Good sign: I am getting unstuck."

It is spiritual law that we are in the process of becoming what we *already* are—perfect creations of a perfect creator. This means that at our most awkward and ill at ease, we are still in divine order and moving ever closer to God's intention. Faith in this process, a belief that we can change and still experience the unchanging support of the universe, is critical to any sense of comfort as we grow.

The lilies of the field began as buds. We are asked to trust that just as they had a glorious and safe unfolding, so will we. In the natural world, we see butterflies emerge from awkward yet protective cocoons. We must remind ourselves to trust that sometimes we, too, are being protected in our growth. Our erraticism, our ungainliness, our panic—these, too, are natural to the passage of change. The Great Creator experiences all his creation in the throes of shifting identity. The unfolding saga of life on all levels is one of constant transformation, constant changing of form. When we cooperate with our need and desire to grow, we

It takes a long time to bring excellence to maturity.

PUBLILIUS SYRUS

are cooperating with spiritual law. Even before we "ask," our coming needs are clear. The trajectory of our growth is not as lonely as it feels. We are experiencing universal growing pains, and our loneliness, alienation, desperation, and doubt have been felt by many before us, survived by many before us—and answered many times before by the Great Creator who made—and is making—us all.

Art, and artful living, is a constant collaboration between what we are made from and what we wish to make of ourselves. As we open ourselves consciously to inspiration and instruction as to our truest current form, we are led not only to creativity but also to comfort.

The bravest are the tenderest—
The loving are the daring.

BAYARD TAYLOR

TASK:
Shape Shifting

When we are changing sizes and shapes as an artist, we often are afraid of looking foolish. We want to be "finished." We want to be "good at it." We want to read the review that exclaims, "Well worth the creative risk!" Unfortunately, change—and the risks that go with it—invite feelings of vulnerability. Sometimes, simply blurting out our secret dream is a tremendous relief, so that's what we will try to do here on paper. Finish the following phrases as fast as you can:

1. If it weren't so foolish, I'd love to try _____.
2. If it weren't so expensive, I'd love to own a _____
   _____.
3. If I were twenty-one again, I would let myself study
   _____.
4. If I could take the next five years off, all expenses paid,
   I'd study _____.
5. If it weren't so nuts, I'd love to try _____.

6. If I gave in to my secret dream, I would let myself
   _____.

7. If I'd had ideal parents and a perfect childhood, I'd be a
   _____.

8. The dream I have never told anyone is _____.

9. The artist I admire and think I am a lot like is _____
   _____.

10. The artist I secretly look down on because I have more
    talent is _____.

Now, rather than feel foolish over what you have just admitted, take pen in hand again and write a letter from your adult self to your inner artist. Spend at least fifteen minutes writing to your inner artist about the dreams it has revealed. Find a concrete form in which you can take an action on your inner artist's behalf.

CHECK-IN

1. **How many days this week did you do your Morning Pages?** If you skipped a day, why did you skip it? How was the experience of writing them for you? Are you experiencing more clarity? A wider range of emotions? A greater sense of detachment, purpose, and calm? Did anything surprise you? Is there a "repeating" issue asking to be dealt with?

2. **Did you do your Artist's Date this week?** Did you note an improved sense of well-being? What did you do and how did it feel? Remember, Artist's Dates can be difficult and you may need to coax yourself into taking them.

3. **Did you get out on your Weekly Walk?** How did that feel? What emotion or insights surfaced for you? Were you able to walk more than once? What did your walk do for your optimism and sense of perspective?

4. **Were there any other issues this week that felt significant to you in your self-discovery?** Describe them.

It requires a direct dispensation from Heaven to become a walker.

HENRY DAVID THOREAU

Discovering a Sense of Perspective

No man is an island, and our creative unfolding occurs within a distinct cultural landscape. Cultural mythology permeates our thinking about art and artists. The readings and tasks of this week aim at detoxifying your thinking regarding the arts and your place as an artist in our society. Art is tonic and medicinal for us all. As an artist, you are a cultural healer.

Medicine

We are all artists—some of us are declared, accomplished, and publicly esteemed artists. Others of us are the private kind, making artful homes and artful lives and shying away from the public practice or pursuit of our art. Some of us—officially "not artists" and "without a creative bone in our body"—are artists nonetheless because creativity is in our blood. In our DNA.

There is one and only one label that seems useful to me in discussing ourselves. That label is "creative." I have been teaching for twenty-five years. (And making art for longer than that.) I have never, *ever* encountered a person who was not creative in some form. Most often, people are creative in many forms. It is the excess of creative energy, not the lack of it, that is what makes people feel—and get labeled—"crazy."

Sarah, a book writer now, was known to family and friends for many years as "high-strung," "nervous," "nutty," even crazy.

She had "too much energy" and it spilled out in making dramas out of daily life. She was always in a pitched battle with something—everything she experienced seemed to be heightened and adversarial. She wasn't precisely depressed, but she did tend to view life in adversarial terms. She moved from therapist to therapist, antidepressant to antidepressant, and "quick-fix" enthusiasm to "quick-fix" enthusiasm. She tried meditation, energy work, and self-help groups. All helped—sort of. Nothing seemed to really make her more comfortable in her skin or in the world we live in. At long last, Sarah began to work with creativity tools. She did Morning Pages, Artist's Dates, and a wide variety of Artist's Way exercises. Her mood lightened. Her energy steadied, and her optimism did not so much return as to make a first appearance on the stage of her adult life.

Creative projects of all stripe began to sprout wings in Sarah's household. She and her children made masks for Halloween, cookies and cut-out snowflakes for Christmas. By New Year's she had a resolution—to try writing the book she had always dreamed of. Carving out a wedge of time for herself during her kids' after-school playtime, Sarah began writing. Her children fielded phone calls: "Mom's writing." And Mom was writing—not only her book, but the distorted dramatics her life had undergone when she had channeled all her creative energy into interpersonal theatrics instead of writing. With plots and dialogue and high stakes on the page, Sarah's tendency toward personal melodrama settled down. Self-expression began to heal her character issues that years of therapy had not touched. At this writing, Sarah has written five books and published four of them. She is not "crazy" anymore, but she is crazy about her work. As she found a way to channel and express her colorful inner selves, her life took on a gentler yet more vibrant shape and her dreams took on Technicolor clarity.

"When I was little, I always wanted to be a writer," she says now. "It's just that for years I didn't think I really could be and

Love is exactly as strong as life.

JOSEPH CAMPBELL

so I abandoned my dream and myself." Finding the courage to dream again, Sarah also found that the parts of herself she had misplaced were alive and well—once they were finally welcome.

I have seen incredible creativity practiced by people in their attempts to avoid their own creativity. A therapist might call those contortions neurosis; I call them "creative knots," as in "I will *not* be creative and so I will be miserable." (In a lot of very creative ways.)

Let's start by getting rid of the nasty labels—"crazy," "grandiose," "flaky," "neurotic." Our true nature is *creative*.

Yes, using our creativity is therapeutic, but that is not because we need to be fixed. What we need is to be expressive. What's inside us is not all nasty and horrid and terrifying, not all shame and secrets and neurosis. Our inner world is a complex, exquisite, and powerful play of colors, lights, and shadows, a cathedral of consciousness as glorious as the natural world itself. This inner wealth is what the artist expresses.

The Great Creator lives within each of us. All of us contain a divine, expressive spark, a creative candle intended to light our path and that of our fellows. We are shiny, not tarnished; large, not small; beautiful, not damaged—although we may be ignorant of our grace, power, and dignity.

The human being, by definition, is a creative being. We are intended to make things and, in the old phrase, to "make something of ourselves." When we lose interest in ourselves and our lives, when we tell ourselves our dreams don't matter or that they are impossible, we are denying our spiritual heritage. When we do this, we become depressed and drained, even physically ill. We become snappish, irritable, high-strung. We call ourselves neurotic—this is not the case. We are not neurotic, we are miserable—miserable because we have stifled our creative selves. Those selves are alive—well—and too large for the cage we have put them in, the cage we call "normal."

In our culture we are trained to hide ourselves and punished

For good and evil, man is a free creative spirit.

JOYCE CARY

when we show ourselves. So we hide ourselves from others and from ourselves. It is the hiding of our true nature that makes us feel or act crazy.

We are trained to pick at ourselves, to rectify ourselves, to label ourselves. Most of our religions emphasize the notion of original sin. Most—not all—of our therapies center on our wounds and not on our gifts. Some, not all, of our 12-Step recovery can center on our character defects and not our assets.

Most of us carry what I call "word wounds"—descriptions of certain qualities that have been conveyed to us as pejorative. I for example have been called both "intense" and "hyperfocused." In our culture we have demonized creativity. We are scared of it and by it. We tell scary stories about artists and how broke, nuts, crazy, drunk, selfish they are. In our culture we are afraid of our creativity. We think it's some nitroglycerin compound that could blow us all up. Nonsense.

Practicing our creativity is healing. Not because we are sick but because we are essentially well. As we express our intrinsic nature, which is beautiful and specific, particular and original, we experience a healing transformation less in ourselves than in our relationship to the world. We are not at fault. We are not powerless. We are very large, and in expressing this truth, healing occurs. What is healed is the rift between our spiritual stature and our mistaken perception of ourselves as flawed.

Creativity is medicine. It is not dangerous or egotistical. It is life-affirming and essential. The more we use it, the more steadily and readily and easily we use it. The more we ground it and regularly access it, the better off we are. The "healthier" we are. Humor and acceptance enter the picture. Far more than self-scrutiny or self-correction, self-expression may be the key to a much more synthesized and effective sense of self.

Yes, we are sometimes unhappy. But this is not because we are neurotic and need to be "adjusted" to the existing norm. This is because we need to express ourselves—which will then change both us *and* the existing norm. Creative change begins in

Out of your vulnerabilities will come your strength.

SIGMUND FREUD

the heart. When we start within ourselves and move outward, expressing what we love and what we value, life gets better, we feel better, and the world gets healthier too.

The tools and process of my book *The Artist's Way* are taught by many therapists. Often, they facilitate Artist's Way groups and report back "miracles of healing." To my eye, the healing is no miracle. The health was always there, waiting to be discovered and expressed as creativity.

I am not interested in debating with people over the reality of mental illness. What I want to focus on is the reality of our considerable mental health. Our society, even our world, might be "sick," but we carry within us the exact medicine to heal it and ourselves.

That medicine is creativity.

Most of us are about as eager to be changed as we were to be born, and go through our changes in a similar state of shock.

JAMES BALDWIN

TASK:
Bless Your Blessings

One of the most medicinal tasks we can undertake is a simple walk. It is difficult to remain mired in negativity and depression when we are "shaking it out" a little.

Walking with an eye to the positive can take a gentle vigilance. As a form of medicine for ourselves, we can consciously turn our thoughts to the ancient practice of practicing gratitude—a footfall at a time. Take yourself out-of-doors and set a goal of a simple twenty-minute walk. Aiming toward the outer world, allow your inner world to fall into a brighter perspective by consciously—and concretely—enumerating your life's blessings. People, events, situations—any of these may be cause for gratitude. As you warm to your task of focusing on the good in your life, both your heart and your step will lighten.

Art Is Therapeutic, Not Therapy

I am still learning.

MICHELANGELO

When we are blocked creatively, we often experience ourselves as miserable—and we then wonder, "How neurotic am I?" Thinking that therapy will supply that answer, or at least alleviate our misery, we often turn to therapy only to find that our misery continues unabated. Of course it does. We are miserable not because we are neurotic but because we are creative and not functioning in our creativity. Therapy may help us to "understand" our blocks. We do better to simply get over them. Art is therapeutic. It is *not* therapy. Therapy aims at transformation through understanding. Art aims at transformation more directly. When we make a piece of art about something we don't understand, we come to understand it, or, at least, our relationship to it through our own experience—which is more full-bodied than merely cerebral. In this sense, art "works" therapeutically whether we understand it or not.

Therapy aims at disarming emotion, placing wounded emotions "in perspective." Art, on the other hand, uses wounded emotions—or any other fuel handy—not to alter our perception of an existing outer reality but to alter that reality through a reality we express. Handel's complex, ecstatic, exultant, and conflicted feelings and perceptions about God created *The Messiah. The Messiah,* in turn, helps others to understand God differently.

Harper Lee wrote one book, *To Kill a Mockingbird,* in 1960. She lives in Manhattan now and still has no plans to write another. And why should she? With one small and "simple" book, she accomplished a great swath of healing. Anyone reading her work comes away from it more whole, more compassionate, more in touch with the interior life of his own vulnerable, childlike self.

Books, poems, plays, symphonies—they aim at healing the soul. They take human emotions and human concerns and, through the alchemy of art, make us somehow feel better about all of it—and us.

Bernice, a Jungian therapist, often sends her patients to music rather than introspection. "Music touches something higher in us," she explains. Music may touch something higher more directly, but all of the arts touch something that is beyond the ordinary machinations of life. It is the overview, this "something higher and more," that makes even the most homespun art somehow therapeutic. Baking a good pie, one feels better for having baked it. The same is true of writing a simple song or even dashing off a quick poem to tell your child she is beloved. When the child calls to say "I got your letter," she is also saying "And it made me feel cherished." Feeling cherished, we feel healed, and, perhaps as much as anything else, the act of making art can be described as the act of cherishing our experience, feelings, and perceptions. This, we are told, is how God regards all of creation. Perhaps it is in this careful attention that we contact the divine spark when we create. Contacting that divine spark is always therapeutic.

Healing is a somewhat automatic by-product of self-expression, not a goal per se. This fact can confuse some people—particularly therapists, who want to "understand" the workings of a process that is both mysterious and spiritual. Intellectually, many doctors and therapists do know that something heals beyond their own skill, but understandably, they want to know what that something is, and control it as part of the healing process that they can administer like a good medicine. Therapy and creative recovery are not mutually exclusive, but they do function differently and come out of two very different sets of assumptions.

We may feel different after making something. We may see something in a different light, but that inner shift of focus comes from expressing what it is we do feel and see rather than striving to feel and see things differently, with more balance and less sting. For an artist—and for the artist in each of us—talking

Music produces a kind of pleasure which human nature cannot do without.

CONFUCIUS

The first and the simplest emotion which we discover in the human mind is curiosity.

EDMUND BURKE

about something may be less useful than painting about it, writing about it, or composing about it. Merely cerebral understanding does not heal. Nor, contrary to many therapeutic models, does the simple expression of emotion, verbally or even physically. Humans are complex, creative beings, and when we create something that expresses our own complexity, we arrive at an inner distillate of clarity through our own *creative* inner process. Many therapists, and many art teachers for that matter, are controlling and intrusive in their premature questioning and direction. They encourage creative clients to cerebrate. This is often the last thing we need. Therapy aims at making us normal. Art aims at expressing our originality. The norm has nothing to do with it.

Enlightened therapies urge us to "accept how we feel." Art teaches us to *express* how we feel and so alchemize it. Art acknowledges that feelings are mutable and that we contain the power to mutate the dross of our wounds into the ore of art. In this sense, art gives us the ability to *always* move out of the victim position. Therapy adjusts us to the world. Art adjusts the world itself.

"Art" is a form of the verb "to be." It is not mere cleverness to point this out. At its core, life is artful and creative, each moment contains choice as much as each brush stroke in a painting, each syllable in a poem, each note in a melodic line. It is because of this, its insistence on choice, choice, choice, that art demolishes the victim position. When bullying life demands of us some injustice: "You want to make something of it?" the artful answer is yes.

When we make something of "it," whatever "it" is, we make something else of it. Art allows us to live freely, even within our restlessness, like Dylan Thomas's green sea singing in its chains. Holocaust victims scratched butterflies on the walls of concentration camps. That assertive creative act spoke plainly: "You cannot kill my spirit." At its core, art is triumphant. At its best, therapy is acquiescent: I accept my influences and accommodate myself to their result. Therapy constructs a self; art presupposes and asserts a self. At bottom, art is rebellious: You cannot name me. I am more than the sum of my parts.

In therapy we seek to examine the impact of those in our life and our resultant wounds and adjustments. We see ourselves in relation to person X or event Y. Our inner workings are understood and understandable in theoretical terms. We deduce why we are what we are. And we often deduce from a flimsy set of stock characters—the nuclear family. Life, even the most impoverished, is far richer than that in its mysterious variables and forces.

Art works in primary colors. We dip our pen, our brush, our hand, directly into the self. "I see it this way," we say. We are the origin of our art. It rises like a river head, asking no one's permission. Art says, "I am." Therapy says, "They were, therefore I am." Therapy may be turbulent, but it is tame compared to art. Therapy may be rewarding, but it makes something of what we *were,* while art makes something of what we *are.* Freud complained, "Whenever I get somewhere, a poet has been there first." Of course. An artist flies direct.

Art is alchemy. It turns the ore of life into gold. Learning to make art rather than drama from a heated imagination is a skill best learned early and practiced fully. If we are to make living art—*and* an art of living—we must be willing to stand knee-deep in the rapids of the human condition, accepting that life, by its nature, is turbulent, powerful, and mysterious. It is the artist's bet that life is better encountered and expressed than diminished and discounted by trying to "fix it" therapeutically. It is the artist's conviction that understanding something intellectually is often far less healing than making something artistically transformative from our shattered selves.

"Keep the drama on the page, the stage, the canvas, the film," an artist learns. It is there that the monsters and beauties, the jewels and junkyard memorabilia of the imagination, can be sorted, shaped, and transformed into art. Dexterity at living

I hate that aesthetic game of the eye and the mind, played by these connoisseurs, these mandarins who "appreciate" beauty. What is beauty, anyway? There's no such thing. I never "appreciate," any more than I "like." I love or I hate.

PABLO PICASSO

with the dramatic shadow play of the creative mind comes with time. A younger artist may mistake intense emotion for a cue to act in his outer life, not his inner one. When turbulent emotions pinch the raw nerves of the creative psyche, there is a choice: Act on this, or act out on this.

With art as our alchemy, the pain of the lost lover becomes the pang of the love song. The misery of a misplaced sense of direction becomes the frantic, seething chords of a dissonant jazz anthem. "Nothing is wrong, nothing is wasted, nothing is neurotic, nothing is disowned, everything is possible in art" must become the artist's credo.

Let the world know you as you are, not as you think you should be, because sooner or later, if you are posing, you will forget the pose, and then where are you?

FANNY BRICE

TASK:
You Want to Make Something of It?

Although therapy may have loftier goals, its most common use is to arrive at a different accommodation of our grudges. "They" did "that" and so we feel bad. The aim of most therapy is that we feel less bad. We come to "understand" why "they" may have done "that" and we make our peace with it. Art is more anarchistic.

Art is more aggressive and more assertive than therapy. It is an action, not a reaction. Dipping directly into ourselves as source, we create something new that would not exist without us as its origin. For this reason art is affirming in a way that therapy is not.

Set aside a stack of magazines with pictures. Buy a piece of poster board and some glue. Locate a scissors, tape if you want it, and give yourself a full hour's time. Scan your consciousness for a situation you would like to understand more fully.

Do you have a mesmerizing personal relationship that seems patently destructive yet you cannot end it? Do you have a tyrant boss to whom you are in feudal bondage? Do you have a bond that is so close to someone that you feel joined at the hip? Are you homesick for the wide open spaces of the West but are living in the vertical canyons of Manhattan? Any of these dilemmas make excellent fuel for the task of collaging.

Holding this theme loosely in mind, spend twenty minutes pulling images that attract you and *may* feel connected to your theme. Spend another twenty minutes arranging your images and gluing them in order. Now spend a final twenty minutes writing about what you've found.

What you discover through this process may surprise and intrigue you. A relationship that seems punitive and one-sided may be revealed to be a source of creative fire. A longing for a "greener" life and environment may be overridden by an actual love of urban images and energy. What you find through making a collage may not even address the specific topic you "worked" on. Instead, a far larger and more holistic sense of healing may emerge.

Anger

When we are angry at being overlooked, it is not arrogance and grandiosity. It is a signal that we have changed sizes and must now act larger.

Very often when we feel small and unheard, it is not because we *are* small and unheard but because we are acting small and unheard. We are not intended to be small. Often we are cornered not into being powerless and puny—as we feel—but into being large.

The problem here is our perspective. When we are angry "out of all proportion," that is a very accurate phrase. We have lost a sense of our true size and power, and the intensity of our feelings makes us feel "hopping mad," another telling phrase, as our mental image of ourselves becomes—or can become—very cartooned. We experience ourselves as puny and tiny and futile. The size of our anger has dwarfed our perspective and our per-

One cool judgment is worth a thousand hasty counsels. The thing to do is supply light and not heat.

WOODROW WILSON

sonality. This is because we do not realize that the power we are perceiving is within us as the power for change. When we are "unspeakably" angry, what we really are is large and unspoken. We are not yet speaking in a way that gives voice and direction to our power. When we feel impotent with rage, we are actually potent with rage—we simply have not yet seen how to effectively use our anger as the fuel that it is.

When we cannot sleep, when we are "eaten alive" by an inequity or slight, the monster that is eating us is our anger over our own displaced power. We are very powerful. That personal power is what we are feeling as a "towering rage," and that artificially externalized wall of rage can make us feel small and puny until we figure out that it is a power within ourselves and not the sheer wall of the "odds" stacked against us. The odds are against us until we are "for" ourselves.

Anger asks us to step up to the plate for ourselves and for others. It points to a path we are trying to avoid. Often we try to act "modest," and that is partially a refusal to be as large, clear, and articulate as we really are. Anger signals us that we are being called to step forward and speak out. We hate this and so we fantasize retreating instead.

Rage at a bully or at a bullying situation is actually a wonderful sign. Once we own it, it is our own rage at allowing ourselves and others to be bullied. If it is our own, we can use it. Yes, this rage feels murderous and distorting, but it is actually a needed corrective. If our rage is that large, so are we.

Our reticence can make us angry. We "know" we should speak up for ourselves but sometimes find we just "cannot."

We do not need to shout, but we do need to act and to speak our truth. A word about that order: Actions do speak louder than words, and so we must take actions that articulate our creative values.

A writer angered by a string of rejections might self-publish— as I did and will always do. A musician frustrated by the "state of the art" in the recording business can more cost-effectively cut

Advice is what we ask for when we already know the answer but wish we didn't.

ERICA JONG

a disc, DAT, or a small CD for far less money and energy than indulging in years of therapy to "accept" his feelings of frustration. A proactive creative act is far less expensive than the health problems and life-shortening caused by stewing in feelings of resentment and bitterness—or the even more expensive waste of retreating from the fray entirely.

Luckily for all of us, artists are stubborn. The best-selling author advised by her psychiatrist that she should aim for a secretarial career kept writing (me). The famous filmmaker fired from a documentary project kept making movies (Martin Scorsese). The talented actress cut from Boston University's acting program kept acting (Oscar-winner Geena Davis). The lawyer who "should have" spent his time "on his cases" won the argument that he should write as well (John Grisham). Something inside spoke clearly enough that these artists listened, and a few outer "someones" whispered, or shouted, that they, too, knew who we were. These discerning outer voices affirm our identities and alter our destinies.

Sometimes when we get angry enough at being treated as if we are small, we get brave enough to trust those who think—and say—we might be big. One slight too many and we finally say our true name, but we "swallow" a lot of anger first.

Center stage belongs to those who are willing to move there, some talented and some not. Rather than angrily decrying the behavior and lack of talent of the "arrogant spotlight-grabbers," we need to use our anger to turn our own voltage up a little despite our fears. We need to say our own names as artists. When we do, we feel self-respect. Self-respect comes from the Self. The market will say what it will, but we need to say our own name as artists.

Anger is a call to action. It is challenging and important to let our light shine. It is important to name ourselves rather than wait for someone else to do it, or pretend that we can continue to bear it when we can't. When we complain that others do not take ourselves and our values seriously, we are actually saying

I'm not a teacher: only a fellow-traveler of whom you asked the way. I pointed ahead—ahead of myself as well as you.

GEORGE BERNARD SHAW

that *we* don't. If our aesthetics matter so much to us, we must act on them in a concrete and specific form.

This is why a failed musical comedy means write another song. This is why a bad review of your novel means write a short story, a poem, anything that signals to your inner world that you still believe in yourself. When we fail to endorse ourselves as artists, others also can undercut us. When we endorse and support ourselves as artists—concretely, in some small form—then others may misread us or mishandle us, but they cannot castrate us or our self-respect.

Anger is a profoundly powerful fuel that we can use to make art and to make more artful lives. When we deny our anger or fritter it away in complaints, we are wasting precious fuel and precious clarity. Anger is a searchlight. It shows us our moral terrain and it shows us the damage we feel done to that terrain by others. It shows us, above all, our choices. If something angers us, we can try to "make do" with stuffing our anger or we can "make something of it" in the literal sense of a piece of art.

Anger causes poems, plays, novels, films. Anger causes symphonies and paintings. When we think of our anger as something that should be excised or denied rather than alchemized, we risk neutering ourselves as artists.

Anger asks us for reservoirs of strength that we often do not know we have. We are galvanized into heroics that we did not feel were a part of our emotional repertoire. We act larger than we feel and end up being larger than we were.

A highly acclaimed classical musician angered by the narrow gauge of highly produced digitalized recordings goes out on a limb to encourage a young and talented musician. *The club is too small, too elite, too canned,* the master musician thinks angrily, and throws the door open a little by lending his prestigious name to a more risky project. Anger has opened his heart and his mind.

Anger is not comfortable. The focused use of it to create art requires emotional maturity we must often reach for to muster—and yet we can. When we do, our world changes by a jot. Anger

No man can know where he is going unless he knows exactly where he has been and exactly how he arrived at his present place.

MAYA ANGELOU

sometimes signals not our immaturity but our maturity, our sea-soned judgment, and outraged temper into form for the sake of healthy change.

TASK:
Use Anger as Fuel

Most of us may feel we "get" angry, but we seldom feel we "are" angry. The tool you are using now is a startling one in this regard: You are probably angrier than you think, and that blocked or unused anger is a powerful source of creative fuel once you are willing to acknowledge it and tap it more directly.

Take pen in hand. Number from 1 to 50. List 50 angering grievances from the historical to the hysterical. Be as petty as possible. You will be astonished at what tiny things "still" anger you. For example:

1. I'm angry the Catholic Church dropped Latin.
2. I'm angry our church uses bad folk songs.
3. I'm angry the candy shop closed.
4. I'm angry my sister is fighting with my brother.

After you have written for a while, you will notice the question popping up: "What can I do about it?" This question pops up like toast. We do not like being victims of so much anger, and so we intuitively look for a positive solution. Jot down the solutions as they come to you. At exercise's end, you will have cleared fifty negatives and come up with a list of do-able positives. Do some of them, using your formerly stuck anger as fuel.

In the beginning was the Word. Man acts it out. He is the act, not the actor.

HENRY MILLER

Cartography

The artist is a cartographer; he maps the world. The world within him, and the world as he sees it. Sometimes that world is very strange. Sometimes our maps are rejected—seen as unrealistic or distorted or unlikely. Magellan sailed with maps made largely of conjecture—as artists, we are always conjuring and conjecturing on the shape of what we see and "know."

A great work of art focuses the imagination of a vast audience on a previously inchoate problem. *The Grapes of Wrath* showed us the Depression. *One Flew Over the Cuckoo's Nest* showed us our democratic horror at institutions run amuck. All novels are "novel" because they are seeking to tell us something new. Known or unknown, famous or anonymous, all art is an attempt to map the territory of the heart.

Let me say it again: As artists, we are cartographers. We draw from our own experience, and we *draw* our experience, sketching in the territory we have encountered and others will encounter. The perceptions of a novel or a musical composition may predate their consensus map of consciousness of their own times. For this reason, artists must have courage, even heroism, to state what they see and hear.

Early in his career, Beethoven enjoyed personal and professional favor. His work was widely heard and widely revered. He was hailed as a large creative talent. His life was sunny and his creative vistas expansive. As his life wore on, Beethoven's cultural fortunes shifted. His work was considered less accessible, too abstract and demanding. As his personal battle with hearing loss deepened his isolation, he was plunged into a harrowing, nearly suicidal depression. He was caught on the horns of a dilemma: He was called to write music and his talent as a musician was called into question by the music he wrote. He could not be true to himself and go back to earlier forms. There seemed to be no audience for his musical work except himself and God. Contemplating suicide, Beethoven chose life and, in one famous letter to God, vowed to continue to write music no matter how ill received it was. He would write "for the glory of God alone." The resultant music, too modern and advanced for Beethoven's peers, has come to be considered masterworks cen-

Whatever creativity is, it is in part a solution to a problem.

BRIAN ALDISS

turies later. A visionary and a leader of musical thought and form, Beethoven wrote for our times and not his own.

Late Beethoven told us more of our century than of his own. As artists, we draw not only consensus reality but the lineaments of approaching reality. This is why Ezra Pound dubbed us "the antennae of the race." This is why our perceptions are so often discounted as "not in reality," when in fact they are a part of a reality that we are not yet in.

George Orwell told us more of the future than *1984*. George Gershwin told us more of the urban—and urbane— revolution than any demographics.

As artists, we explore the territory of the human heart, braving the dark woods to report to our human tribe that a trail can be found, and we will survive. As artists, we are scouts of consciousness, trailblazers for community and culture.

Of necessity, artists report dangers we might wish to ignore. Like the scout who returns to report an unpassable gorge requiring an unforeseen detour, the artist may report perceptions that feel unbearable to others. From Sam Shepard to Samuel Beckett, the artist may encounter and encapsulate the loneliness of missed connections. The heart of darkness *is,* all too often, the human heart. As artists, we must muster self-respect and compassion for the difficulty of our own calling. The great adventure of the creative life lies not only in the territory seen but in the fact that much of what we see has not been seen before. Human stories are as old as the earth, but human consciousness is always the edge of the known world, like fine telescopes focused on deep space. As artists, we routinely step beyond, straining our eyes and vision to discern and record the shapes heaving into birth from darkness.

We function on nerve, daring, stamina, vision, and persistence. Mountains appear where no mountains are known to be. Lakes shine in the light where there are no lakes. The artist does not see as others see. His imagination yokes together disparate images, some fanciful, some frightening, some enlightening.

Thou didst create the night,
but I made the lamp.
Thou didst create clay,
but I made the cup.
Thou didst create the deserts,
mountains and forests,
I produced the orchards,
gardens and groves.
It is I who made the glass out
of stone,
And it is I who turn a poison
into an antidote.

SIR MUHAMMAD IQBAL

The artist's inner world may resemble a fairy tale—there are ogres, trolls, monsters, witches. Everything is heightened, intensified, dramatized. This pitch of intensity forges art from the raw materials of the imagination. As an artist matures, so does his skill at encompassing such pitched emotion.

Does this mean that we cannibalize our lives? Emphatically, no. It does mean that we own them, shaping and reshaping the acreage of our personal experience into a philosophical habitat that expresses accurately our view of the world.

Make visible what, without you, might perhaps never have been seen.

ROBERT BRESSON

"Look at it this way," the artist says, and shows the world what his inner world has revealed to him. Franz Kafka was Kafka before we had the term Kafka-esque. George Orwell predated Orwellian. Each of us carries an internal lens through which we view the world. The willingness to reveal what that lens sees is what determines an artist. And an artist must continually open that lens to take in new and wider realities.

A woman in her mid-fifties gets up daily to write a song. She has been musically inclined since childhood, but it took her until her forties to muster the emotional courage to express her songs in more than her inner ear.

"I think I am too old for this," she tells me, yet her year's moneys are budgeted to include the expense of cutting a CD of her work. She could be buying expensive clothes or meals out or gifts for her children, but she has learned that what matters most to her is the process of expressing her heart through art.

"If I don't tell my parents' story, who will?" a writer asks me, explaining a decade's diligence on a long family saga.

"My computer class is very exciting," a woman artist tells me. "I am so much less limited now in the ways that I can see. I was defining myself so narrowly as a fine artist."

For each of these artists, the act of making art is the act of revelation. First to themselves and then to the world: "Listen! Look! It looks like this!" they are saying.

Like Audubon sketching his birds, great art is sometimes

made by the simple act of witness rendered to the world: "I saw this beautiful thing." Of course, not all of what we see as artists is beautiful, nor do we render it beautifully, yet just as a crude and handmade map gives us a sense of direction, so, too, the mapmaking of art points the human compass straighter toward home.

Everything vanishes around me, and works are born as if out of the void. Ripe, graphic fruits fall off. My hand has become the obedient instrument of a remote will.

PAUL KLEE

TASK:
Mapping Your Interests

Maps begin as the roughest of sketches, approximately whole continents. We can similarly sketch in our areas of creative interest, working in the loosest terms.

Take pen in hand. Finish the following:

Five topics that interest me are
1.
2.
3.
4.
5.

Five people who interest me are
1.
2.
3.
4.
5.

Five art forms that interest me are
1.
2.
3.

4.

5.

Five projects I could try out are

1.

2.

3.

4.

5.

Come forth into the light of things, Let nature be your teacher.

WILLIAM WORDSWORTH

When we map out our "coulds" instead of our "shoulds," we shift from the realm of probability into the more interesting realm of possibility. When we name and claim an interest, we seem to magnetize that area, drawing to ourselves people, places, and things that speak to our emerging interests.

CHECK-IN

1. **How many days this week did you do your Morning Pages?** If you skipped a day, why did you skip it? How was the experience of writing them for you? Are you experiencing more clarity? A wider range of emotions? A greater sense of detachment, purpose, and calm? Did anything surprise you? Is there a "repeating" issue asking to be dealt with?

2. **Did you do your Artist's Date this week?** Did you note an improved sense of well-being? What did you do and how did you feel? Remember, Artist's Dates can be difficult and you may need to coax yourself into taking them.

3. **Did you get out on your Weekly Walk?** How did that feel? What emotions or insights surfaced for you? Were you able to walk more than once? What did your walk do for your optimism and sense of perspective?

4. **Were there any other issues this week that felt significant to you in your self-discovery?** Describe them.

Discovering a Sense of Adventure

This week you are asked to jettison some of
your personal baggage. The essays and tasks are
aimed at helping you claim a greater sense of freedom.
You will be asked to consciously experiment with open-
mindedness. You will dismantle many unconscious
mechanisms that may have impeded your artistic
expression. You will focus on self-acceptance
as a route to self-expression.

Adventure

Too often, we think we know what we love. It is more accurate
to admit we know only some of what we love, and that the "sum"
of what we love can grow larger. This requires an open mind.

An hour's adventure in a nineteenth-century photography
exhibit may do more to spark your visual artist than six months
in a sensible computer-graphics program. A visit to the zoo may
mean more to your creative animal than a virtuous visit to an art
supply store.

Humans are by nature adventurous. Watch a toddler expand
his territory a wobbly step at a time. Watch a teenager test cur-
few. Watch an eighty-year-old grandmother sign up for an art
tour of Russia. The soul thrives on adventure. Deprived of adventure, our optimism fails us. Adventure is a nutrient, not a fri-
volity. When we ignore our need for adventure, we ignore our

very nature. Often we do exactly that, calling it "adulthood" or "discipline." When we are too adult and too disciplined, our impish, childlike innovator yearns to rebel. Too often, that rebellion takes the form of a stubborn, self-involved crankiness rather than an exuberant and expansive risk. Risks, we tell ourselves, are too risky. When we avoid risk, we court depression.

Depression is emotional quicksand. Once we get stuck, it's hard to pull free. Our struggles exhaust us and depress us further. It is easier to avoid depression than overcome it, and, yes, we avoid it by taking risks. If we remember that we need to court, woo, and romance our creative selves, we begin to have a notion of what sort of risk best serves us.

Adele lives in Manhattan. On her good days she loves the vigor of the city. She finds the rich red tones of the buildings on her Upper West Side street adult and invigorating. She loves the window boxes and the glimpses of richly painted rooms beyond. On her bad days Adele feels trapped by the city. She is a westerner at heart and she longs for wide open spaces and wide horizons. The city feels claustrophobic. "Tame." And so, on her worst days, Adele calls the Claremont Riding Academy, reserves a horse, and goes riding.

Claremont is not the wide open spaces, but it does have horses and the stench of horse sweat and it is somehow so daring—three stories of horses wedged into a Manhattan brownstone—that it feels anarchistic and rebellious even to crack open the door and step into the hidden world of horseflesh and leather. And so, when Adele feels too dull and too domesticated, she gets on a horse and feels like she's sitting a lot taller in the saddle, living in a world of risk and adventure.

Caroline, a hothouse flower, needs to have a taste of luxury when her world feels too much like a treadmill. She has taught herself that few things lift her spirits more rapidly than a visit to a really good florist shop, where beauty in all its delicacy and daring can be found intertwined amid wicker baskets and faux vertigris vases. Although she seldom spends much—settling on

To die will be an awfully big adventure.

JAMES M. BARRIE

a truly shocking color of Gerber daisy can give her tiny kitchen a transfusion of color—Caroline always feels her money and time is well spent when she buys herself not merely a bouquet but the optimistic sense that this earth is, or can be, a garden of earthly delights.

Adam, a mild-mannered writer, gets his sense of worthy risk by taking himself to travel stores. He cannot always up and leave his job, but he can take daring mental vacations. He sometimes buys a guidebook, *Most-Used Egyptian Phrases,* and learns a few key words to get him to and from a pyramid. Other times he plans a trip he actually can take, *A Pocket Guide to Day Trips in the Greater Boston Area.* What is pivotal to him is not so much leaving life as he knows it as knowing that he could.

"Most of the time my life is fine, but I need to know that I have psychic permission to get away from it all," Adam explains. A stop in a sports store to look at a new model cross-training shoe, a pamphlet from the bike store about a bicycle vacation in France, these imaginary risks add a needed risk to Adam's Mr. Nice Guy persona. "And I love Indiana Jones movies," he adds.

The creative imagination is a will-o'-the-wisp. Wooed best by enticement and not by aggressive assault, the imagination responds to being coaxed and cajoled. Just as in romance, too serious, too fast, and the fun fizzles out. We need to flirt with an interest, approach it with a sidelong glance. Children's books might be a better first date with a new interest than enrolling in a master's program. If you want to write a novel about an automotive inventor and need to know how an automobile engine works, a good children's book may tell you just what you need to know, while a scholarly tome on the laws of physical dynamics may tell you just enough to squelch your budding interest entirely. More is very nice as something to look forward to and not so nice as part of the phrase "More than I could handle or absorb." Adventures should be manageable, not overwhelming.

It is not so much that the creative imagination is shallow; rather, it is selective. Dumping a huge load of facts into your

It's like driving a car at night. You never see further than your headlights, but you can make the whole trip that way.

E. L. DOCTOROW

imagination can stall its gears rather than start them humming. A biographer sifts the truth from a quarry full of facts. A poet or novelist intuits a quarry full of truth from a single fact. Too many facts, too fast, and the artistic attic gets both stuffy and overstuffed. The imagination feels stifled, not stimulated. Creative heights are best reached when we are not overburdened by an overly intellectual freight of facts.

It is one of the paradoxes of the sustained creative life that the more lightly we take ourselves, the more serious work we will probably be able to do. The more we bear down on ourselves, the more constricted we will feel, and the more vulnerable we will be to creative injury.

Very often, consummate artists are consummate enthusiasts. Director Mike Nichols breeds Arabian horses. Coppola grows great grapes. Novelist John Nichols is an avid bird-watcher. Sculptor Kevin Cannon plays formidable jazz guitar. They have taken a cue from the Great Creator and developed a playful appetite for life itself.

If you play softball once a week, it's a little easier to handle the curve ball of a vicious review. If you let yourself bake an apple pie or two, it's a little harder to think the artist's life, or life in general, is so rotten. If you go salsa dancing once a week, or even once a month, it's a little harder to think that the purpose of your art is to make you rich and famous, and that if it hasn't, it's worthless and so are you.

In light of all this, I am not sure where we got the idea that in order to be "real" artists we had to do things perfectly. The minute we see that word "perfect" (and I think critics are the ones who drag it in the door), spontaneity goes out the window. We get so sure that we can't be a great composer that we never let ourselves write our kids a goofy lullaby or play improvisational noodles at the piano. We're so respectful of "great" art that we always, chronically, sell ourselves short. We're so worried about whether we can play in the "big leagues" that we refuse to let ourselves play at all.

To create, you must empty yourself of every artistic thought.

GILBERT (OF GILBERT AND GEORGE)

Here's what I like about God: Trees are crooked, mountains are lumpy, a lot of his creatures are funny-looking, and he made it all anyway. He didn't let the aardvark convince him he had no business designing creatures. He didn't make a puffer fish and get discouraged. No, the maker made things—and still does.

European film directors often enjoy creative careers, during which their films mature from the manifestos of angry young men to the rueful wisdom of great works by creative masters. Is an afternoon siesta the secret? Is their *vita* just a little more *dolce?* We've taken espresso to our American hearts, but we haven't quite taken to the "break" in our coffee breaks. Worried about playing the fool, we forget how to simply play. We try to make our creativity linear and goal oriented. We want our "work" to lead somewhere. We forget that diversions do more than merely divert us.

How did all this sternness get in here? We let it in. We dragged it in. We even begged it to please come in. And why? Our own natural antic and animal high spirits scare us silly. There are few things more fun than exercising our talents, and since most of us keep them on a pretty tight leash, we are scared that if we let them off, we will need a lion tamer.

As little kids, we might fool around rhapsodically on the piano. We might improvise for hours, pouring out our hearts and our adolescent angst. We play so much and so often that people might say we're good, have a talent, could even have a career— "if we're serious enough about it." Then what happens? We get serious. We begin to "practice," not play. We begin to seek perfection like the Holy Grail. We begin to compete. We go to school, music school, and to master classes, and to intensives and . . . and we may end up with quite a hot career. Meanwhile, some of our ardor cools. Music becomes something we "master." We become musical acrobats capable of flying across the keys with amazing ease, performing astounding stunts—but we have forgotten the sheer thrill of flying.

Anything worth doing is worth doing badly.

An original is a creation motivated by desire.

Man Ray

How we hate *that* idea. We know it as beginners but forget it as we advance. Trial-and-error becomes beneath our dignity. Of course it does. It pulls the rug out from underneath our seriousness. We don't really have a nice big block to stand behind while we "figure things out." What's to figure out? God was humble enough to just doodle, to just noodle, to fool around—why are we so serious?

'Tis an ill cook that cannot lick his own fingers.

WILLIAM SHAKESPEARE

When making art becomes about making a career, it has the same deadening impact as when making love becomes about making a baby. Rather than enjoy the process, we become focused on the result, everything else is just foreplay. There's a rush to get it over with and move on to the main thrust of things, our Brilliant Career.

Focused on career goals—prosperity, security, celebrity—we remove ourselves from the sensuality of process. The delight of a first published poem becomes First Published, not "Nice paper. Like how they laid it out." The exciting event becomes "I wonder how it will be received" instead of "What do *I* think of it?"

It becomes about perfection and other people's perception, not the joy of creation, the play of ideas.

When our art boils down to a calculated career move, we ourselves tend to become hard-boiled and calculated. Not bad traits for the hero of a detective novel, but we might need one to detect any fun in our lives.

The creative imagination leaps crag to crag and does not chug up the mountain like an automated chairlift. If we treat the creative self like a young and curious animal, we will get the right idea. A young animal pokes its curious nose here and there. Our creative animal must be allowed the same freedom. Nothing—or something—may come to your sortie into reading about the Norman Conquest, and the "something" that might come may be nothing like the "something" you first envisioned. You *could* start out with an interest in Robin Hood, only to find yourself writing the diary of Maid Marian. The greater your appetite for adventure, the more adventuresome the creative elements at hand when you turn to working on something. It does not take much to spark the imagination, but just what will do it is always the question, and the answers can be very queer indeed. Georgia O'Keeffe wrote home: "I got half-a-dozen paintings from that shattered plate." Someone else may simply have gotten a cleaning job. Do not be too hasty to name your soul's delights.

Sticks and stones, marbles and peacock feathers, a smooth gray river rock—what we take to heart is what speaks to us uniquely. As artists, we are like beachcombers, walking the tide line, pocketing the oddments washed ashore—some small stray thing will tell us a story to tell the world. There is a reason we call art a "calling"—but we do have to answer the call. Intuition speaks to us as impulse. We must learn to explore, not repress, our intuition. Intuition is key to creative unfolding.

"I wanted to learn more about the city," Kenton remembers. "After all, I lived there, but I didn't know much about it. I didn't really know how old things were. I didn't know which parts of town were built first. I didn't know significant historical turning points. I was occupying the great new job in the great new town and I was kind of lonely—but lonely for a sense of roots as well."

On impulse, Kenton began browsing the architecture section of his new neighborhood's swank Barnes and Noble. He found a book on Victorian architecture and realized his neighborhood was filled with vintage homes that were only passing for modern. Detecting here a new cornice, there a portico, Kenton began to feel there was a lot more to his neighborhood than met the eye. He next went to a secondhand bookstore and there found a shelf of "local authors." Amid the texts was a how-to-renovate guide that he picked up for fifty cents. A free Saturday afternoon found him showing up for a lecture at the neighborhood library, "Our Historic District and What We Don't Know About It." At the lecture, Kenton found himself picking up a

There is not a sprig of grass that shoots uninteresting to me.

Thomas Jefferson

All are needed by each one:
Nothing is fair or good alone.

RALPH WALDO EMERSON

flyer for a neighborhood garden tour. On that garden tour, thinking, *What am I doing here?* Kenton met two pieces of destiny. He got an idea for a photojournalism essay he would place with a local underground paper and he met a very interesting young woman—who is now his fiancée.

Opening to our intuition *is* like opening to a new love affair. Our first adventure may be a coffee date that feels a little stiff but has a few memorable possibilities. Our second flyer may be a little more bold—say, a kiss good-bye on the cheek. Our third venture may mark the beginning of a budding passion, an interest that we can't quite shake, that companions us through our days. An intuitive leading is a lead we must follow. "Destiny" arrives as a humble lunch, not a fanfare.

TASK:
Draw Yourself to Scale

An adventure does not need to be large or intense to be adventurous and nutritious for our artist. Arguably, most of us lead lives with too much adventure in it. The nightly news and daily headlines are packed with extremes of all sorts. For this reason, this tool, the "adventuring tool," is a gentle one. We all have adventurous lives, but we must see them to know it.

Go to an office supply or art supply shop. Acquire a small blank notebook suitable for sketching. Carry this notebook with you and carry, too, a sketching pencil or pen so that you can begin to capture the many small adventures of life as you actually live it.

When you enter the adventure of each moment by sketching the office where you are waiting for the doctor, sketching the bus stop where the bus is taking "forever," sketching the coffee mug while your friend is powdering her nose, you begin to gain a sense of yourself as leading a life that is crammed with interesting character and characters the moment you take the time to focus. You do not need to sketch well to enjoy sketching.

The summer I was twenty-one, I carried such a sketchbook with me all over New York. I still have the awkward sketch that I made waiting in what was to become my first literary agent's office. I have a drawing of the gawky plant and hard-to-sit-on chair. One glance at the sketch and I am "back there," alive to the great adventure of launching what was to become my literary career. A few pages later in the same sketchbook, I have a drawing of my friend Nick Cariello. "You make me look too old," he complained as I sketched him—he has since aged into and through the Nick I saw as I drew him.

So much of the adventure of the life we lead rushes past us in a blur. Velocity is the culprit. Velocity and pressure. A sketchbook freezes time. It is an instantaneous form of meditation focusing us on the worth of every passing moment. So often the great adventure of life lies between the lines, in how we felt at a certain time and at a certain place. This tool will help you to remember and savor the passing parade.

To me every hour of the light and dark is a miracle.

WALT WHITMAN

The Verb "To Be"

It is all too easy to think of art as something we aspire to, an ideal by which to measure our efforts and find them falling woefully short. Well, that is one way to think of art, and God knows we have bludgeoned ourselves with it pretty thoroughly. Our concepts of "great art" and "great artists" are often less something we aspire to than something we use to denigrate our own effort. We might want to try thinking about art a little differently.

Catherine was a highly acclaimed young singer. She had a very pure and very "scopey" operatic voice. She responded like a Maserati to direction and could corner on a dime, making her a director's favorite. She had been to the finest conservatory in America, studied with the most rigorous and respected teachers, won competitions and fine notices. She seemed set for a career in the world of opera, except for just one thing: Broadway was what made her heart sing. Like *Madame Butterfly* suffering the pangs of unrequited love, Catherine sang opera but dreamed Broadway—until her health broke down.

The time of the singing of birds is come.

SONG OF SOLOMON

"I just didn't have the heart to sing one more tragic aria. I may have the gift for it, but I wanted to return it unopened. Opera was heavy lifting for me, not vocally but emotionally. I was being groomed for a career I didn't want and I was going along with the agenda. As a result, my heart was broken and so was my health."

Fortunately, Catherine encountered a wise older woman who asked her what she wanted in life, to be admired or to be happy? Catherine saw that her motives for pursuing an operatic career were based in a snobbery she herself did not respect. Screwing up her courage, Catherine admitted her heart's desire. "I deviated from being a diva and became a happy hoofer instead." Turning her ambitions and her talents toward Broadway, Catherine has been working steadily ever since. She laughs, "If the shoe fits, you're supposed to wear it—even if it's tap."

"Art" is less about what we could be and more about what we are than we normally acknowledge. When we are fixated on getting better, we miss what it is we already are—and this is dangerous because we—as we are—are the origin of our art. "We" are what makes our art original. If we are always striving to be something more and something different, we dilute the power of what it is we actually are. Doing that, we dilute our art.

A musician with a profound gift for melody decides that dissonance and minimalism are preferable to his flowing musicality. A sculptor who prefers small-format work feels that without a towering and aggressive masterwork he is diminutive in talent. A filmmaker born to cinema verité admires the drawing-room comedy he will never be able to perfect. An artist whose line drawings make people weep with their stunning simplicity decides that only oil painting is high art.

Arthur Kretchmer, a great editor, once remarked to me, "What is it about writers? If something is easy for them, they don't respect it. Instead, they find their métier and kick it in the teeth."

Sometimes as artists, we practice a self-rejecting aesthetic that is like what adolescents do in terms of their physicality. This is a self-loathing that sets in and says whatever we are, it is not as good or as beautiful as whatever it is the other one has. If we are small, dark, and exotic, we want to be tall and bland and blond. If we are a Nordic goddess, we wish our eyes were brown and not cobalt and that our skin looked like a sultry Gauguin. In other words, whatever we are is not what we wish ourselves to be. Comedians yearn for drama; dramatic actors crave comedy. Born short-story writers lust for the National Book Award for their novels; natural novelists scream for the stage. Not that we can't do more than one thing, but one of the things we should let ourselves do is what comes naturally and easily. So why don't we?

Art is not programmatic. We cannot "improve" ourselves into great artists by doing creative sit-ups. Great artists are actually the greatest amateurs—from the Latin verb *amare,* "to love." They have learned to wriggle out of the seriousness of rigid categorization and allow themselves to pursue the Pied Piper of delight. Picasso is a fine case in point. He found beauty in a tin can, in a rusted coiled spring, in a junkyard. Delighted with his roadside finds, he delighted the world by assembling great art out of his simple love of found objects. What a loss if he had said instead, "Pablo, get a grip! You are the maestro! No tin cans for you. Think Guernica! Think serious!"

No surprise that it was Picasso himself who remarked, "We are all born children. The trick is how to remain one." Mozart, we are told, remained one. Why do we get so damn adult?

If we stop trying to improve ourselves and start trying to delight ourselves, we get further as artists. If we lean into what we

Be ye lamps unto yourselves.
Be your own reliance.
Hold to the truth within
yourselves
As to the only lamp.

BUDDHA

love instead of soldiering toward what we "should," our pace quickens, our energy rises, optimism sets in. What we love is nutritious for us. If you are crazy about Schubert, play a little Schubert. Your Liszt will be less listless. If you are wild about yellow right now for no apparent reason, paint something yellow and call that closet the sunroom. Instead of resisting yourself, try finding yourself irresistible. Try out the idea that you might be onto something when you catch sight of an amaryllis in the florist's window and think, *Oh, I'd love to have that.*

Children learn at a prodigious rate. If you watch a child learning, you see that he will move from interest to interest, hungrily grazing among multiple appetites: the blocks, the crayons, the Legos, this way and that, experimenting. When we set to structure a curriculum for our artist, we forget that the artist within is childlike and cantankerous. Enticement works better than entrapment. Curiosity gets us further than curriculum. Serious art requires serious play—and play, by definition, is anarchic, naughty.

To be an artist you must learn to let yourself be. Stop getting better. Start appreciating what you are. Do something that simply delights you for no apparent reason. Give in to a little temptation, poke into a strange doorway, buy the weird scrap of silk in a color you never wear. Make it an altar cloth, set your geranium on it, frame it—try letting yourself be that nasty, derogatory little word, "arty." Drop the rock. A lot of great artists work in their pajamas. Ernest Hemingway and Oscar Hammerstein both worked standing up because they liked that.

Sometimes we get a lot further in our art and in our lives when we let ourselves do a little of what comes easily and naturally. If you like to draw horses, stop drawing chairs. If you would love to take ballet, do it and let modern jazz be someone else's winter sport. If you have a deep love for Broadway, tell Chopin you'll be back.

Painting your kitchen is creative. Putting bells on your kid's school shoes is creative. Restructuring the office is creative. Get-

It is the addition of strangeness to beauty that constitutes the romantic character of art.

WALTER PATER

ting the bad stuff tossed from the closet is creative. None of that's going to blow up Western civilization, and it *is* going to cheer us up, our world up, and, by the tiny overflow joie de vivre, help Western civilization by one tiny jot. It is self-expression, not self-scrutiny and "correction," that brings healing and happiness. Bells on the shoelaces, sonnets in the schools. These are not so far apart. Writing a novel and doing something novel on a Saturday afternoon are *both* creative leaps—one large and one small, but each is grounded in the right to express creative choice.

Very often a little friendly and easy art can send us back up those other slithery slopes with a bit more humor and optimism.

Artists of all stripe tend to equate difficulty with virtue and ease with slumming. We do not lean into our ease and enjoy the ride of our gift. Instead, we make firm resolves to work on our areas of difficulty. We call this improving ourselves—okay, sometimes we do improve a wobbly area, but if we do not practice the joy of using our talents where they fall easily, we rob ourselves of self-expression. The "self" has a few things it "selfishly" enjoys—and it is dangerous, as an artist, to ignore these natural affections and predilections.

This is not to say you have to "give up" high art. Instead, I am saying to try "Hi, Art!" like you are waving to someone friendly out the window of your pickup truck.

Today isn't any other day, you know.

LEWIS CARROLL

TASK:
Allow Yourself to Be

Seriousness is the enemy of spontaneity. What we "should" love and what we do love are often two different things. Allow yourself to admit to some of your more anarchistic forbidden pleasures. (Many French romantic liaisons last longer than marriages. Why? Because they are officially a "forbidden delight.")

Take pen in hand and finish this phrase 10 times:

Secretly, I would love to _____.

You have just cast the net of dreams and scooped from your subconscious some secret and hidden desires. Take pen in hand again and for fifteen minutes allow yourself to fully inhabit one of your secret desires. How does it feel to be doing it? Where are you when you do it? Who cheers you on? What surprises you? Make this mental movie as vivid as possible. Be sure to flesh out your supporting cast and color in your setting. Initiative often begins in the imagination. As Stella Merrill Mann summarizes it, "Ask, believe, receive." Give yourself the initial gift of conceptualizing a fully inhabited secret desire.

Invention vs. Convention

As artists, we are innovators. We experiment and explore. We make things new—at the very least, we make things anew. Every painting edges us forward a hair in skill and experience, even if we are in a workshop class that copies an old master. Every time a pianist tackles Franck or Beethoven, interprets Debussy—there is still some personal nuance that the artist brings to the work. A new staging of an old ballet, the millionth high school production of *Romeo and Juliet*—each expression of art breathes new breath into the work and into the world. Even when we are doing something that "has been done," we bring to bear fresh creative energy. And when we deliberately explore and extend our creative territory, we innovate even further and even more.

Some people are innovators by temperament and trade. Other people are conservers. As artists, we are most often innovators. Those who work with our work—agents, managers, publishers, gallery owners, curators, producers—are most often conservers. As innovators, we must not be *so* innovative that we burn our bridges, but we must not allow our conservers to be so conservative that we spend entire careers shoring up the bridges we have already built. Conservers focus not on the forward-

It is the first part of intelligence to recognize our precarious estate in life, and the first part of courage to be not at all abashed before the fact.

ROBERT LOUIS STEVENSON

moving edge but on the known territory of "how it's done" and "the way it is in the business" and "what will sell." They tell us not how to skin the creative cat a new way but how the cat has already been skinned. They talk about "what works" rather than "what *could* work." They say things like "That's not how the business runs."

Conservers want artists to believe that "how it is done" is how it has to be done. They often talk about the odds against accomplishment of an artistic dream. They often come up with the numbers that "prove" the impossible odds stacked against us. They often forget what we as artists know—the odds are not impossible. They never are and they never will be. They may look impossible. They may sound impossible, but those are largely scare tactics. The phrase "scared out of our wits" is a very precise phrase. As artists, when we allow conservers to terrorize us, we *are* being scared out of our wits—wits being those innovative and inventive smarts that allow us to figure out, always, one more way to skin a cat.

As an artist and an innovator, we must always ask, "How *can* we?" We must always look for, and find, still *another* way to skin the cat, publish the book, shoot the film, stage the play—as artists, we are practitioners not of how it *is* done, but of how it could be done. We are charged with finding not the problems but the solutions. As artists, we are concerned with making things, while conservers are often concerned with making do with the world as they find it.

When Jean met and married Gordon, she was a working artist with a lively and varied career. Painting, sculpture, and photography were her favorite pursuits. She moved nimbly among the three, making a brisk and interesting career for herself. "You've got to specialize—you've got to market yourself," Gordon solemnly advised her. "You can't just chase whatever whim catches your fancy. It's not good business."

Impressed and intimidated by her husband's "expertise," Jean shaped her career to his wishes instead of to her own. For the

You never know what is enough unless you know what is more than enough.

WILLIAM BLAKE

decade that their marriage lasted, she largely did as she was told, focusing as her husband told her she should. Instead of flourishing, she felt her career growing "successful"—but stagnant and stale. Depression set in before divorce. When her husband abruptly left her, claiming *he* felt stifled, Jean found herself suddenly free. After a few months of dizzy disorientation, she began exploring a variety of creative interests.

"I'd been defining myself so narrowly, as just a painter. I've got all sorts of creative skills I love using." Long a "closet techie," Jean explored new computer skills, studied layout and newsletters. To her delight, people loved paying her to do exactly that. A lively design business was born.

As artists, we are more like inventors than we are like those who mass-produce the inventions. We may do both, of course, and often do, but we are at heart those who make what others may make more of. We create a painting that may later become a greeting card, a poster, or a calendar piece, but the kernel of invention remains with us. We try to see if an idea "flies." Like the Wright brothers, we make the gadget that then becomes the staple of the industry. As artists, we are interested in what can be done rather than how it can't be done.

Some agents, some managers, some producers and dealers and curators, are themselves innovators and creators. They bring to our work their own inventive daring—most do not. As conservers, they are oriented toward what has sold rather than what could sell. They look more often for the downside than the upside. They may additionally be looking most often for the known sale and the proven return and where they can make the most financial reward in the short term rather than thinking of the long-term creative rewards of making a superior work and trusting the market to respond to that.

As artists, we know very well that something can "not be done," only until someone does it. Some artist, somewhere, decides to shove the fence back a little and extend his or her and all of our range. *Showboat* brought serious concerns to musical

Any profound view of the world is mysticism.

ALBERT SCHWEITZER

theater. *Oklahoma!* and *Carousel* brought "real" stories and characters and plays that could stand in their own right as dramatic material. The musical was no longer defined merely as boy-meets-girl—from Rodgers and Hammerstein on out, it tackled real issues and ideas. They had moved the fence, buying everyone more creative acreage.

As examples like these make pointedly clear, as artists, we must listen most carefully to our inner guidance and secondarily to our outer advisers. This isn't just spiritual law—trusting the still, small voice to guide us—it's good business practice as well. The interaction of commerce and creativity is a tricky dance, and we as artists must lead it. Show a new direction in your painting to a dealer who is being asked for more of last year's series and you may hear a worried and dispiriting "Mmmm." Do not be fooled. He cannot see what you as an artist may sense, that your direction is the new direction the market will soon be following. For an artist willing to have a learning curve, all directions lead to somewhere worthy.

"Nothing succeeds like success" is a truism for a life in the arts. The problem lies in parsing out what constitutes a success—and for an artist that may be making something new and challenging rather than repeating a known success. It may be having a body of work that is personally respectable, following not merely the market but our own very changing interests. I have been told "short stories don't sell" and then found yes, they did. I have been told "memory plays don't work" and won prizes for the same play. I have been told "never use first person for a novel" and published the same novel to good reviews, good reception, and personal satisfaction.

The business of art is a machine, but an artist is the live, animating spark that runs it. That spark can be extinguished by too much "realism" and too much "I know you don't want to hear this, but . . ." Well-meaning advisers can advise us straight into a creative slump, straight into a fallow period, straight into a wall of inner resistance. They forget that they cannot sell what we do not

Trifles make perfection—and perfection is no trifle.

MICHELANGELO

make and so often urge us to make what they know they can sell, forgetting that if they deaden our spirits too often and too much, the work will deaden as well and there will be nothing to sell.

As artists, we have a form of inner power the advisers can never extinguish or ultimately thwart. And this is always the key.

It is the question of "odds" that always baffles conservers when they deal with artists. Conservers like to think they know the odds. They like to think they know what sells—and they do know until another artist invents another memorable and unpredictable something and thus creates a market for that. As artists, we are first and foremost the origins of our work. Since each of us is one-of-a-kind, the market, for all its supposed predictability, is actually vulnerable to falling in love with any of us at any time.

I say this and I know this because I believe and know creativity to be a spiritual issue. "Faith moves mountains"—Christ told us that, and he may have meant that literally.

We speak of the Great Creator, we speak of Christ but seldom make the connection that the spiritual laws he taught are actually the spiritual laws related to creativity. "Knock and it shall be opened." "Ask and you shall receive"—these are not mere spiritual bromide, they are spiritual laws as they relate to manifestation.

- Ask
- Believe
- Receive

As artists, we routinely ask for inspiration. We need to learn from Christ's example that we can also ask for the material manifestation of our visions to come to us as money, support, opportunity. Our faith, which is a request coupled with an expectation of its successful fulfillment, is no different from the faith of a navigator setting out to prove the world is round. Creative dreams come to us as visions that we are charged with ful-

I find that I have painted my life—things happening in my life—without knowing.

GEORGIA O'KEEFFE

filling. When we allow the Great Creator to do this to us, through us, then we are aligning ourselves with the spiritual power necessary to negate the "odds."

TASK:
Strike Up a Dialogue

In addition to the outer conservers that we encounter in a creative career, we all also carry an inner conserver, who functions as a gatekeeper on our more expansive impulses. The best creative careers are built by a fruitful inner dialogue between our inner innovator and our inner conserver. It is a practical skill that can be practiced. Take pen in hand and allow your two sides to strike up a dialogue. It might look like this:

What a man thinks of himself . . . determines, or rather indicates, his fate.

HENRY DAVID THOREAU

INNOVATOR
*I'd love to go back to school
full-time. I've been shut up
in my painting studio a decade
and I'm lonely and bored.*

CONSERVER
*You make your living from the
work you do in that studio. You
can't just quit.*

INNOVATOR
Well, I'd like to, that's for sure.

CONSERVER
*What about a once-a-week class?
You'd have time to do that and,
if you pick the right one, it's
a lot of stimulus.*

INNOVATOR
*That's a good idea and less of
a radical free fall. Thank you.*

All successful creative careers are built upon dialogues like the one above. As we both move forward and solidify where we've been, "solid" careers take shape. They are like gardens that require patient nurturance, where no one plant runs wild.

CHECK-IN

1. **How many days this week did you do your Morning Pages?** If you skipped a day, why did you skip it? How was the experience of writing them for you? Are you experiencing more clarity? A wider range of emotions? A greater sense of detachment, purpose, and calm? Did anything surprise you? Is there a "repeating" issue asking to be dealt with?

2. **Did you do your Artist's Date this week?** Did you note an improved sense of well-being? What did you do and how did it feel? Remember, Artist's Dates can be difficult and you may need to coax yourself into taking them.

3. **Did you get out on your Weekly Walk?** How did that feel? What emotions or insights surfaced for you? Were you able to walk more than once? What did your walk do for your optimism and sense of perspective?

4. **Were there any other issues this week that felt significant to you in your self-discovery?** Describe them.

Discovering a Sense of Personal Territory

Saying yes to our creative selves may
involve saying no to our significant others.
This week focuses on boundaries. The essays
and tasks aim at helping us to define our creative
identities as opposed to our many other roles.
Expect to feel heightened emotions as
energy rebounds into your
own court.

Sexuality vs. Caretaking

As artists, our sexual energy and our creative energy are very closely intertwined. This is why we have love songs. Love sonnets. Torch songs. And the phrase "Carrying a torch," because as unrequited lovers we still carry a bright enough spark to speak of being "shot down in flames."

When someone who ignites our creative imagination crosses our path, that person is a "fuse lighter." Our creative engine kicks over. We suddenly have things to say and long for new ways to say them. We say them in paint, in dance, in poetry, in plasticine sculpture. We suddenly "come alive to the possibility." We are galvanized. People ask, "Are you in love?"

In a sense, we are in love—and we are also in love with our own artist, who is suddenly mirrored back to us as exciting and adventurous, powerful, perhaps even dangerous. We experience more energy. We burn the candle at both ends, staying up late to work on a project. Getting up early to grab an hour at the easel, like a stolen bout of lovemaking on the way to work.

Creative energy and sexual energy are both our personal energy. Our use of them is private, and to pretend otherwise is debilitating and abusive. In point of fact, the two energies are so closely intertwined, they may be experienced as nearly identical. We conceive children and we conceive creative projects. Both energies are sacred. They spring from the same source, our inner core. Our creative energy, like our sexual energy, must not be squandered. And yet, we are often asked to do just that.

As artists, we must be alert to what people ask us for and reward us for being. Our partners and friends do condition us into behaviors quite unconsciously. We must be alert to what they reward us for with their thanks and reciprocity. And to what ways they are withholding and manipulative in their lack of approval and generosity. These things condition us, and they are also the conditions in which our art will or will not be made.

Festivity breeds creativity. Rigidity breeds despair. When our high spirits are straitjacketed in the name of virtue or discipline, the vital and youthful spark in us that enjoys adventure and is game for invention begins to flicker like a flame in a draft.

Creativity responds to nourishment and warmth. If we are forbidden to be childlike—told perhaps that it is "childish" or "selfish"—if we are urged to be too sensible, we react as gifted students do to an authoritarian teacher—we refuse to learn and grow. Our considerable energy is channeled into resistance and over time solidifies into a hard-to-penetrate shell of feigned indifference.

The universe is alive with energy. It is fertile, abundant, even raucous—so are we. Most of us are high spirited, humorous, even pranksterish with the least encouragement. What is lacking for so many of us is precisely the least encouragement. We buy in to the notion that life is dreary and difficult and something to be soldiered through. We tell ourselves, "Oh, well, what did I expect?"

The truth is that as children, many of us expected much

It is only with the heart that one can see rightly; what is essential is invisible to the eye.

ANTOINE DE SAINT-EXUPÉRY

more. We had dreams and desires and inklings of delight and full-blown passions. We practiced ballet in the living room, we sang wildly, we loved the goo of finger painting. We loved, period—and love is a passionate and energizing force. In order for our creativity to flourish, we must reclaim our right both to love and to be loved. We must become a little nuts about ourselves, about our notions, whimsies, and ambitions. Instead of chiding ourselves or allowing ourselves to be chided into an "adult" solemnity, we must regain our right to be goofy, earthy, even silly. In lovemaking we speak of "foreplay," and we must allow ourselves to play at the things we love. This means that if our partner is restrictive, we must get a little clever at daring to be ourselves in private. Instead of yanking on our bootlaces and asking ourselves to get better, we need to loosen up the shoelaces, take off the shoes, and wiggle our feet in the green grass of earth.

Be it life or death, we crave only reality.

HENRY DAVID THOREAU

Creativity is sensual, and so are we. As we celebrate rather than repress our passion, we are rewarded by more passion, and that is the fuel for art.

If our romantic partner insists on always using us to process with, never taking us out to something simply fun, we will begin to feel snappish and hostile. The same is true of our creative partnerships. We may be caring, we may be acute, we may be an invaluable sounding board, but that's not romance, and that's not creative collaboration either. Nurturing is a part of a partnership—overnurturing is the usurping of your creative energy for someone else's agendas.

When we are asked to overcaretake, to "mother" or "father" our friends or lovers or colleagues, our artist reacts with depression and also with rage. Both as artists and as people, such demands can make us feel curiously desexualized, as if we are truly being neutered, castrated, and used.

A woman writer married to an omnivorously needy partner was astounded to discover that after her divorce, both her creative energy and her sexual energy came springing back to life like a lioness waking up after years of medication and depression from living in a too-small zoo cage. As she sharply realized, creative and sexual energy are connected. Dampen our creative ardor and our sexual selves dampen as well. Dampen our sexual selves by demanding we overnurture and parentalize ourselves, and our creativity suffers.

It is no coincidence that artistic annals are filled with the tales of incendiary romantic intrigues, yielding blazing creative work. Our muses *are* fuse lighters, and the blaze they ignite may be passionate, creative, or both. Does this mean we must sexualize all our relationships or creative collaborations? Emphatically, *no*. But it *does* mean that we must be alert to avoid those bonds and entanglements that neuter our exuberance, hence our sexuality and creativity. If someone refuses to share our humor, we are cast as grim parents to their infantile demands. Artists can marry, but they must marry well. And, I would argue, there must be merriment in their marriage for their work to continue to flourish. And if the work is dead, the relationship will soon follow suit. If our energy must always be all-nurturing or stern, our creative keyboard is stuck on middle C.

In artist-to-artist relationships, *both* artists need to be nurtured and seen. Neither partner should be neutered or neutralized by excessive caretaking. Agendas cannot replace adventures.

If a man wants to be mothered, he will not respond with enthusiasm to your sexy new dress—*or* your new song. Similarly, a woman artist might demand an all-caretaking daddy from her spouse, saying her "artist child" needs pampering.

Neither sex is immune to creative castration by relationships that drain creative reservoirs without the tenderness to refill them.

Sexuality can be sublimated in the name of art, but it need not be. Damaging sexual entanglements *do* damage our creativity, but enlivening ones nurture and spark it.

Married to a narcissistic and greedy actress, Daniel felt increasingly drained, and his work life withered. Later, involved with a woman artist who found both him and his work attrac-

I cannot understand; I love.

ALFRED, LORD TENNYSON

tive, Daniel's creative life rebounded robustly with plays, novels, films—all the creative brainchildren of a happy coupling.

Our mythology around artists and sexuality tends to dwell on the negative, on the promiscuity of artists, on their self-destructive sexual binging. Far more pernicious is the subtle leeching of creativity and sexuality through overcaretaking, and far less often mentioned is the happy blossoming artists may experience when settled in a relationship that is alive to their creative and sexual energies.

If there is an art to romance, it can equally be said that there must be romance to art.

The aim, if reached or not, makes great the life; Try to be Shakespeare, leave the rest to fate.

ROBERT BROWNING

TASK:
Putting a Tiger Back in Your Tank

When we are in love, we find our partners fascinating and ourselves with them. When we are in a creative recovery, we find *ourselves* fascinating. We fall in love with our own ideas, insights, inspirations, and impulses. We are interested by what we have to say and think. We feel alive, alert, and vibrant—and, if we don't feel that way, we know it and resent it. Admitting those who leave us cold, we warm to our own interests.

Take pen in hand and finish the following phrases as rapidly as you can:

1. Among my friends, a "fuse lighter" who makes me feel creative and powerful is _____.
2. Among my friends, a "wet blanket" who drains and dampens me is _____.
3. Historically, a relationship that left me depleted from overcaretaking was _____.
4. Realistically, a current relationship that leaves me feeling neutered is _____.
5. My most reciprocal, mutually nurturing creative friendship is with _____.

Once you have sorted through your acquaintances and intimates for those who allow you to be fiery, ask yourself the same question: "Do I allow myself to have passion?" Take pen in hand and write yourself a love letter. Be as specific and as affectionate as you can imagine.

Stop Being "Nice," Be Honest

When you are content to be simply yourself and don't compare or compete, everybody will respect you.

LAO-TZU

"Charity begins at home" is not a bromide. It is a direction. It means start with being nice to yourself, your authentic self, then try being nice to everyone else. When we place ourselves too low in the pecking order, we feel henpecked and, yes, we feel peckish. We neglect our work or do it distractedly. Soon our work may develop a querulous tone, sour and dyspeptic, like ourselves. When we undervalue ourselves, we literally bury ourselves in lives not our own. Meeting the expectations of others, we may misplace our own values.

Value systems are as individual as fingerprints. Each of us has a set of priorities that may be baffling to others but absolutely necessary to ourselves. Violating our true selves, we soon feel worthless and undeserving. This in turn prevents our acting on our own behalf, and so we suffer further.

When I was a young single mother, I felt guilty because I craved time away from my daughter. I wanted silence. I needed to hear my own thoughts. I also needed to take my own soul by the hand occasionally and not have to worry about keeping my daughter's tiny hand clutched. Whatever dreams I harbored had better take the back burner, I lectured myself—although I never stopped writing—and so I tried putting my dreams on the back burner, where they proceeded to boil—and so did my temper. Domenica was a delightful child. I began to find her not so delightful. I was snappish, irritable, and guilty. Yearning for more writing time, a luxury of my premotherhood years, I felt cornered and trapped. Wasn't my child more important than my brainchildren? I lectured myself. I could see no way out.

"Take a night off," an older woman friend, an actress, advised me. "Take care of your artist. That will make you a much better mother. You need to get in reality here. Society tells you motherhood comes first, but—with you—it doesn't. If you're honest about that and put your artist first, you might be quite a good mother. Lie to yourself about it—and did you know most child abuse comes from too much togetherness?"

We get our lives wrong because we get our questions wrong. We get our questions wrong because we have been raised in a culture that is punishing to the forms of freedom necessary for artists to flourish. These freedoms are the ones that allow us to be a little less nice so that we can be a little more genuine. Richard Rodgers needed piano time and took it every morning—*then* he was a devoted father—only then.

I had not known that too much "nice" caused child abuse, but I could believe it. Taking my friend's radical advice, I began getting up an hour earlier to write Morning Pages while my daughter slept. I also began a practice of taking Artist's Dates, getting me and my creative consciousness a few of the sort of festive adventures that I had been devising—and resenting—for my daughter. I was rewarded with this self-care by a movie idea—I wrote a script and sold it to Paramount.

What was even more "paramount" was this: I found that my mother had been quite right to post over her kitchen sink a small poem I had always dismissed as doggerel. It read:

> *If your nose is held to the grindstone rough*
> *and you hold it down there long enough*
> *soon you'll say there's no such thing*
> *as brooks that babble and birds that sing.*
> *Three things will all your world compose—*
> *just you, the grindstone, and your darned old nose.*

That which we understand
we can't blame.

JOHANN WOLFGANG
VON GOETHE

Jump.

JOSEPH CAMPBELL

I've taught for twenty-five years. I've had a great many students worry that they were selfish. It is my considered opinion that most creative people are actually too selfless. Instead of asking "Julia, am I selfish?" they should ask, "Julia, am I selfish enough?" "Selfish enough" gives us the self for self-expression.

As artists, when we are too nice for too long, we stop being nice at all. "I just need to get to the goddamn piano," we say correctly, or "I haven't written in days and it's driving me crazy," correctly, or "If I don't get to the easel, these kids are gonna walk the plank." Our slowly stoked fires of resentment—caused by too many yesses where a timely no would have been more honest and given us time and space to work—begin to set our tempers to a simmer and then to a boil. If we persist in still being nice, we get to cook ourselves an ulcer or develop high blood pressure. For an artist, being too virtuous is no virtue at all. It is destructive and counterproductive. Have I mentioned that it is no fun?

A sustained artistic career is made of two variables—talent and character. By "character" I do not mean the good or bad kind, I simply mean the character or tone of a personality, its exact nature. Great talent linked to an erratic character will yield an erratic career—bursts of promise subverted, flashes of glorious clarity and brilliance lost or muddled by the "flaw" in the stone of resolve. A sustained creative career requires discipline— the courage to evict what does not serve the goal of excellence. This is what it means to have character.

"What does not serve" varies person to person. For one it may be an overly dramatic friend. For another, too many high-octane dinner parties full of boast-and-toast talk. Whatever ungrounds an artist ungrounds his or her work. Whatever ungrounds an artist must be curtailed, avoided, or indulged in with care. As artists, we learn this from bitter experience. A virtuoso concert violinist learns that even a single scotch the night before playing certain works costs in terms of the necessary manual dexterity to safely undertake musical flight. Indulgence has a price. Airline pilots know the same thing as does the FAA. Pilots are checked for abuse of alcohol and other substances. If they overindulge, lives are endangered. For an artist, the life of his work is endangered. Self-indulgence spells self-endangerment. Our large self falls prey to our petty vices. It is enlightened self-interest to be selfish enough to be self-protective. Being self-protective may not seem "nice." We may say no to invitations that do not serve us.

I love those who yearn for the impossible.

JOHANN WOLFGANG VON GOETHE

As an artist, being nice is not nearly as important as being authentic. When we are what we truly are and say what we truly mean, we stop shouldering the responsibility for everyone else's shortfalls and become accountable to ourselves. When we do, astonishing shifts occur. We become aligned with our true higher power, and creative grace flows freely.

When we stop playing God, God can play through us. When I stopped rescuing my blocked writer-boyfriend, I moved from writing articles and short stories to writing books. That's how much energy he had consumed. When a composer dropped his high-maintenance girlfriend, he finally finished an album that had simmered a decade. An officially "burned-out" woman painter stopped volunteering her time to the all-consuming neighborhood environmental group and found she suddenly had time to both paint and teach, solidly increasing both her productivity and her income. Her volunteerism had long felt involuntary. Willing to seem less saintly, she felt herself far more free.

Teaching those around us what our priorities are—and remembering them ourselves—makes for harmonious relationships. Clarifying ourselves to others brings honest connections that are grounded in mutual respect. Honesty starts with us. Identifying those who habitually abuse our time and energies is pivotal, but identifying them is only step one. Avoiding them is step two, and this is where a lot of us stumble. It is as if we doubt we have a right to tranquility, respect, and good humor. Shouldn't we really suffer? Shouldn't we find it more spiritual not to upset the status quo? Artificial acceptance of people and circumstances we resent makes us ill tempered. A little honest self-love does wonders for our personality, and for our art.

"But, Julia," I've heard people wail, "are you saying we should be selfish?"

Personally, I prefer selfish to simmering, cranky, hostile, and long-suffering. And is it really selfish to take time to have a self? You need a self for self-expression—and you need a self for a lot of other things as well. If the unexamined life is not worth living, the unlived life is not worth examining, or painting, or sculpting, or acting.

Too often, the rich world that feeds career-making work gives way to a hothouse world, and later works that feel recycled. For artists at every level, the necessity for nutritive inflow remains. Ironically, that inflow may be impeded by success itself, with the multiple demands made on our creative time.

A man at the very top of his art form professionally found himself so overbooked and so overburdened with advising others and lending his prestigious name to worthy causes that his life was no longer his own. The prestigious institutions with which he had aligned himself seemed to possess omnivorous appetites. Each request was "reasonable," each cause was "worthy." What he was was exhausted, burned-out, and baffled. "I'm at the top," he told me, "where I was always supposed to get, but I don't like it very much." Of course not. He had no time for his personal art, the beloved vehicle that had taken him to the top.

It is impossible to say yes to ourselves and our art until we learn to say no to others. People do not mean us harm, but they do harm us when they ask for more than we can give. When we go ahead and give it to them, we are harming ourselves as well.

"I knew I should have said no," we wail—until we start to actually do it. No, we cannot take on the one extra student. No, we cannot take on the one more committee. No, we cannot allow ourselves to be used—or we stop being useful.

Virtue—and the false virtue of being too virtuous—is very

Knowing what you can not do is more important than knowing what you can do. In fact, that's good taste.

LUCILLE BALL

tempting. The problem with worthy causes is that they are worthy.

"You cannot be healthy and popular all at the same time," an accomplished older actress once warned me. "People want what they want and if you don't give it to them, they will get angry."

True enough, but our artist also wants what it wants and if we don't give it to our artist, our very core gets angry. If we think of the part of our self that creates as being like a vibrant and gifted inner youngster, we begin to imagine how dispirited a series of "Not now, be nice, just be a good sport and wait until later" dismissiveness on our part can make it.

When we start saying "Can't, because I am working," our life starts to work again. We start to feel our artist begin to trust us again and to ante up more ideas. Again, think of the artist as being quite young. What does a child do if disciplined too rigidly? It sulks. It lapses into silence. It acts out—our artist can be fairly depended upon to do some or all of these behaviors when we insist on being "nice" instead of honest.

It is never too late to start over. It is never past the point of no return for our artist to recover. We can heap years, decades, a lifetime of insult upon our artist and it is so resilient, so powerful, and so stubborn that it will come back to life when we give it the smallest opportunity. Instead of being coaxed into one more overextension of our energies in the name of helping others, we can help ourselves by coaxing our artist out with the promise of some protected time to be listened to, talked with, and interacted with. If we actively love our artist, our artist will love us in return. Lovers tell secrets and share dreams. Lovers meet no matter how adverse the circumstances, sneaking off for a rendezvous. As we woo our artist with our focused attention and private time, it will reward us with art.

To live well is to work well, to show a good activity.

THOMAS AQUINAS

TASK:
Be Nice to Yourself
(There's a Self in Self-Expression)

Did you know that secret? The awful thing is that beauty is mysterious.

FYODOR DOSTOYEVSKY

Many of us work too hard on being selfless. We forget that we actually need a self for self-expression. Take pen in hand and do a little archaeology—dig through your "shoulds" until you arrive at some "coulds." Complete the following sentences with 5 wishes. Write rapidly to evade your inner censor.

If it weren't so selfish, I'd love to try . . .
1.
2.
3.
4.
5.

If it weren't so expensive, I'd love to try . . .
1.
2.
3.
4.
5.

If it weren't so frivolous, I'd love to own . . .
1.
2.
3.
4.
5.

If it weren't so scary, I'd love to tell . . .
1.
2.
3.
4.
5.

If I had five other lives, I'd love to be . . .

1.

2.

3.

4.

5.

These lists are powerful dreams. They may manifest in your life rapidly and unexpectedly. For this reason, you may want to put these lists into your God Jar for safekeeping. Do not be surprised if "parts" of your "other" lives begin to show up in the life you've actually got.

Energy Debts

All actions require creative energy. We seldom acknowledge this. As artists, we must learn to think of our energy the way a person thinks about money—am I spending my energy wisely here, investing in this person, this situation, this use of my time? As a rule, artists are temperamentally generous, even spendthrift. This natural inclination must be consciously monitored. An artist must return enough to the inner well to feel a sense of well-being.

A phone call with a tedious creative colleague is draining. What is getting drained is our creative bank account. A phone call or conversation in which our feedback is asked, used, and unacknowledged is like coaching someone on their stock market investments and not getting a thank-you for their big win. Conversely, a phone call that feels reciprocal is a win–win for both parties. You aren't just a site where someone is downloading information. You are a partner in a genuine dialogue that expands you both. I have a musician friend whose conversations are so rewarding, they send me racing to the page to write. Something in our give-and-take just plain gives.

As people and as artists, we crave to be seen for who and

Whatever is worth doing at all is worth doing well.

LORD CHESTERFIELD

what we really are. If we are in relationships where the dividends we need are never extended back to us, that is a bad investment. Too many of those, and we bankrupt our creative stores. We must ask not only "Do I love this person?" but "Is this relationship self-loving?" Any relationship that risks your artist's identity is not.

A creative person is intended to be fed and supported by both divine and human sources, but none of those needed nutrients can reach us if we have turned ourselves into a food source for others, allowing them to dine freely on our time, our talents and our reserves. If we give someone who is without scruples and needy full access to our time and attention, it is like giving them our creative checkbook. They will spend us willy-nilly, and when we turn to use our own reserves, we will find them missing.

Creativity expands in an atmosphere encouraging to it, and constricts self-protectively in an atmosphere that is cynical or hostile. This is why artists can have a difficult time accessing their best work in academia. This is why our close friends must be safe and smart, but not so smart-aleck that our creative child is afraid to speak up. When we lose our voice or our energy creatively, it is not some mysterious malady. It can usually be traced directly to an encounter in which our energy was abused.

If someone squanders our time by refusing to be pinned down as to when rehearsals or writing sessions or deadlines can be accomplished, we are put on hold. We cannot invest in other directions because we are always aware that we might be "suddenly" called on to invest when the erratic person is available. If we put our life and our planning on hold to accommodate another, too often we will feel tapped out because we cannot really claim any time and energy as safely and positively as our own. We are "on call." It is like having the door to your creative house unlocked and not knowing when someone will enter.

Think of your energy as money. Does this person tie up too much of your time and energy for you to invest it elsewhere? Is he the human equivalent of an investment you cannot liquidate

The art of being wise is the art of knowing what to overlook.

WILLIAM JAMES

when you need to? If so, he is then not only expensive in himself, he is also costing you finding and making other more emotionally and creatively remunerative relationships.

Our creative energy is our divine inheritance. If people insist on squandering it and we cooperate, we will find ourselves creatively bankrupt, drained of goodwill and good feelings, short-tempered and short-fused. If our energy is squandered on their poor judgment, our continuing to invest in them robs us of the power to effectively invest elsewhere or in ourselves.

As artists, we must husband our energy as carefully as our money. We must spend it along lines that are personally and creatively rewarding. We must invest it wisely in people and projects that return our investment with measurable satisfaction, growth, and achievement.

Every exit is an entry somewhere else.

TOM STOPPARD

Just as we expect and demand a fair return on our investments, we have a right to expect and receive a fair return on our investments of energy—both personally and professionally. Does this mean that we will never—or should never—extend ourselves in generosity toward our friends, family, and work? No. But it does mean that we must be alert to when and where our investment of energy is valued in return.

We must also be clear that "valued in return" may involve—and must involve—a return that is in some way compatible with what we extend. If a great apple pie is extended as a sign of love, "Could I have the recipe?" is not acknowledgment. It is ignoring the key ingredient—the love in the recipe. Similarly, if intellectual acuity is extended to a friend or a spouse or a colleague, that true ingredient must be acknowledged as well.

As an artist with thirty-five years of experience, I am the equivalent of the senior partner at a law firm. That is not ego, it is simply the level of my practice. While I may gladly undertake a "let's parse this out" political discussion on a close friend's creative career, I cannot undertake a regime of lunches involving creative counseling. I would come home both too fat and too thin, overnourished and undernurtured.

I am closer to the work than to anything on earth. That's the marriage.

LOUISE NEVELSON

As artists, all of us need to invest wisely in ourselves and in others. We deserve recognition and respect and acknowledgment for the actual worth of our investments of time, talent, and keen observation.

In our personal friendships, we require peers who see and acknowledge the skills we bring to the table. It is perfectly fine to talk with friends about our career situations and our fiscal dilemmas, but if those friends are giving us advice from their own considerable professional acuity and attainment, that should get some small nod from us, as ours hopefully does from them. This reciprocity of respect may be largely tacit, but it must be there or we may feel slighted or used.

Artists routinely apprentice and even adopt younger artists, but if you examine such arrangements closely, there is a reciprocal flow of energy from elder to younger, younger to elder. The apprentice helps, not merely helps himself. Such relationships can be controversial but mutually catalytic. Georgia O'Keeffe was both benefactor to—and benefitted by—her young protégé Juan Hamilton. Musical mentorships are commonplace. Aaron Copland helped Bernstein, who helped Copland. "Part of what I think we teach younger artists is professionalism," explains one master musician.

For the elder artists who teach and mentor, the rewards are real, but the demands can be unrealistic. In their desire to give, they may expend more than they can refund to themselves. A student who thoughtlessly misses lessons and expects and demands rescheduling can tip the balance from possible to impossible in a teacher's busy schedule.

If our teaching or mentoring feels thankless, we are either overextended or unthanked or both. As older, established artists, the company we keep may very well be underlings, and sometimes people help themselves to our help. When we are unhappy in a relationship, when we "blow things out of proportion," it is because the proportions within the relationship, and perhaps in our life as a whole, are somehow skewed. We are not crazy, but something is. We feel drained because we *are* drained. If the person who emptied the tank cannot help to fill it, well then, we must fill it elsewhere—and put a little red flag next to the person's name in our consciousness. When overtaxed by a friend, we must ask, Is this an understandable, rare situation—a death in the family, a job loss—that requires our marshaling extra help, or is this person habitually taxing, habitually dramatic and accident prone, a chronic abuser of our time and attention, a chronic undernurturer, or in between?

As artists, we have antennae sensitive to the thoughts and feelings of those around us. We can be chilled by indifference, hurt by lack of consideration, and we can be exhausted and diminished if we are in the company of those who talk down to us or treat us subtly like the identified patient: "Oh, you and your crazy ideas." As artists, we *need* our crazy ideas, and we need those who don't think they're too crazy. Symphonies and screenplays begin as crazy ideas. So do novels and nocturnes, bronzes and ballets.

Writers must write. Piano players must play pianos. Painters must paint and singers must sing. We can use our creative energy in the support of others, but if our artist gets lost in the transaction, if our aid and support is treated as generic cheerleading, if we are not acknowledged and nurtured in return in a way that fits our actual personal needs, then we are being inadvertently battered.

Alan sold a book and was required to do a substantial rewrite in order to bring the book fully into form. Rather than appreciating the pressure he was under, Alan's wife chose this "quiet time. You're just rewriting" to invite her extended family for a large and noisy visit. Wanting to be a good sport, wanting not to seem like a prima donna, Alan struggled with his growing anger as loud voices and interruptions cost him time and focus. Finally, exasperated and hurt, Alan rented a room in a nearby motel and retreated there with his computer and his unfinished book. It wasn't that he didn't love his wife and her family, it was that they

There are so many selves in everybody and to explore and exploit just one is wrong, dead wrong, for the creative person.

JAMES DICKEY

were unable to see that he was at the glass-mountain phase of a project—the heartbreakingly hard make-it-or-break-it period when an artist knows he just may not be quite good enough to bring to bear the excellence he knows he is required to.

One of the most difficult things that happens to an artist is the sorrow that occurs when misperceived in the public arena. This makes it doubly important that in our private arena our artist be acknowledged and respected. I am not saying that we should swoon around the house—or march around the house—wearing the air "I am a great artist." What I am saying is that if you are a writer and someone doesn't respect your writing time, she is not respecting you. If you are a pianist and someone doesn't respect your need to practice, he is not respecting your personal and professional priorities.

Some people batter us often and for agendas of their own. Other people, excellent ones, may bruise us as they racket through a set of terrifying personal rapids. Learning to decipher which is which takes practice. As artists, we must practice generosity not only toward others but also toward ourselves.

Early in a creative career, sainthood isn't too common. But as we become revered and respected for our work, we can develop a weakness for being revered and respected. Our Achilles' heel can be the compliment that makes us feel that we alone can properly mentor a talented youngster. This seemingly harmless form of hubris actually undercuts our own usefulness to the young artists we tutor. Yes, yes, it's wonderful to be a wonderful teacher, a generous friend, but it's healthier to be ourselves, active artists acting on our own behalf. "You cannot transmit what you haven't got," 12-Step programs warn, and unless we make room for art, we resent making room for everything else. And some people—the gifted but needy student or colleague—always ask us to make too much room for them. And we cooperate!

Rather than speak our mind to someone else, we turn up the voice-over in our own head. This is that chiding voice that says

The world is made up of stories, not of atoms.

MURIEL RUKEYSER

"Now, now. Be nice. Be reasonable. Be whatever is convenient for everyone else."

Ours is a culture that tells us "bigger is always better" and that "more" is better too. As artists, big is not always better and more is sometimes less. As artists, when we overdiversify, we also grow diffused. The name we have worked so hard to make means less as it is stretched too thin—along with our energies—in the name of being a "good sport," a "good guy," a "mensch." As artists, we know all too well how a helping hand at a timely intersection can move us up the ladder. Is it any wonder that as we first feel the rush of success, we often rush to help too many others? Directors may overcommit to "executive-producing" to help younger directors. They become a creative umbrella for less developed talents and often fail to see when that umbrella is so big that it puts their own work into the shade. Committing to help others, we may undercommit to ourselves. Instead of investing our energies wisely in husbanding what we have gained and making a modest expansion, we "go for broke"—a telling phrase—and in the end we break our own hearts by being overtired, overextended, and bankrupt of our own creative energies. When we "energy-debt" to others, the worst debt we incur is to ourselves.

Without sufficient containment for our own temperaments to thrive, without physical and psychic walls to shield us from the demands and dramas of others, we become overstressed. Our nerves short-circuit and our ideas lash like live wires—we are filled with energy, but it's not grounded and usable. Our art suffers and so do we. When we begin to set boundaries—no calls after eleven, no calls before eight, no work on Saturdays, and no on-demand makeup lessons for missed classes—we begin to experience a sense of faith. Why? Because we feel safe. It is hard to have faith in the future when we have no charity for ourselves in the present. When we ourselves feel like the food source, it is hard to find food for thought.

Creativity is really the structuring of magic.

ANN KENT RUSH

We cannot chronically and repeatedly make up the shortfalls of our colleagues without exhausting ourselves and our resources. We cannot chronically and repeatedly allow others to spend our time and our energy foolishly without discovering eventually that we have been robbed of our creative lives—and given the burglars the keys. We cannot take on "difficult" people and situations to prove our heroism and realistically expect to be either heroic or triumphant in the long run. Saving the day too often means that at the end of the day we have nothing left for ourselves, our own lives, loves, and passions. What we have is a life squandered and not cherished, misspent and not invested.

When we insist on playing God by trying to be all-powerful and all-understanding and all-giving and all things to all people, God can work no miracles in our own lives, because we never allow the time or space to let a divine hand enter our affairs. While it is true the divine source is an inexhaustible flow, as humans we are finite. We do tire, and we tire most easily from tiresome people.

TASK:
Invest in Yourself Energetically

Sometimes, it takes a little sleuthing to actually see our self-destructive patterns. We are so enculturated to "not be selfish" that we may have difficulty setting aside the demands and expectations of others. Our own artist may be so concerned with helping to caretake other artists, we may find our stores of optimism depleted. When we reach for our inner resources, we find that our inner well has run dry, quite simply tapped too many times to help others.

Set aside a solid half hour's writing time. You are going to write—and receive—a letter from your artist's best friend suggesting that you make a few simple changes. The writer of your letter intends nothing but good and has been watching you and how you lead your life for a long time. There will be some simple suggestions—"Get more sleep"—and some complicated suggestions—"See less of Annie." Some of the ideas are going to be surprisingly do-able—"Take a life-drawing class"—and others will require some thought—"You need new friends." Allow your letter writer to say whatever is needed to bring you to reality in ways that you chronically sell yourself short. At the end of a half hour, read your letter carefully and place it in your God Jar. If you have carefully selected a "believing mirror," you may additionally wish to share the letter with that friend.

I am what is around me.

WALLACE STEVENS

CHECK-IN

1. **How many days this week did you do your Morning Pages?** If you skipped a day, why did you skip it? How was the experience of writing them for you? Are you experiencing more clarity? A wider range of emotions? A greater sense of detachment, purpose, and calm? Did anything surprise you? Is there a "repeating" issue asking to be dealt with?

2. **Did you do your Artist's Date this week?** Did you note an improved sense of well-being? What did you do and how did it feel? Remember, Artist's Dates can be difficult and you may need to coax yourself into taking them.

3. **Did you get out on your Weekly Walk?** How did that feel? What emotions or insights surfaced for you? Were you able to walk more than once? What did your walk do for your optimism and sense of perspective?

4. **Were there any other issues this week that felt significant to you in your self-discovery?** Describe them.

Discovering a
Sense of Boundaries

*Creativity requires vigilant self-nurturing.
The damaging impact of toxic inflow must
be countered and neutralized. This week's readings
and tasks focus on helping us to interact with the
world in ways that minimize negativity and
maximize productive stimulation.*

Containment

My favorite Tarot card is the Magician. I think of it as the artist's card. He stands alone, holding one arm aloft, summoning the power of the heavens. He has no audience. His power—and our own—lies in our connection, personal and private, to the divine. As artists, we may perform in public, we may publish or show in public, but we must invoke and rehearse and practice and incubate and first execute within a circle of safety and privacy—or else.

Or else what?

Making a piece of art requires two very different forms of intelligence—the largeness of vision to conceptualize a project and the precision and specificity to bring that project fully and carefully to focused form. Often a project will reveal itself in large swaths very rapidly—like a series of lightning strikes. An artist will see clearly and quickly the large thing she is going to build. Then, years may follow as she labors to bring in what it is she saw. During those years, focus can be lost or diffused by distracting and destructive influences.

When you are conceptualizing something large, sketching in the lineaments of a book or play, a picky and inappropriate question can derail your process, sometimes catastrophically. If you say, "I have started to write a new novel" and the person across the table asks, "What's your closer?" that can be a very destructive question. You may not know that yet—nor should you. Material needs time to evolve and find its own feet. As you live with a piece, writing it and "finding" it, it will tell you the answers to those questions—however, if you overplot a piece of work first, trying to dictate its shape, you can run into the same problem a parent might have deciding at a child's birth that he should be a mathematician, doctor, lawyer, or opera singer—the child may not agree. Given a long enough creative childhood—and enough privacy—your project will reveal itself eventually to you as its parent. But a protective parent we must learn to be.

As artists, we must be very careful to protect ourselves and our work from premature questions and assumptions. It is not appropriate to describe our work in a few short sentences, watching the look of interest turn into one of "I'll pass" on the listener's face. Talk uses creative power. Talk dilutes our feelings and passions. Not always, but usually. It is only talk with the right person and at the right time that is useful.

As artists, we must learn to practice containment. Our ideas are valuable. Sharing them with someone who is not discerning is like being talked out of a precious stone—you knew it was a diamond until someone tossed it aside. Most of us do not have the self-worth to yell, "Hey, that's the Hope diamond you just discussed!" But it might have been.

In order for persons or projects to grow, they require a safe container. Both a person and a project need a roof over their head. Both a person and a project need walls for privacy. Just as it is uncomfortable to have people enter your home when it is

An essential portion of any artist's labor is not creation so much as invocation.

LEWIS HYDE

in chaotic disarray ("Oh, my Lord! What is my red lace bra do-ing on the piano?!"), it creates embarrassment and discomfort to show a project too early to too many people. What's worse, it's risky. Projects are brainchildren. They deserve our protection.

As the world of commerce has overrun the world of art, artists in all fields are routinely asked to "pitch" their work, or "write up a quick proposal." Any seasoned editor will tell you that a book proposal seldom bears much resemblance to the fi-nal book. An honest editor or studio executive will tell you that a great pitch does not often deliver a great book or a great film. This is no mystery. The energy that belonged in making the book or film was wasted and diffused by the "selling" of an idea that wasn't yet in solid form.

Just as we wouldn't wake the baby so that the party guests could all coo and chortle and loom at her, we don't want to trot our projects out like performing seals. We all know the horror stories about toddlers who were told "Sing, darling!" Well, projects prematurely exposed to scrutiny tend also to develop a certain sullenness about growing up. We call our projects "brain-children," and that word can be instructive. Just as it is traumatic to talented youngsters to trot them out and demand they per-form for the dinner guests, with later psychotherapy and stage fright as a result, so, too, our projects can develop mysterious tics and phobias if they are prematurely auditioned and critiqued.

Writers' conferences are dark with the stories of books that miscarried by being read too soon and by the wrong eyes. "I showed an early draft to a friend who was a blocked writer. The comments were so negative, I never got the book back on track."

As a young writer, I, too, made the mistake of showing an early draft of a novel to a friend who wanted to write but wasn't writing. "Nothing happens in this novel," my friend com-plained, meaning no murder, no mayhem, no bloodcurdling drama of the kind she longed to write. The drama in my book was psychological—as I am sure was the writer's block that sent

Art is not a pastime but a priesthood.

JEAN COCTEAU

Always the wish that you may find patience enough in yourself to endure, and simplicity enough to believe; that you may acquire more and more confidence in that which is difficult, and in your solitude among others.

RAINER MARIA RILKE

the novel straight to a bottom desk drawer, where it lived out the rest of its days despite an encouraging note from the one other reader I had sent it to, a New York editor who liked it.

Before we became so modern, many marriages began with meeting a friend of a friend. People vouched for the person they felt you might find interesting. And people vouched for you. In the arts, we need to be alert to the need for such checks and balances. If someone says to you, as to me, "So-and-so could help you with your musical," then you'd better find out if they have ever had any actual success helping anyone with a musical, or if they are an "expert" with nothing to share but their largely unworkable theories.

As artists, we are open-minded but we need not be gullible. Many of the people purporting to be able to help us shape our craft have very little experience with crafting something themselves. What we are looking for is people who have done what we want to do—not someone who has watched others do it. It feels different to be in the cockpit at Cape Canaveral than it does to watch from the ground. A great writer like Tom Wolfe may be able to accurately convey the experience, or damn nearly, but many "experts" in your art may not have enough knowledge of creative liftoff to safely teach you how to withstand its rigors.

It is experience that teaches what a tremor means and what it does not. As artists, we must find people who can share actual experience rather than a sanitized, dramatized, glorified, or press-filtered version. When "help" is volunteered, we must be certain it is timely and actually helpful. We must ask ourselves always, "Am I opening myself or my art to early and improper input, input that is ungrounded or inappropriate?" Another way to put it is: "Do they really know more about what I am doing than I do?"

The sacred circle of privacy is like the seal on a bell jar. It keeps the contents fresh. It keeps germs from getting in. It's unpleasant to say friends can be germs—but they certainly can be.

They can "spoil" a batch of paintings or a perfectly good play by their few ill-considered or even malicious remarks.

Cooking images are very apt and very clear: "Too many cooks spoil the broth" being a homelier way of saying "Practice containment." Keep your creative ingredients your own.

You do not want people prematurely tasting your project and making worried little murmurs. You do not want their ingredients added before you have done what you want with the ingredients you yourself chose.

You may not have added your spice yet when they say "Terribly flat." Instead of catching on, *Oops, this applesauce needs cinnamon,* you may think, *Oh, dear, bad applesauce,* and toss the whole batch out.

One of the most useful creative laws I know is this: "The first rule of magic is containment."

All in all, the creative act is not performed by the artist alone; the spectator brings the work in contact with the external world.

Marcel Duchamp

TASK:
Practicing Containment

Most blocked creatives are blocked not by a lack of talent but by a lack of containment. Rather than practice discernment and discretion in whom we choose to show a project to, we throw open the doors and welcome comments from all corners. If we look closely at why we have abandoned certain projects and dreams, we can often find the offender—the ruthless commentator that caused us to lose heart.

TASK:
Rescue and Recall

Entire novels, movies, and musicals have been rescued, resuscitated, and restored through this simple reclamation tool. One best-selling nonfiction book owes its publication to this too. You might want to try it.

Take pen in hand and answer these questions as quickly as you can. That will give you the information with minimal pain; the information will give you back your power.

1. Have you ever spoiled a creative project by indiscriminate input too early?
2. What was the project?
3. What was the input?
4. What about that input especially confused or threw you?
5. How long did it take you to realize what had happened to you and your project?
6. Have you looked at the project again?
7. Can you commit to looking at the project again?
8. Choose a friend to whom you can commit that you will reexamine your project.
9. Reexamine your project. (Do this process as gently as you can.)
10. Call your friend and debrief your findings.

If you do not already own a God Jar, select or designate one now. A God Jar is a container for your sacred hopes and dreams. It might be a ginger jar, a cookie tin, a Chinese porcelain vase. My God Jar is Chinese porcelain and features two intertwining dragons, the symbols for creativity in Chinese lore. Into your God Jar should go the name and description of anything you are trying to incubate or protect. The play I am hatching goes into the God Jar—not into group discussion. The difficulty I am having in my rewrite also goes into the God Jar, as do my hopes for a successful resolution.

In addition to a physical God Jar, it also helps to select one person as a personal "believing mirror." A believing mirror is a carefully chosen individual who helps a project's growth by be-

A miracle is an event which creates faith. That is the purpose and nature of miracles.

GEORGE BERNARD SHAW

lieving in it even in embryonic stages. A believing mirror ideally practices a form of shared containment. The seed of an idea is protected and incubated by the warmth of their shared belief. Another way to think of a believing mirror is the old expression "secret sharer." It is a form of containment to select a trustworthy companion for our dreams and to confide their shape there only. Most of us need to talk to someone, sometime, about our creative aspirations. The right person to talk to is a believing mirror.

Inflow

Ours is a stimulating world—often an overstimulating one. We have cell phones, car phones, radios, televisions, and the constant barrage of media in all forms. Beyond this, we have our families, our friends, our jobs, and our other pursuits—all potential sources of stress and sensory overload. As our phones shrill, we, too, become shrill and rung out.

"I can't hear myself think," we sometimes say, and we are not lying about that. If "still waters run deep," the noisy rapids of our lives make it hard to be anything but shallow. Our deeper selves are muffled, overtaxed, and overextended. Our sensibilities are stripped of their fine tuning. We become numb to our own responses and reactions. Life is "too much" for many of us.

The act of making art requires sensitivity, and when we cultivate sufficient sensitivity for our art, we often find that the tumult of life takes a very high toll on our psyches. We become overwrought and overtired. Our energies are drained not by coping with our output of creative energy but from coping with the ceaseless inflow of distractions and distresses that bid for our time, attention, and emotional involvement. As artists, we are great listeners, and as the volume is pitched too high, our inner ear and our inner work suffers.

When a creative artist is fatigued, it is often from too much inflow, *not* too much outflow. When we are making something,

It always comes down to the same necessity; go deep enough and there is a bedrock of truth, however hard.

MAY SARTON

we are listening to an inner voice that has many things to tell us—if we will listen. It is hard to listen amid chatter. It is hard to listen amid chaos. It is hard to listen amid the static of ungrounded and demanding energy.

Contrary to mythology about us, artists are generous, often overly generous. We listen to others deeply, sometimes too deeply for our own good. We are susceptible to their hurt feelings and their pouting when we withdraw, and so sometimes we do listen to them even as our creative energy ebbs out of our own life and into theirs. This creates exhaustion, irritation, and, finally, <u>rage.</u>

It's not that we are unwilling to share our time and attention. It is that people must give us the courtesy of listening accurately to our needs about when and how we can do it. We may have huge energy stores, but they are *our* energy stores and we have the right to determine along what lines we want our energies to flow. For this reason, we may need to draw more boundaries than many people, and those who love us must be conscious that unless they can respect this, they are not a friend at all.

As artists, our inflow level must be kept manageable and we must "train" our friends and families and colleagues at work when and how we need our space, both physical and psychic. This may mean no calls in the morning before eleven. Or voice-mail calls returned every day after three. It may mean "Patience. No contact on demand."

For many artists, expressing is almost a matter of emptying themselves to let inspiration move through them. We do not want to be in our human personalities and concerns when we are in the midst of creating. This is why busy executives have secretaries—to monitor their inflow and keep it from becoming overwhelming to their creative process. As artists, we may need this same protective shield and have to erect it ourselves.

Virginia Woolf said all artists need a room of their own—I think that room may be at Starbucks, or in the basement, or in the bathroom, sitting on the floor. It may be the words "Not now."

And when is there time to remember, to sift, to weigh, to estimate, to total?

TILLIE OLSEN

An artist requires solitude and quiet—which is different from solemnity and isolation. Artists require respect for their thoughts and their process, but that respect must start with us. An artist needs to be treated well—but often we are the ones who must begin that treatment, and one way we do it is by carefully setting our own valve on how much inflow is allowed to come into us. When we are embedded in family life, or in a sea of students, this can be difficult. If our phone rings constantly, we can't hear ourselves think. When something "gets to us," that is often quite literal because it *gets* to us. We want to "be reasonable." We want to not "fly off the handle." But it can be too much to handle the building up of something yearning to be expressed (inner pressure) and the nudging to conform (outer pressure) to what a "normal" person might act like. Creativity is a process of birth. Labor pain is not a time for manners.

Labor is intense and it is intimate. The whole psyche is turned inward to cooperate with what is being born. Similarly, when I write a book, I am listening to what I must write. When I am writing music, I am following a melody line that I must hear in my head. That takes attention. Attention requires focus. If we have friends and colleagues who, when we don't take their calls, do not get that we're busy, that is a form of abuse to us as artists. "Are you working?" must be asked and answered truthfully. Why? Because when we create, we are psychically very open. We can be flooded by energies. Creative energy—and psychic energy—can flow in many directions. When our friends interrupt our creative time to ask us to problem-solve for them, they are often inadvertently squandering our creative energies. They are deflecting our creative energy into flow lines that will illuminate their work and their lives and not our own. When people simply call and download in great detail, our creative energy gets depleted by trying to solve their problems. "So, don't do it," you might say. Easier said than done.

Creative work is often invisible to other people. If they see you typing, they may know you're writing. If they hear the pi-

Living in process is being open to insight and encounter. Creativity is becoming intensively absorbed in the process and giving it form.

SUSAN SMITH

ano picking out a tune, they may realize music is afoot, but even the threat of interruption may strike them as bearable.

"This will take just a minute," they say without realizing that they are breaking the thread of your concentration and that finding the thread again may be very, very hard.

It is difficult enough to make a piece of art without the added burden of being available while you are doing it. For many very creative people it is hard to muster the self-worth to say "I will get back to you" or "I cannot talk now." As simple as such boundaries sound in the telling, you need only listen for a few minutes to the perceived "selfishness" of a creative parent to recognize that we have a culture where on-tap and on-demand attention are equated with love, and deferred gratification is equated with coldness.

"My father wrote first thing in the morning," the daughter of a famed creator recalls with scarcely banked fury. "Only afterward was he available to be a parent. . . ."

Perhaps, because much creative work is done in the home, the necessity of boundaries is more resented than, say, a banker father's work hours away from the house. Perhaps, too, there is a certain sibling rivalry as "brainchildren" are perceived as competition for parental or espousal attention.

A hardworking portrait artist whose commissioned work required long studio hours and great discipline to meet client deadlines like birthdays and Christmas ruefully recalled that "studio time was considered fair game. My friends would call from their office, unaware that they were, in effect, interrupting me at my office—and I had no secretary to deflect the calls."

For many of us, turning the phone off is an option we have never considered. TV and radio are also automatic—almost a form of civic duty. We "have to" be informed. Silence can be very threatening, but it is a threat worth trying in half-hour increments. Practice turning everything off—for one half hour— and tuning into yourself. A half hour is time enough for a bath,

Just a tender sense of my own inner process, that holds something of my connection with the divine.

PERCY BYSSHE SHELLEY

a letter, a bit of reading, a manicure, some meditation. It is just long enough to hear yourself think or catch a catnap. What you do with your half hour matters less than the fact that it is *yours*. Setting even such small boundaries is a huge step toward self-care—which leads to the self in self-expression.

TASK:
A Room of Your Own

For most of us, privacy takes a little planning. We love our friends, our family, and our art. In order to be alone together, "just the two of us," you and your art—you may need to sneak off like illicit lovers, or plan a weekend away like a married couple trying to keep the zing of romance in their relationship. Take pen in hand and list 10 ways and places you can have privacy with your art. For example:

Love the moment, and the energy of that moment will spread beyond all boundaries.

CORITA KENT

1. I could get up an hour early.
2. I could stay up an hour late.
3. I could take my artist to Starbucks for a writing date.
4. I could borrow the key to a friend's apartment and go do my art there.
5. I could take a sketchbook or notebook and go sit in the back of a church.
6. I could take a train ride.
7. I could find a quiet reading room at a library.
8. I could arrange with friends to hide out and house-sit while they're out of town.
9. I could go home to my family; it could drive me to the page, the easel, the sketchbook.
10. I could plan and execute a tiny vacation. Even a day and a half of solitude could reorder my thoughts and priorities.

Day Jobs

If we do not limit our inflow, we become swamped by the life demands of others. If we practice too much solitude, we risk being flooded by stagnation and a moody narcissism as our life and our art become emptied of all but the big question "How am I doing?" What we are after is a balance, enough containment and autonomy to make our art, enough involvement and immersion in community to have someone and something to make art for.

Raymond Chandler sold insurance. T. S. Eliot worked in a bank. Virginia Woolf ran a printing press with her husband, Leonard. What gives us the idea that people with "day jobs" can't be real artists? Very often our day jobs feed our consciousness. They bring us people and ideas, stories and subjects, opportunities as much as obstacles. A day job is not something to "outgrow." It is something to consider, especially if your art feels stale. You may have cannibalized your own creative stores and need to restore them with contact from new sources. As artists, we need life, or our art is lifeless.

Art thrives on life. Life feeds it, enriches it, enlarges it. Cloistering ourselves away from life in the name of being artists causes us to run the risk of producing art that is arid, artless, and, yes, heartless.

For most artists, there is something risky about too much unstructured time, too much freedom to make nothing but art. We talk about self-expression, but we must develop a self to express. A self is developed not only alone, but in community. Community functions like resistance in weight-training—the contact with others makes us stronger and more defined. Day jobs help not only to pay the rent but also to build stamina and structure. Artists need both stamina and structure. Often, a day job provides both. A novel can be a vast savannah in which I wander alone—a musical may mean six years sailing across uncharted seas. Navigators needed the stars to structure their voyages. We artists, too, need other points of reference to stay on course.

Chekhov advised young actors: "If you want to work on your art, work on yourself." He did not mean "Contemplate yourself." He meant we ought to do those things that develop in us creative sinew. A day job can do that. So can some committed community service. So can taking the time to practice the art of listening to something other than our own concerns. A day job requires that skill.

Although we might like to think of ourselves as more rarified, artists are people, and people *do* need people. And things. And hobbies. And, yes, fun. If you strip your life down to get serious about your art, you will find that you get serious, period. If all you think about is your Art with a capital A, then it's always there, twitching and heaving like a space alien having its death throes in the middle of your stark, serene, and artsy loft. You begin to wonder how you will ever lift that thing or even get it out of the house for a walk. Your serious career begins to become your serious problem, which you can talk about, seriously, to other "serious" artists and, perhaps, to an endlessly empathetic therapist who understands how sensitive you are. None of this will get much art done.

The concept "I am a serious full-time artist" can get a little dreary—like one of those oversized New York artist lofts does in a chill winter light. What do you fill a space like that, a concept like that, with? Lofts are supposed to be empty to be chic. And if you start emptying your life of normal human pursuits so it looks like a "serious" artist's life "should," pretty soon you've got the same problem as that drafty acre of chic industrial space: groovy, but do you really want to live there? Doesn't all that empty hipness make you want to visit your aunt Rachel's homey, overstuffed three rooms, where there is a lot of bric-a-brac and comforting clutter and food in the refrigerator?

In our cash-conscious culture, we have a mythology that says you must be a full-time artist to be a real artist. We hear this to

A clay pot sitting in the sun will always be a clay pot. It has to go though the white heat of the furnace to become porcelain.

MILDRED WITTE STOUVEN

mean "no day jobs." The actual truth is we are all full-time artists. Art is a matter of consciousness.

A friend of mine gets cranky when he is separated too long from his piano. He also gets cranky when he is closeted too long with his piano. Our love affair with our art is like any other love affair—it needs separation as much as it needs togetherness.

Our life is supposed to be our life and our art is supposed to be something we do *in* it and with it. Our life must be larger than our art. It must be the container that holds it.

Life is not linear. Our Artist's Way is a long and winding road, and we travel it best in the company of others, engaged not in the inner movie of the ego but in the outer-directed attention that fills the well with images and stocks the imagination with stories. Rather than yearning to be "full-time artists," we might aspire to being full-time humans. When we do, art is the overflow of a heart filled with life.

That day job may not be a millstone after all. It might be a life-support system.

It is the soul's duty to be loyal to its own desires. It must abandon itself to its master passion.

REBECCA WEST

TASK:
Commune with Your Community

We have a great deal of "artist-as-loner mythology." It is as false as our mythology regarding the American West. Cowboys didn't settle the West. Families did. Communities did. Similarly, art is made by artists who know and love other artists and other people. When we think about who and what we love, we get ideas about who and what we would love to make. When we think about what my aunt Bernice would enjoy seeing, we begin to see in a new way, more focused and particular. Modern life is restless. We often move from city to city and in moving we lose touch with parts of ourselves and whole communities. We encompass a great many "chosen losses," and to make it up to ourselves, we must also learn to encompass "chosen gains." Ritual and regularity are a part of how we commit to community.

Take pen in hand and answer the following questions:

1. A daily ritual I could take in community is _____ _____ .

2. A community paper I could read is _____ .

3. A community store I could support is _____ .

4. A community concern I could support is _____ _____ .

5. A community service I could volunteer is _____ _____ .

While you are upon earth, enjoy the good things that are here.

JOHN SELDEN

Sometimes our commitment is as small as a daily cup of coffee in the same coffee shop. Our community reading might be the local underground paper or a networking paper in our field, let us say *Back Stage* for actors or *The Village Voice Literary Supplement* for writers. We might buy our Christmas and birthday presents at the local independent children's bookstore. We might join a cleanup crew on "park day" or spend one hour a week reading to the elderly. None of these community commitments requires training, and they all offer us an anchor in the changing seas of life. All of us need a good dose of daily sweetness—the goodwill we put into life and the good cheer we draw from cherished familiar faces. Artists may need community and companionship more, not less, than other people. Our projects can take a long time to incubate, develop, and mature. In the meanwhile, we need a life and life needs us.

CHECK-IN

1. **How many days this week did you do your Morning Pages?** If you skipped a day, why did you skip it? How was

the experience of writing them for you? Are you experiencing more clarity? A wider range of emotions? A greater sense of detachment, purpose, and calm? Did anything surprise you? Is there a "repeating" issue asking to be dealt with?

2. **Did you do your Artist's Date this week?** Did you note an improved sense of well-being? What did you do and how did it feel? Remember, Artist's Dates can be difficult and you may need to coax yourself into taking them.

3. **Did you get out on your Weekly Walk?** How did that feel? What emotions or insights surfaced for you? Were you able to walk more than once? What did your walk do for your optimism and sense of perspective?

4. **Were there any other issues this week that felt significant to you in your self-discovery?** Describe them.

Discovering a Sense of Momentum

Creativity thrives on small, do-able actions.
This week dismantles procrastination as a major
creative block. The readings and tasks aim at a sense of
personal accountability and accomplishment. The key
to a creative life is sustained, consistent, positive
action. This is possible for all of us.

Easy Does It, but Do It: Flow

Most artists get blocked not because they have too few ideas but because they have too many. Our competing ideas create a sort of logjam—and that is why we feel stuck. When we think about a project, we think, *I could try this and this and this and maybe I could try this and this and this and, oh, I could try that and then and what if and oh, dear!*

When we get to the *Oh, dear!* the mental gears either clutch up and freeze, leaving them stuck and immobilized, or they start to whir frantically, like a bike pedal when the chain has slipped. Is it any wonder we get confused and frightened? Sometimes, our friends unintentionally panic us, even our closest friends. I remember a testy, difficult lunch with my beloved friend and frequent director, John Newland. I had just started work on a new musical—songs and concepts felt like they were being dumped down a chimney into the top of my head—a little like Santa Claus gone berserk and just pouring the presents willy-nilly from the rooftop. John innocently asked, "What's your act one closer?" I didn't know. I had so many ideas, I couldn't even read the menu much less plot the show's proper build.

"Don't ask me that!" I wailed. "I don't know!" I snapped.

"It's just *me*," John chided, "your old *friend*. Why are you so angry?"

I was angry because I was overwhelmed, I was overwhelmed because I had so many ideas about what I *could* do that I was panicked.

Whenever you feel stymied, stuck, or frantic, remind yourself, this is the result of having too many good ideas—even if it feels like you have no good ideas at all.

The trick is to establish a gentle flow, to keep that gentle flow trickling forward. This keeps the dammed-up ideas from bursting through and flooding you. It keeps the pressure from becoming so great, it clogs your mental system and shuts down your flow, leaving you even more tense, like an overfilled balloon.

Remember, creativity is not fickle, finite, or limited. There are always ideas. Good ideas. Workable ideas, brave and revolutionary ideas. Calm and serviceable ideas. The trick is to gently access them and allow them to flow. In other words, it's time for that 12-Step adage "Easy does it," because the truth is, easy *does* do it, and frantic, forced, and frenetic does not.

You must take some small step or the ideas will remain jammed up and the creative pressure behind the jam will continue to escalate. When it does, it will often manifest as attacks of self-doubt and self-loathing. "I am so stupid!" you might wail, when the actual problem is "I am so smart!"

What you are trying to do is move energy out of you. That is what starts the logjam gently moving. That is why you cannot achieve calm by listening to talk radio or watching TV—or listening to your friends' helpful suggestions for that matter. You want to quiet your mind by gently siphoning off its overflow, not adding to it.

The season is changeable, fitful, and maddening as I am myself these days that are cloaked with too many demands and engagements.

MAY SARTON

In our culture, we are trained to deal with anxiety by always putting more in. A drink, a shopping spree, a rendezvous with Häagen-Dazs—we tend to medicate our anxieties, not listen to them. The trick is to flow more out, not add more in.

This is where you can serve others and yourself. Instead of zoning out with the news, write your elderly uncle a letter. The operative word is "write." Do not call to talk. You do not want to tip the balance further by adding in more. You need to release thoughts. Think of a balloon that's too full. If you let air out, it zips ahead. If you blow more air in, things pop. When you feel tense and stuck, your life is like that too-taut, overfilled balloon. You are stretched too tight. This is why you cannot let in the well-meaning words of friends. This is why the chatter of a neighbor drives you suddenly so crazy. This is why you are a hair trigger. You are too full of creative energy and you need to gently siphon some off. Take a walk and remind yourself:

It is in the knowledge of the genuine conditions of our lives that we must draw our strength to live and our reasons for living.

SIMONE DE BEAUVOIR

1. I do have good ideas.
2. I have many good ideas.
3. Slowly and gently, one at a time, I can execute them.

People become addicted to talk therapy because it does temporarily siphon energy off. People become addicted to over-medicating because it wins them momentary relief from their too-full state. So does overexercising. What is needed is to make forward motion creatively. The truer the dream, the more creative pressure it has, and the more important it is to begin with small actions to keep them from getting frozen up. Don't just talk. *Do.* You need to express yourself in some concrete, small way.

If your head is awhirl and you "cannot think straight," then start by straightening something up. Fold your laundry. Sort your drawers. Go through your closet and hang things more neatly. Straighten your bed. Go get the lemon Pledge and dust and shine your bookcase and your dresser—often, when we are engaged in such small, homely tasks, a sense of being "at home" will steal over us. When we take the time to husband the details of our lives, we may encounter a sense of grace. In 12-Step slang, "God" has often been said to stand for "Good Orderly Direction." Often, in making a sense of order, we encounter a direction we can valuably express ourselves in.

A letter, a memo, a stack of valentine's cards. This will prime the pump. In my creative practice, I write daily. Every day. Three pages in the morning. Almost always some more writing follows later in the day. When I began writing music, I at first binged on it and wore myself out. Then I was afraid to start again, and pressure built up. When I learned that it, too, yielded to the "a little daily keeps it flowing" technique, I slowed way down, and my productivity speeded way up.

No matter how stupid and overwhelmed you may feel in the face of the complexities and terrors of change, the problem is not—not *ever*—that you are stupid. It is simply that your excellent mind is working overtime and so you need to calm it down. Instead of discounting your anxiety or labeling your anxiety, use it as creative fuel.

You need to claim the events of your life to make yourself yours. When you truly possess all you have been and done, which may take some time, you are fierce with reality.

FLONDA SCOTT MAXWELL

TASK:
Easy Does It, but Do Do It

A close friend of mine accuses me of practicing the Martha Stewart school of creativity. A man who lives with his wife and servants, he has all but forgotten the sense of well-being that comes from doing one small something to sort our world and our own place in it. Most of us have many small areas where we could benefit from a little housekeeping. Take pen in hand and list five areas that you could neaten up. Choose one area and execute a little cleanliness-is-next-to-godliness energy—does this experiment put you in touch with a greater sense of benevolence?

A few examples of possible chores:

1. Polish my shoes.
2. Clear the surface of my desk.
3. Straighten out my bookshelves.
4. Sort my receipts into good order.
5. Throw out old magazines.

What we are after with this task is the experience of using stuck energy in a productive way, however small. Once we realize that our sense of being stymied by the outer world can actually be altered by simple and small actions on our own part, we begin to have more faith in the benevolence of the universe itself. In other words, if God is in the details, we had better be there ourselves!

Breakthroughs

One of the difficulties with the creative life is that when we have creative breakthroughs, they may look and even be experienced as breakdowns. Our normal, ordinary way of seeing ourselves and the world suddenly goes on tilt, and as it does, a new way of seeing and looking at things comes toward us. Sometimes this "new vision" can seem almost hallucinogenic in its persuasive shifting of perspective. What seemed certain now seems uncertain. What seemed out of the question now seems possible, even probable. It is as though we have had a strobe light sweep across our experience and freeze into bas relief a certain previously unquestioned assumption.

Creativity is grounded not in dreamy vagueness but in piercing clarity. We "see" a piece of work and then we work to shape it. We "envision" a new direction and then we move toward it. The creative journey is characterized not by a muzzy and hazy retreat from reality but by the continual sorting and reordering and structuring of reality into new forms and new relationships.

Life ought to be a struggle of desire toward adventures whose nobility will fertilize the soul.

REBECCA WEST

As artists, we "see things differently." In part, this is because we are looking.

When we are willing to look—and willing to see what we see—we open ourselves to losing comfortable assumptions about the nature of "things." Those things may be creative—we paint a chair at skewed angles because that seems more "chair" to us suddenly—and this new viewing may apply to our human relationships as well. Suddenly and unexpectedly, we may apprehend them in a new and startling light. Sometimes such breakthroughs are frightening. When they are, we might call them "strobe-light clarity."

We might realize equally, "This relationship is going nowhere" or "My God, I am going to marry this man." Suddenly, our future has different casting than we imagined. We got a clear glimpse of ourselves solo or in an unexpected coupling. Such glimpses, a kind of "flash forward to your future," can be very disorienting. We "see" the shape of things to come, but that doesn't mean they are "there" yet. The bad relationship still needs to finish falling apart. The new relationship needs to finish coming together. We "know" what's going to happen, but we cannot force time to match our perceptions—and we ourselves actually need time to become grounded and able to handle the change we have foreseen.

When strobe-light clarity hits an area of our life or our work, we suddenly see the outlines of that arena with startling and heightened drama. "Why, I could paint this way!" we gasp, or "My God, she has no intention of ever standing on her own two feet. I am not helping her, I am enabling her!" When strobe-light clarity hits, it is harsh but distorted. We get a quick and terrifying glimpse of an unfamiliar truth that has the same disorienting effect as a strobe light flashed across the dance floor—everything jerks into new positions without our seeing the transitions. It can be tempting—in the flash of strobe-light clarity—to dismiss our former work or our former understanding as false. It is not false. It is simply outmoded. The way we

Courage—fear that has said its prayers.

DOROTHY BERNARD

used to paint was fine for then. And our friend may well have been authentically helped and is now only trying to create a wrong dependency. Strobe-light clarity is so sudden and so sharp that it is discontinuous. It is something we catch out of the corner of our eye: "What was that?!"

When we have such dramatic breakthroughs in our creative and personal reality, we must take care to integrate and absorb their meaning before acting on them. It is not that all of our prior understandings are inauthentic. It is more that they were incomplete. Our new insight offers a corrective to our prior understanding but it is a corrective that needs to be lived with a little before we act on it.

Strobe-light clarity is the creative equivalent of "This relationship is over." That may well be, but we do not need to move all of our belongings into the street. We can take a beat and assess our future options. When we decide, *I am bored with this art form as I have practiced it,* we are posing a question—"What next?"—that the universe is already in the process of answering. Creativity is always an interactive dance between our inner world and our outer world. Opportunity does not knock only as soon as we are willing to hear it. Arguably, it has been knocking for some time, and we have turned a deaf ear, a blind eye, to what our accepted consciousness had screened out and now is open to receiving.

Sudden breakthroughs *can* feel like breakdowns. It is helpful to think of them not as "breaking down" but as "breaking up." Think of your consciousness like a frozen river that breaks up in spring from a solid sheet to many floes. This is what is happening to your creative consciousness—what was solid is becoming fluid, new forms and new structures are becoming possible. New growth is afoot.

Instead of being unable "to see the forest for the trees," we suddenly see both the forest and the trees. *My God, I could include photographic snippets in my painting surfaces,* we think. We have shifted our mental furniture, repainted the old bureau a beau-

The great thing about getting older is that you don't lose all the other ages you've been.

MADELEINE L'ENGLE

tiful robin's-egg blue and given ourselves a whole new vista and venue.

The narrator should be first person and a male, we suddenly "know." And we "know," too, that it doesn't matter that we are female and writing this character. *Memoirs of a Geisha* is a brilliantly conceived and executed first-person narrative of an Oriental woman—written entirely by an Occidental man.

When we get a flash of strobe-light clarity, walls fall away. We see suddenly that we "can" do what we "couldn't" a moment before. We have a "flash" of invention and, like glimpsing the bright underfeathers of a bird, we suddenly realize our creative life is not colorless and lackluster, as we thought.

"I didn't realize what I was doing," we may gasp when we see that behind our own back and through our own hand, the Great Creator has orchestrated something new and original that we had no idea we were making. "Why, if I string all those heartbreak poems together, I have got the spine of a great performance piece. What a great idea!"

Strobe-light clarity is like a glimpse of yourself in a new and for-once-flattering mirror. It's like catching a glimpse of an attractive stranger and then going, "My God, I am that stylish woman." We look so different, so impossibly possible to ourselves that we are caught off guard. Our age falls away and we are abruptly young at heart, caught by the throat with the sudden emotion that says "This is real. . . ." We suddenly get just a glimmer of where we are heading and that new growth is possible, even impending at our advanced age—whatever it is.

Strobe-light clarity tells us this new growth will be terrifying. There is a "monster movie" drama to a sudden flash of insight. "Oh, dear God! What was that?!" we gasp. Seen so quickly and sharply, the most normal things can appear frightening. So it is with our new growth. The thought *I have got to go back to grad school* can be as scary as an ax murderer looming at us from the corner. As the light of reality grows around this sudden thought, the ax murderer begins to look more like a teacher and less like

Life was meant to be lived and curiosity must be kept alive. One must never, for whatever reason, turn his [sic] back on life.

ELEANOR ROOSEVELT

someone who is out to dismember our known reality. When you are in the grips of a sudden and startling flash of clarity, move slowly and gently with yourself so that you do not bolt in terror, tripping on the furniture of your consciousness.

Breakthroughs are not breakdowns. They just feel that way. Remember, you, too, are breakable. Be gentle with yourself while you grow accustomed to your new mental and emotional terrain.

We are not human beings trying to be spiritual. We are spiritual beings trying to be human.

JACQUELYN SMALL

TASK:
Geography

As a child, my favorite subject in school was geography. I loved the images of foreign cultures that startled my eyes—baskets and balls of rubber balanced atop heads; the plane dipping low over the head of the falls; hidden in the jungle highlands; the long, slender wands used by Egyptian healer priests to trace the body's energy meridians; the art and artifacts of other ages called across time and distance.

Begin by considering the following questions.

1. What culture other than your own speaks to you?
2. What age other than the one we're in resonates with your sensibilities?
3. What foreign cuisine feels like home to your palate?
4. What exotic smells give you a sense of expansion and well-being?
5. What spiritual tradition intrigues you beyond your own?
6. What music from another culture plucks your heartstrings?
7. In another age, what physical age do you see yourself being?
8. In another culture and time, what is your sex?
9. Do you enjoy period movies? Or movies, period?

10.   If you were to write a film, what age and time, what place and predicament, would you choose to explore?

Now, collect a large and colorful stash of magazines and, if possible, catalogues. Find a good photo of yourself and place it in the center of a large sheet of posterboard. Working rapidly, select images from your magazines and catalogues and use them to establish your leading character—you—in an imaginary world filled with beloved objects and interests.

Finish Something

As artists, we often complain about our inability to begin. *If only I had the nerve to start X*—a novel, a short story, the rewrite on our play, the photo series we're "thinking" of. I would like to suggest that you start somewhere else—start with finishing something.

There must be some obscure law of physics that revs into action when artists finish something. And that something can be reorganizing the medicine cabinet, cleaning out the glove compartment, or taping your cherished road maps back into usable companions. The moment we finish something, we get a sort of celestial pat—sometimes even a shove—a small booster rocket of energy to be applied elsewhere.

How can you begin your thesis if you can't finish your mending? How can you fill out your grad school applications if your shower curtain is stained and torn, half on and half off its rings, while the new curtain waits expectantly folded on the toilet tank?

Most of us have households and studios filled with half-done projects: sorting the photos of our portfolio, a project half in albums, half in shoe boxes; realphabetizing the business Rolodex—another project half done; organizing the consecutive drafts of your last play, yet another "when I get back to it"

My favorite thing is to go where I've never been.

DIANE ARBUS

agenda—the list goes on. No wonder we drag our feet at the thought of starting something else. We've had too many false starts, too many half-finished, halfhearted projects.

Christian, a young composer, had great enthusiasm and a great many projects. He was always racing ahead on some new musical theme, going full steam until something else caught his eye and that something became the focus of a new burst of energy. Christian was the kind of young artist often called "promising," but he was too fragmented to deliver on that promise.

"Clean up your arranging room," an older composer advised him. "Make systems. Put everything in order and give every scrap of work its proper place."

Although he felt that he was wasting time and energy that he could be using on writing music, Christian grudgingly complied. As he began to assemble three-ring binders and put all of the work on each project carefully into place, a curious thing happened: self-respect began to rear its noble head.

I certainly have done a lot of work, Christian caught himself thinking. He saw that several projects were very near completion and that he had been denying himself the satisfaction of a job well done. Predictably, he almost did the same avoidant behavior on organizing the room itself. He worked on it until it was two-thirds done and then he stopped.

"How's that arranging room coming?" his friend, the savvy older composer, asked him. Christian confessed that he had stopped before finishing his clean-up.

"It's much better," he said defensively. "I know where almost everything is and you wouldn't believe how much work I have done, really. I had no idea how many projects I had come so far on."

"Finish that room. Get every last bit of it in order. You are close to the reward but not there yet. Finish it and see what happens."

Grudgingly, working under half steam, almost laughing at how he lollygagged and dawdled, Christian finally finished the clean-up of his little room. There was a place for everything.

It is good to have an end to journey towards; but it is the journey that matters in the end.

Ursula K. Le Guin

Every project stood squarely in place, sorted and simple to see. Christian felt a buzz of new energy. It felt like optimism but a bit more focused than optimism. It took him a while to name this new emotional component, but when he did he saw it was something different from inspiration, something more solid and firm than hope.

"I felt determination," Christian recalls. Many things that had seemed vague and illusory now seemed squarely within his grasp. A project at a time, moving folder to folder, Christian began completing work. Within a month of arranging his arranging room, Christian had multiple projects in final form, able to be moved to the next step, submitted for grants and competitions.

"I suddenly showed something more than 'promise,'" Christian relates. "I had actual finished projects. I wasn't just 'talented' anymore. I was something much better—productive."

There seems to be an unwritten spiritual law that if we want our good to increase, we must focus on appreciating and husbanding the good that we already experience. This can be done by writing gratitude lists enumerating the many things in our current life that are fruitful and rewarding. On a concrete level, it can be done by the careful husbanding of what we have. This means that buttons get sewn on, hems get tacked up, smudges get scrubbed off doorjambs. We make the very best of exactly what we have and we find that almost behind our back the Great Creator redoubles and reinforces our efforts and makes something even better. This is where the old adage "God helps those who help themselves" can be tested and found to be true.

A body in motion remains in motion, and nowhere is this law more true than in creative endeavors. When we want to grease the creative wheels, we do very well to muster a little elbow grease elsewhere. Mend the trousers. Hang the curtains. I do not know why hemming the droopy pant leg gives you the juice to get to the easel, but it does. I cannot tell you what it is about detoxing the mud closet that makes you see more clearly how to end a short story—or start one—but it does.

Finishing almost anything—sorting your CD collection, pumping up a bike tire, matching and mating your socks— creates both order and an inner order: "Now, start something," finishing something says.

TASK:
Learning to Navigate the Learning Curve

This is an exercise in encouragement. Faced with doing something new, we often forget we have successfully done many "somethings" old. Take pen in hand and list 10 things you have learned to do despite your doubt they could be mastered.

For example:

In order to carry out great enterprises, one must live as if one will never have to die.

MARQUIS DE VAUVENARGUES

1. Spanikopita—I can actually make it and it's good.
2. Spanish—I can actually speak it well enough to communicate more than "How are you?"
3. The backstroke—I didn't drown, and now I like it.
4. How to change oil
5. How to operate my new computer
6. Calculus—another calculated risk I succeeded at
7. Ear training—yes, I *can* notate simple melodies more and more accurately.
8. Reading at open mic—I can speak into the microphone and hold my own most of the time.
9. I did learn how to work Photoshop on my computer.
10. I am able to give my dog heartworm pills without losing my hand.

Skills can be learned, and we can learn that the learning curve always involves excitement, discouragement, dismay, misery, and, eventually, mastery.

No one needs to know that you've shut the world out and are meditating as you stroll down the street. Twenty minutes to a half-hour every day is a good amount of time to restore a sense of serenity.

SARAH BAN BREATHNACH

CHECK-IN

1. **How many days this week did you do your Morning Pages?** If you skipped a day, why did you skip it? How was the experience of writing them for you? Are you experiencing more clarity? A wider range of emotions? A greater sense of detachment, purpose, and calm? Did anything surprise you? Is there a "repeating" issue asking to be dealt with?

2. **Did you do your Artist's Date this week?** Did you note an improved sense of well-being? What did you do and how did you feel? Remember, Artist's Dates can be difficult and you may need to coax yourself into taking them.

3. **Did you get out on your Weekly Walk?** How did that feel? What emotions or insights surfaced for you? Were you able to walk more than once? What did your walk do for your optimism and sense of perspective?

4. **Were there any other issues this week that felt significant to you in your self-discovery?** Describe them.

Discovering a Sense of Discernment

This week poses a challenge: Are we actually able to go the distance? To answer in the affirmative, we must learn to keep certain demons at bay, most notably success, "the unseen enemy." The readings and tasks of this week aim at naming and declawing the creative monsters that lurk at higher altitudes. Anger is a frequent companion of this week's explorations. As we unmask our villains, we often feel a sense of betrayal and grief. This is replaced by a sense of safety as we name our true supporters more accurately.

Making Art, Not "Making It"

In the study of overeating, it has been discovered that certain foods are "trigger foods"—the first bite leads to the craving for more, more, and more. For many artists, fame is a trigger food, or can be. When fame is sought for itself, we always will want more, more, and more. When it occurs as the by-product of our work—which it does and often will—then it is more easily metabolized. But we must stay focused on *what* we are doing, not *how*.

When we are in the midst of making something, in the actual creative act, we know we are who and what we are because we forget our public reception for a minute. We become the art itself instead of the artist who makes it. In the actual moment of making art, we are blessedly anonymous. Even when done in public, the act of making art is a private act. Creativity is always between us and our creative energy, us and the creative power working through us. When we are able to stay clearly and cleanly focused on that, then we are able to do very well.

We can always make art. What we cannot always do is make it in the venues we might choose or even in the field that we consider our rightful playing field. Actors who are not acting tend to forget that they can still learn a monologue, still try their hand at writing a one-person show, still try learning piano, watercolor, or clay. When we insist that we will express our creativity in only one field, or even in one corner of one field, we lose sight of two things: our versatility and our opportunity. We tend to isolate and to brood, resentful over not being appreciated, resentful over not being chosen when we can actually make choices of our own that put our creative power, if not our "career," squarely back in our own hands.

It is difficult to be depressed and in action at the same time. Actors forget that the key word is "act." Waiting to be chosen by an agent, waiting to be cast in a part, waiting to be well reviewed, they forget they can put on a show by reading at an open mic, recording monologues on a home video, throwing a benefit for their church group, going to old-age homes and performing. In a word, they can *act*.

Musicians can learn a new music, whether or not it can be seen as applicable to their particular métier. They can remember that the term is "play music," not "work at their career." Broadway melodies are enjoyable to play on the violin. The Beatles can be a welcome change from Bach. If we are really serious about our art, then we need to be serious about making it—not about being perceived as "a serious artist."

Self-respect lies in the writing and the playing, not in the reviews. Not even in the mental review of what has been done. Or how it was perceived in the public eye.

Creative minds have always been known to survive any kind of bad training.

ANNA FREUD

That phrase "the public eye" tells us the danger of focusing on "How am I doing?" instead of "What am I doing?" What exactly is the public eye? And why does it seem to always be closed or winking during our solos?

When making art becomes about making a career and making a profit—not that we don't enjoy those as benefits—then making our art is someone else's responsibility, not our own. We need a "lucky break," we say. We fall into talking about the way it is "in the business," and the odds against us, and the next thing that happens is that we feel powerless and depressed and mad—mad because we're not "making it" fast enough. And we don't mean art.

Clarence was a talented musician, so talented that "big things" had always been predicted for him. He played for "big names" on "big albums" and was always on the verge of his "big break." A chronic dissatisfaction that "it"—the really big break—hadn't happened yet kept Clarence from ever noticing and enjoying the many marvelous and exciting things that did happen. He had played with Bob Dylan and other idols of his. He had appeared on David Letterman's show and toured Europe with a red-hot band. His life looked glamorous from the outside but felt glamourless on the inside. He didn't play music for the joy of it. He played it to impress a producer or to rack up another Grammy nomination.

There has to be more to making art than this, Clarence caught himself thinking, and it was at this point that he saw the flyer calling for parents' help with the school music pageant. No one had contacted him directly. He was too big a fish for that. Looking at the little flyer, Clarence thought, *This might be fun. And the kids would be happy if I got involved.*

Clarence did get involved. Very involved. He had an extensive and expensive home studio where he could record tracks. The "little music pageant" began to have some very glossy and professional musical help. Next Clarence enlisted his wife—

We flood our minds with words! They mesmerize and manipulate us, masking the truth even when it's set down squarely in front of us. To discover the underlying reality, I've learned to listen only to the action.

JUDITH M. KNOWLTON

talented both as a costume designer and as a fine backup singer. Soon the entire house was filled with lively children's music and draped with brightly colored costumes.

"It's like Santa's workshop over here," Clarence told his friends, laughing. Laughter became a regular guest in the household as Clarence was relieved of his "serious focus" on his "serious career." Never before had the little school had such a sophisticated and happy production. There were even videotapes of the kids' star turns as they sang out to Clarence's professional music tracks.

"I think they got a lot out of it," Clarence said with satisfaction, "and I know I did."

Using his art artfully in the service of his family, community, and friends, Clarence reconnected to the joy that had made him an artist in the first place. He again came in contact with the generous part of himself that spilled out into music and self-expression. His art became about making something instead of about "making it." He now makes time every year for the children's music pageant. It gave him back the gift of giving by putting the "heart" back into his art.

Focused on success as a business goal, we often lose sight of success in terms of our personal spiritual well-being. We focus "out there" rather than on our own inner experience. Doing that, we can become lost.

"I always knew I was supposed to make good," says Joy. "Everyone was betting on me."

Joy had been a performer since childhood, when her parents first pushed her center stage. A talented actress with good comedic skills, she quickly got regularly cast in her small midwestern city, and when she made the "big move" out to Hollywood, she found regular casting there as well. She worked more than any of her friends and "really had very little to complain about" except for the fact that she just wasn't happy.

Entering a creativity recovery, she began writing Morning Pages and, as she did, began to wonder how much of her center-

Those who lose dreaming are lost.

AUSTRALIAN ABORIGINAL
PROVERB

stage personality was really her own idea. "You're a born actress," her mother had always told her—but was she? Acting got her a lot of attention but brought little satisfaction.

As her self-exploration progressed, Joy noticed she really loved writing. Writing was what her serious "brilliant" sister did for a living, and it had always been off limits for her. She was the family cut-up and "star." Telling herself she was "just exploring," Joy began to let herself write. As she did, she found that she felt more comfortable in her own skin, more at home with herself creatively. She continued to work as an actor, but her writing held more and more of her attention. After a solid bout of urging from her best friend, she tried her hand at a monologue. It flew from her pen. She tried another. Then another. Then another. Before six months had passed, she had enough monologues for a one-woman show and the same best friend volunteered to direct it.

"I was terrified, stepping forward as a writer," Joy recalls, but her friend printed flyers, found a good venue, and was convinced that Joy's actor was just the midwife to her real talent as a writer.

"I didn't give up my actress, but I stopped acting as though acting were all of me," Joy remembers. Her one-woman show was a modest hit. Her friend next suggested she try a one-act play.

"With friends like you, who needs an agent?" Joy complained, but she set pen to page, and page to stage soon followed. It is several years later now, and Joy enjoys her success as a "hot" young playwright. She enjoys the process of making her art and finds "making it" a happy coincidence, not her goal.

"Once I let go of my idea that making art was about making it, meaning fame, I began to make the art I wanted to make and that gave me something that looks an awful lot like the life I always wanted to have."

When we surrender to becoming what we are meant to be instead of trying to convince the world of who we think we are, we find our proper creative shoes and can walk in them com-

One of the marks of an intelligent person is to be able to distinguish what is worth doing and what isn't and to be able to set priorities.

ANNE WILSON SCHAEF

fortably. Not surprisingly, they sometimes take us far. Moving comfortably and at a less driven pace, we also enjoy the journey, finding pleasure in our companions and our "view" each step of the way.

TASK:
Make Something for Someone Else, Not to Be Somebody

They do not know that ideas come slowly, and that the more clear, tranquil and unstimulated you are, the slower the ideas come, but the better they are.

BRENDA UELAND

When we are focused on making a career in the arts, we often forget that our artful nature is a gift we can bring to the personal as well as the professional realm. We write for a living but do not take the time to write letters to our friends. We draw for a living but use our artistic skills only on paid commissions. Hobbies are out the window as "too frivolous," and as we focus seriously on our art, we become very serious indeed.

Take pen in hand, number from 1 to 5. List 5 people to whom you feel closely connected. Next to each name, devise one creative project you could undertake to show them your love and gratitude for their friendship. Select one project and execute it. For example:

1. My daughter—write out memories of raising her.
2. My sister—write out "artist" stories of her courage.
3. Carolina—draw her as a child and now as a friend.
4. Emma—make a photo album of our creative adventures.
5. Connie—make an "arts and crafts" recipe box for her.

We don't need to devote years, months, days, or even hours to a connection project, but it is often true that art made from the heart leads us to more and more art. As we free ourselves from our "get serious" mold, we often encounter new energies and new interests. When art becomes a part of our greater life, we often discover greater life in our art.

Velocity and Vulnerability

Any sudden change in velocity creates vulnerability for an artist. Two things come at us—opportunity and diversion or, more bluntly, useful things and opportunities to be used. When your life changes speed, it is often difficult to discern what is a genuine opportunity and what, on closer inspection, is an opportunity for someone else at your expense.

As our success and visibility as artists rise, so does the flow of two often difficult to distinguish things: opportunities and diversions. It is no coincidence that in Chinese the hexagram for "opportunity" and "crisis" are the same. As we become brighter and stronger as artists, others are attracted by that clarity and glow. Some of them will help us on our way, while others will try to help themselves, diverting our creative light to their own path. Those who actually offer us invitations and work in alignment with our true values and goals are opportunities to be cherished, and colleagues to bond with. Those who covertly present their own agendas in the disguise of a lucky break for us are opportunists, not opportunities. They represent a creative crisis in the making. They are what I call "piggybackers," and they must be identified and weeded out of our creative garden.

Piggybackers have a project they want to attach to your name, fame, reputation, and energy, and they seldom say "You could really help me," which would give you a chance to think about it on a clear level. Instead, they say, "I could really help you . . ." and they present their agenda cloaked in ways that make it look as though it could be compatible with your own. Maybe it is. Maybe it isn't.

When a piggybacker wants a share of your creative trough, he can be *very* persuasive. Flattery can flatten your will to resist. This is dangerous. Just as weeds and flowers can look a lot alike, a piggybacker can often successfully pose as something nicer.

Success can make you go one of two ways. It can make you a prima donna, or it can smooth the edges, take away the insecurities, let the nice things come out.

BARBARA WALTERS

It is distraction, not meditation, that becomes habitual; interruption, not continuity; spasmodic, not constant toil.

TILLIE OLSEN

Weeds are greedy, and choke out the garden by claiming too much territory. A piggybacker will do the same—and often, that is how you know them. Piggybackers often use flowery phrases: "I got this wonderful opportunity and I immediately thought of you, you're so wonderful, so gifted, so talented, so blah-blah-blah. . . ."

Piggybackers do not really care what your actual goal is. They care about harnessing your time, energy, and expertise to pursue goals of their own.

Piggybackers may have goals and agendas quite different from your own—although they are loath to reveal it. They may send you something fairly repellent to your values and yet insist you have huge swaths of common ground and that, therefore, you should endorse it. It is my experience that every time you are "generous" against your better judgment, you end up embarrassed.

Piggybackers like to offer you an opportunity and then, once you have signed on, try to run off with the project. Your "opportunity" gets trampled under their opportunism. In their race to win—and win big—artistic values get lost.

Arthur scored a substantial success with a best-selling book. For the first time in his adult life, he had money, recognition, and a seemingly assured future. Agents were eager to represent him, and publishing companies were eager to bid on his next project. Everyone was betting that Arthur would go on to bigger and better things—including Arthur himself. He had a winning personality and he was on a winning streak. It seemed nothing was beyond his reach—until he began to grab for all of it at once, telling himself that each opportunity was too good to pass up.

First, there was the infomercial. "It will sell who you already are and tell people who you are becoming." The filmmaker was persuasive and Arthur parted with 25,000 of his newly earned dollars, telling himself what the filmmaker told him, that it was "an investment in his future."

Next, there was the decision to join a prestigious think tank. All it took to "get in" was another $25,000. Most of the people involved had corporate sponsors, but since Arthur was really his own corporation . . . After listening to how much the prestigious credential would help him look more solid, Arthur was "in" again.

After a short while, it began to look like the line formed to the right. Everyone had a wonderful opportunity for Arthur to help himself and help them in the bargain. He really needed a high-powered and well-paid assistant. "They" really needed a better office than just a room in the house. "It"—the new big book—deserved a glossy, professionally designed proposal to "properly package" Arthur's good ideas. And, too, where was the Arthur Web site? Someone of his stature needed a "presence on the Web" to tell interested consumers who and what he was.

And what was that?

Arthur found himself overcommitted, overtired, overworked, and underpaid. His money and name underwrote a great many opportunities that simply didn't pan out in his real favor.

"I'd have done a lot better to buy nothing, bank my money, and wait for all of the furor around my 'fame' to die down." Instead, Arthur found himself struggling to meet his mortgage on his newly bought designer bachelor pad, meet the credit card payments on his newly acquired designer suits, and, as to getting any real writing done, he lacked the focus even to try. Ironically, his success had cost him everything that helped him make a success of himself in the first place—solitude, mulling time, the space and concentration necessary to forge some genuinely original thinking. Now Arthur fit the mold. He looked like many another Armani-clad huckster and he sounded the same— frantic and desperate to score.

As artistic visibility increases, so does artistic vulnerability. Velocity creates porosity—things and people whiz past our defenses and, if they breach our walls—"This will take only a minute"—they can create havoc. Their "minute" can take a

What I am actually saying is that we each need to let our intuition guide us, and then be willing to follow that guidance directly and fearlessly.

SHAKTI GAWAIN

*To have realized your dream
makes you feel lost.*

ORIANA FALLACI

great deal of time to detox from. It may cost us hours from our writing or our practice time. Like any other human being, we need time to metabolize our lives, our gains, and our losses. Blinded by our celebrity—we look like a shiny nickel to a lot of people—they can ignore our humanity. They attack our boundaries rather than understand them.

Three times in the last three decades I have unwisely involved myself with creative people and projects about whom I had reservations. In each case, the human flaw I had suspected resulted in a flawed project as well. Piggybackers are after the glory of the "win" more than the good of the project. In their rush for success they may rush a project and, like hothouse tomatoes forced to grow too fast, such projects emerge cardboard and tasteless—attractive enough looking but not succulent or nourishing—nowhere nearly as creatively tasty as the real thing.

A creative name and reputation has weight and width. If we lend our name and reputation to ventures of questionable merit, we lose both our credibility and our chances of continuing to gain ground ourselves.

No matter what level we make our art on—community theater to Broadway, small town open mic to major poetry venues—the question "Is this an opportunity or an opportunity to be used?" must be asked.

We all want to be generous. We all want to find colleagues. We all want to work. We must be alert to the caliber not only of our own work but of those whom we align ourselves with.

As an artist, some risks are worth taking and some risks are not. This is not snobbery. This is not exclusivity. This is discretion, discernment, and accountability to ourselves and our gifts.

The phrase "more trouble than it is worth" is something to ask about any venture. Some difficult and daring things are worth expenditure, worth the risk. Lesser projects and troublesome collaborators are creative quicksand—we get stuck and go down with them. As artists, we must learn to stick to our art and not sticky situations.

As artists, we are open in a way that differs from many people's, so we are very vulnerable at being caught off guard. Inspiration can be caught out of the corner of the eye and on the fly, and so can opportunity, but this openness to creative possibility can also make us open to creative exploitation. Caught off center and off guard, we might agree to help someone do something that takes us far from our own work and priorities. Anytime your career shifts gears into something faster, think of what happens when you are driving a car: The shift from fifty-five to sixty-five is often the difference between seeing and enjoying the scenery and whizzing past things, saying, "Was that a gas station I just passed or a convenience store? Did I miss the exit?"

As artists, we easily miss the exit or get off at the wrong interchange. If you have someone else deflecting your attention, it is even easier. Think of trying to read the turnpike signs at a complicated interchange when someone is chatting in your ear about things not of bearing to the matter at hand: "How do we get there?" As artists, the "there" we are trying to get to is the work we can respect ourselves for and hopefully be respected for. The fame and hoopla are diversions, and after an expensive one, if someone—say, your agent or manager—is constantly calling you with opportunities that may serve them but not you, you will lose your focus, stop seeing clearly, and miss your opportunity to take a route through your own career that you like.

Opportunity knocks with a Christmas-morning feeling. There is often, for me, a hushed sense of awe as an opportunity slides into place: "Oh, this is so neat!" Sometimes we go just a little numb, as in "Pinch me. Can this be real?" Opportunists, by contrast, have more of a pressured feeling of last-minute shopping, the kind of impulse buy where you know you shouldn't but you do.

The simplest way to put it may be this: Facts are sober. Re-

I don't want to get to the end of my life and find that I just lived the length of it. I want to have lived the width of it as well.

DIANE ACKERMAN

assurances are not. Facts are what we are after in sorting the difference between an opportunist and an opportunity. Facts are "Well, let's see, I've worked on five Broadway shows and three national tours." Hype is "I have lots of experience working with singers." ("Lots," like what?)

When we are embarrassed by our own lack of credentials, when we feel lucky to be getting any help at all with our dreams, we may forget that we have a right to prices and accountability. As we begin to ask about both, either our sense of ease or our sense of unease will continue to grow. Discernment is a combination of gut instinct and a little careful reportorial work. We don't want to be told "There, there, don't you worry." We want to be told "I've done this six times and I've got three good friends I could call if I get in trouble."

As artists, we must be alert not only to our lucky breaks but also to our unlucky choices. We must learn when and how—pull the plug on people and ventures that do not serve our authentic goals and aspirations. All too often, the "big chance" offered us by another may be a big chance to be used.

Since you are like no other being ever created since the beginning of time, you are incomparable.

BRENDA UELAND

TASK:
Slow Down and Feel Strong

Speed creates an illusion of invincibility. We hurry through our days numbing ourselves to the deeper flow of our lives. We feel shallow and push ourselves to live harder when what we need is to live more deeply and quietly. A potent mantra for calming down is to repeat to yourself the phrase "There are no emergencies." If there are no emergencies in your life, what situation could you allow to unfold more gently?

Take pen in hand. Number from 1 to 5. List 5 areas in your life where you feel a sense of haste and pressure. Ask yourself if your sense of urgency is misplaced. Often we simply have anxiety about something unfolding naturally. We want to force our own growth like hothouse plants rather than allow situations—and ourselves—to ripen.

Turn again to your list of 5 haste-makes-waste areas. Can you reset your time line in each area so that you live more gracefully with ambiguity? One of the most common slogans in 12-Step work is "Easy does it." Too often, we hear this phrase to mean "Oh, calm down." The phrase means much more than that. It is the distillate of a vast network of spiritual wisdom that has learned that "Easy does it" actually means "Easy accomplishes it."

No person, place, or situation benefits from our harried pushing forward. Everything and everyone benefits from our slowing down—letting go and letting God—so that a natural pace and progression can be discovered.

A phrase from the drug culture, "Speed kills," warns us of the danger of too much velocity. We are vulnerable and exquisite creatures, complex mechanisms intended to move at a human and humane pace. We elect that pace every time we slow down to gather—and feel—our strength.

It is the creative potential itself in human beings that is the image of God.

MARY DALY

Creative Saboteurs

Most environments have some undesirable elements—mosquito season in the hot, wet South. Winter chills diving far below zero in the cold, ice-locked winter in Minnesota. Even idyllic environments have their hostile elements and, as artists, we need to know and name the elements in our environment that are clear and present dangers of the trail. In the Southwest, where I live half of every year, I have learned to walk with an eye peeled for rattlesnakes and even the stray tarantula. As an artist, I must pay equal heed to the psychologically dangerous denizens of my environment. I call these characters "creative saboteurs," and the appearance of any of them—just like the sighting of a baby rattler on an evening's stroll—can focus our attention on survival and off the beauty of whatever it was we were making. A creative saboteur doesn't always rattle before it strikes, so we do need a measure of self-protective alertness.

Because all environments have some negative elements, it is a fantasy to think we can completely escape creative saboteurs. I have found it more useful to take the same approach I take toward the more dangerous high-desert dwellers—know them, name them, and avoid them. A creative saboteur is not a friendly animal, and no matter how innocent it may try to appear, its very presence means you must be alert to impeding damage to you and your dreams.

A playful name for a creative saboteur allows us to retain a sense of our own power. "Why, it's just a Wet Blanket Matador," we can say to ourselves when hit with the dampening impact of their uninvited and often ill-considered opinions and advice. The following is a typical exchange with a Wet Blanket Matador:

> ARTIST: *I'm so excited. I think I've finally cracked the top of act two.*
> WET BLANKET MATADOR: *Well, I'm sure it'll shift once you get it on its feet anyway. Structure really can't be determined solely by the playwright. It's also in the playing. Theater is a collaborative art, after all, blah-blah-blah. . . .*

This character will use an energetic wet blanket to deflect, dampen, and confuse your creative thrust.

As the artist/playwright, an exchange like this can dampen your enthusiasm. We are usually too well mannered to respond "Of course it's a collaborative art, but you have to have something to collaborate on, dim bulb."

Wet Blanket Matadors like to employ an air of sad superiority, as if they have seen you and your like come and go countless times before. Their tone is that of a worried camp counselor listening to an ill-advised twelve-year-old planning a picnic

Don't let them tame you!

ISADORA DUNCAN

amid grizzlies. Wet Blanket Matadors will typically tell you, "Oh, no! South!" the minute that you say, "I've decided to go north." Their contrariness is comic once you catch on to their ability to *never* co-sign your perceptions. Successfully identified, a Wet Blanket Matador becomes less a saboteur than an occasion for comic relief.

Now let's look at a related character: the Amateur Expert. Like the Wet Blanket Matador, this citizen dwells in negativity but bolsters his opinions with the company of facts and figures that may have no relevance whatsoever to the actual success of your progress. Long on theory, short on experience, an Amateur Expert can give you a million reasons why something *won't* work but no functional advice to help something work. Amateur Experts are trivia freaks—they resemble fan club presidents in that they know what shampoo Rita Hayworth preferred but are unable to recognize a Hayworth in the making.

Both the Wet Blanket Matador and the Amateur Expert bludgeon creatives by their presumed superiority. They just "know" they "know better" than we do. . . . This persona is intended to deflect such pointed questions as "Exactly what have *you* ever done anyway?"

The next destructive character knows worse and cannot wait to tell us. Like a malaria-bearing mosquito, the Bad-News Fairy delivers a sting and a lingering malady. Rather than speak from her personal negativity, she carries—and delivers—the negativity of others. This is a typical exchange:

> ARTIST: *I've just finished my new operetta and I'm pretty damn excited.*
>
> BAD-NEWS FAIRY: *Of course, you know that operetta funding has just been cut by a million percent and, as my close friend Nigel Nix told me just yesterday, operettas as an art form are really of no interest to anyone anymore, especially him and Percy Pursestrings, who controls all funding you might be interested in.*

Grace does not pressure— but offers.

JOHN BOWEN COBURN

*The thing that makes you
exceptional, if you are at all,
is inevitably that which must
also make you lonely.*

LORRAINE HANSBERRY

Notice that this saboteur always washes his hands. It's never *his* nasty little bacteria that are causing your creative cold. It's someone else's he just "happens" to pass on to you.

No roundup of creative saboteurs would be complete without mentioning that art snobs come in two primary colors: Very Important People and Very Serious People. VIPs like their clothes labeled and their art the same way. When they meet you, they want to check out your creative passport to make sure your skills have been stamped in all the right places. For them it's not that you can play the piano, but that you got into Juilliard. It's not that you can paint but that the Whitney owns one of your paintings. Forget that you're a writer, do you have an A-list agent or mere talent? These people are about who's who and not what's what. If you're Beethoven, you'd better be able to prove it. Contact with a VIP normally leaves an artist feeling very unimportant.

Now let's look at their close cousins, Very Serious People. The exchange here has to do with the notion that *you* are a mere artist, while *they* are a lover of *ART.* Your work, whatever it is, pales by comparison to the "great works" they ultimately know. To hear them tell it—and they will—art is a matter of life and death. And, of course, dead artists fare better than the living at "making the art" of *their* informed perceptions. Like oenophiles who horde vintage wines but won't drink it, the very serious art crowd can't be bothered with mere enjoyment and appreciation. What they "know" is "no."

As artists, we are often, far more often, more insecure than grandiose. We are stubborn as crabgrass, yes, but we are just as easily stepped on. Yes, we spring back—but sometimes only after years of discouragement. As we move our art into public venues, what we need is to find a few friends who encourage us by mirroring our competency—that, and the inner resolve to post a few signs that say "Keep off the grass."

Surviving a creative saboteur is like surviving a snakebite. It can be done and it makes a good story afterward. However, the first step—as with any snakebite—is to name and contain the poison. We cannot afford our own or anyone else's denial. We have been bitten. We have been poisoned. Damage has been done and the delicate and fine nerve endings of our art are badly hurt. Step one is to get away so that you are not bitten again. Do not stand stock-still in astonishment, poking the snake to see if it might want to bite again. Snakes bite. They bite once and they do bite again. If you think you have been bitten, assume you have been bitten and jump back. Don't listen to people who want you to "find the lesson" in your experience. There will be plenty of time for that afterward. For right now, put distance between you and the snake.

Do not engage with the people who want to talk with you about how rare this particular kind of poisonous snake is. Do not start to feel that the odds of your having been bitten make any difference in the fact that you have been bitten. Later on, after you have a few weeks' recuperation, you can enjoy lunch with someone who says, "Oh, he's always a viper and he bit me too," but such talk is for later, not right now.

First administer first aid. That means you acknowledge you have been bitten, don't pretend you have not, and reach for the antidote. The antidote is someone who supports you before, during, and after your creative injuries. This is a friend who doesn't say anything much besides "That's awful" and "What can I do to help?"

The answer to "What can I do to help?" is very straightforward: "Love me." That, and "Help me to forgive myself for having gotten fooled, hurt, bitten. Help me to let myself off the hook and not blame me for someone else's bad behavior. Help me to stop calling myself stupid. Tell me, accidents happen. There are snakes out here. Why, any one of us could have run into a nasty creature like you did."

It is spiritual law that if we cannot always avoid injury, we can always later turn it to good use. The silver lining of surviving snakebite is the compassion that it brings to bear both toward

Integrity is so perishable in the summer months of success.

VANESSA REDGRAVE

ourselves and later toward others. There will always be creative saboteurs. Their bite will always sting and, as we learn to identify them and avoid them, we can share our experience, strength, and hope with others: Creative saboteurs hurt us, but they can be survived.

TASK:
Perform an Exorcism

The beginning of compunction is the beginning of a new life.

GEORGE ELIOT

Creativity is a spiritual issue and that means we can invoke forces to cast out our demons. A spiritual-creativity injury is an excellent opportunity for a spiritual ritual of your own devising. Here are two of my favorites. They are both powerful and playful, a potent combination:

1. Exorcize a creative demon: Reflect on your injury and make a creativity monster embodying all the nasty elements of your tormentor. Making this monster is cathartic, but destroying it is more so. Burn it, bury it, abandon it in the wilderness twenty miles from your house, throw it over the gorge bridge, and send it downriver. Get rid of it. One student made a "word monster" using all the controlling rules of grammar and usage. She wrote more freely later.

2. Create a creativity totem: Make a being that embodies all the spiritual forces you would like to muster to your support. This can be a doll, a sculpture, a painted image, a piece of music, even a collage. Place it prominently and protectively in your environment. It is the act of making art that heals the broken creative heart.

CHECK-IN

1. **How many days this week did you do your Morning Pages?** If you skipped a day, why did you skip it? How was the experience of writing them for you? Are you experiencing more clarity? A wider range of emotions? A greater sense of detachment, purpose and calm? Did anything surprise you? Is there a "repeating" issue asking to be dealt with?

2. **Did you do your Artist's Date this week?** Did you note an improved sense of well-being? What did you do and how did you feel? Remember, Artist's Dates can be difficult and you may need to coax yourself into taking them.

3. **Did you get out on your Weekly Walk?** How did that feel? What emotions or insights surfaced for you? Were you able to walk more than once? What did your walk do for your optimism and sense of perspective?

4. **Were there any other issues this week that felt significant to you in your self-discovery?** Describe them.

In solitude we give passionate attention to our lives, to our memories, to the details around us.

VIRGINIA WOOLF

Discovering a Sense of Resiliency

This week dismantles the myth of
artist as superhero. No artist is immune
to negative emotions. The key to surviving such
emotions is accepting them as necessary, a known and
expectable part of the creative trail. The readings and
tasks of this week invite a sense of compassion for
the difficulties of our elected creative journey.
As the week focuses on the inner trials faced
by artists, it assures us that while the dark
night of the soul comes to all of us, by
accepting this we are able to
move through it.

Worry

It is valuable to think of creative artists as being like skittish race-horses, nervous until they are out the gate and actually running.

In my experience, no artist is ever immune to or beyond apprehension in many forms. Successful artists have learned to identify and deal successfully with these close-sibling emotions. It helps to make a few important distinctions, distill a few working definitions. Here they are:

Panic is an escalating sense of terror that can feel as if we are being flooded and immobilized by the glare of change. Panic is what you feel on the way to the altar or to the theater on opening night, or to the airport for a book tour. It is rooted in "I know where I want to go, but how am I going to get there?"

Worry has an anxious and unfocused quality. It skitters subject to subject, fixating first on one thing, then on another. Like a noisy vacuum cleaner, its chief function is to distract us from what we really are afraid of. Worry is a kind of emotional anteater poking into *all* corners for trouble.

Fear is not obsessive like worry and not escalating like panic. Fear is more reality based. It asks us to check something out. Unpleasant as it is, fear is our ally. Ignore it and the fear escalates. A sense of loneliness joins its clamor. At its root, fear is based in a sense of isolation. We feel like David facing Goliath with no help from his cronies and a concern that this time, his trusty slingshot might not work.

The more active—and even more negative—your imagination is, the more it is a sign of creative energy. Think of yourself as a racehorse—all that agitated animation as you prance from paddock to track bodes well for your ability to actually run.

In both my teaching and collaborative experience, I have often found that the most "fearful" and "neurotic" people are actually those with the best imaginations. They have simply channeled their imaginations down the routes of their cultural conditioning. The News at Five is never the good news, and so when they play the possible movie of their future they routinely screen the one with danger and dire outcomes. They do the same with creative projects.

Worry is the imagination's negative stepsister. Instead of making things, we make trouble. Culturally, we are trained to worry.

We are trained to prepare for any negative possibility. The news tutors us daily in the many possible catastrophes available to us all. Is it any wonder that our imaginations routinely turn to worry? We do not hear about the many old people who make it

I think these difficult times have helped me to understand better than before how infinitely rich and beautiful life is in every way and that so many things that one goes around worrying about are of no importance whatsoever.

ISAK DINESEN

safely home; we hear of the grandmother who did not. On the brink of opening a play, we therefore expect critical snipers, not raves. One reason Morning Pages work so well for artists is that they give a way to siphon off worry at the very beginning of our creative day. Similarly, the spot-check inventory of blasting through our blocks by the naming, claiming, and dumping of any worries, angers, and fears related to a project can also get an artist out the starting gate effectively.

Fears for our own safety and the safety of others, the sudden suspicion of brain tumors and neurological disorders, the "real-ization" that we are going blind or deaf, any and all of these worrisome symptoms indicate we are on the brink of a large creative *breakthrough,* not breakdown, although the resemblance between the two can feel striking.

Poised to shoot a feature film, I found myself abruptly plagued by the "conviction" that a sniper was about to shoot me in the eye. Where this phobia came from, I don't know, but it plagued me on the city streets. That it arrived on the brink of my shooting a film, I consider no coincidence. Also, noncoinci-dentally, once the camera was running, my sniper ran away.

Authors leave on book tours, huffing on their inhalers. Film-makers populate the ER, suddenly beset by hives. Pianists know the terror of imminent arthritic crippling. Dancers develop club feet, stubbing their "en pointe" toes walking to the bathroom. We survive these maladies and the success that they presage more easily if we remember not to worry about worry.

After thirty-five years in the arts and twenty-five years of teaching creative unblocking, I sometimes think of myself as a creative dowsing rod. I will meet someone and my radar will start to twitch. Creative energy is clear and palpable energy, dis-guised perhaps as neurosis or fretfulness, but real and usable en-ergy nonetheless. I feel a little like a tracker—the bent twig of someone's undue anxiety tells me that person has an active imagination that needs to be focused and channeled and that when it is we will have quite a flowering.

Any disaster you can survive is an improvement in your character, your stature, and your life. What a privilege!

JOSEPH CAMPBELL

One of my daughter's high school friends was a hyperactive teenager with bright, avid eyes and a restless energy that jogged him foot to foot as he exclaimed, "Look at that! Look at that!" his attention darting here, then there. Nothing escaped his worried attention. He literally looked for trouble.

That boy needs a camera, I thought, and gave him one for his high school graduation present. It's ten years later and he's a filmmaker. No surprise to me. His worrisome intensity lacked only the right channel.

When we focus our imaginations to inhabit the positive, the same creative energy that was worry can become something else. I have written poems, songs, entire plays with "anxiety." When worry strikes, remind yourself your gift for worry and negativity is merely a sure sign of your considerable creative powers. It is the proof of the creative potential you have for making your life better, not worse.

As performers, we *must* learn, and the rest of us *can* learn: We can learn to throw the switch that channels our energy out of worry and into invention. If we are to expand our lives, we must be open to positive possibilities and outcomes as well as negative ones. By learning to embrace our worried energy, we are able to translate it from fear into fuel. "Just use it, just use it," an accomplished actress chants to herself when the worried willies strike. This is a learned process.

In my experience, artists never completely outgrow worry. We simply become more adroit at recognizing it as misplaced creative energy.

I have sat in the back of movie theaters with accomplished directors who suffered attacks of asthma and nausea as their movies were screened for preview audiences. As a playwright, I have watched in horror as my leading lady stood heaving like a carthorse, hyperventilating in the wings before stepping onstage to perform brilliantly.

It is palpable nonsense to believe that "real artists" are somehow beyond fear, and yet that is the version of "real artists" so

Ideas have come from the strangest places.

JOYCE CAROL OATES

often sold to us by the press. We learn of an artist's nerviness—"Steven acquired his first camera at age seven"—but we seldom hear of an artist's nerves. It is for this reason that I like to tell the stories I was privy to in my twenties, when I was married to young Martin Scorsese, who was friends with young Steven Spielberg, George Lucas, Brian DePalma, and Francis Ford Coppola. From my privileged position as wife and insider, I witnessed fits of nerves and bouts of insecurity suffered through with the help of friends. Because all of the men in our intimate circle matured into very famous artists, these stories are quite valuable—not because they drop names but because they drop information. They tell us in no uncertain terms that great artists suffer great fears like the rest of us. They do not make art without fear but despite fear. They are not worry free but they are free to both worry and create. They are not superhuman and we need not expect ourselves to be so either. We need not disqualify ourselves from trying to make art by saying "Since it's so terrifying for me, I must not be supposed to do it."

Let me say it again: Some of the most terrified people I ever met are some of the greatest American artists. They have achieved their careers by walking through their fears, not by running away from them. The very active imaginations that led them into jittery terrors are the same imaginations that have allowed them to thrill us, enthrall us, and enchant us. Your own worries may similarly be the pilot fish that accompany your great talent. They are certainly no reason not to swim deeper into the waters of your own creative consciousness.

The really great writers are people like Emily Brontë who sit in a room and write out of their limited experience and unlimited imagination.

JAMES A. MICHENER

TASK:
Let the "Reel" Be an Ideal

Our imagination is skilled at inhabiting the negative. We must train it to inhabit the positive. On the brink of a creative breakthrough, we often rehearse our bad reviews—or, at least, our bad day. We imagine how foolish we will look ever to have hoped to have our dreams. We are adroit at picturing our creative downfalls.

Fortunately, success sometimes comes to us whether we can imagine it or not. Still, it comes to us more easily and stays more comfortably if it feels like a welcome guest, something looked forward to with anticipation, not apprehension. This tool is an exercise in optimism, and that word "exercise" is well chosen. Some of us may have to strain to constructively imagine our ideal day. But let's try it.

Take pen in hand. Set aside at least one half hour for writing freely. Imagine yourself at the beginning of your ideal day, a day in which all of your dreams have come true and you are living smack in the middle of your own glorious accomplishments. How does it feel? How good can you imagine feeling? Moment by moment, hour by hour, happening by happening, and person by person, give yourself the pleasure in your own mind's eye of the precise day you would like to have. For example:

"I wake up early, just as a beautiful morning light spills into the room and focuses on the wall where I have hung the covers of my best original cast albums for my Broadway shows. My bedroom has a fireplace and my row of Oscars and Tony awards balance happily on the mantel. I slip from bed so as not to wake my beloved, who is happily still asleep. It is a big day, day one of rehearsals for a new show. Casting has gone well. The director is superb. Everyone is eager and excited to be at work, and so am I. I have worked with many of these people before. We have a loyal, constructive, and brilliantly talented core group of talent that was working in what they call "Broadway reborn," as the melodic songs of our work echo the best of Rodgers and Hammerstein. . . ."

Let your imagination be a real "ham." Spare no expense and consider nothing too frivolous. Do you have telegrams of congratulations wreathing your makeup mirror? Did somebody send you two dozen roses, and a dozen fresh bagels for breakfast?

One word frees us of all the weight and pain of life: That word is love.

SOPHOCLES

When the phone rings with great news, who is calling to say "That's great!" Is it your favorite sister or the president? This is your day and you have it exactly as you want.

Allow yourself to inhabit your absolute ideal from morning until nightfall. Include your family and friends, your pets, time for a nap or high tea. Enjoy scones and excellent reviews. Accept a lucrative and prestigious film deal. Make arrangements to tithe a percentage of your megaprofits to charity. Stretch your mind and your emotional boundaries to encompass the very best day you can imagine and allow yourself a sense of peace, calm, and self-respect for a job well done.

There's only one corner of the universe you can be certain of improving and that's your own self.

ALDOUS HUXLEY

Fear

If you'll pardon the levity, most of us are afraid of fear. We think it's a bad thing. We *know* it's a scary thing. We're afraid of becoming afraid, scared of becoming scared. We know all too well how our fears can escalate into terror, and how our terror can either translate into frantic action or into paralyzing inertia. Because so many of our experiences with fear have been negative, we fail to see fear as positive or useful. It is both. Let me repeat: Fear is positive and useful. Fear says things like "I'm afraid that second movement is boring, and you might want to look at shifting a little of the harmony" or "I'm afraid my characters talk too much at the top of act two without the stakes being clear" or "I'm afraid there's something wrong with the bridge on my viola and I need to get it checked" or "I'm afraid I've overdosed on vermilion in this series and need my eye to fall in love with something else."

Fear is a blip on the radar screen of our consciousness. Fear tells us "Check this out." It is something we catch out of the corner of our eye. It enters our thoughts the way a dark shadow looms across a doorway. "Is someone there?" we may gasp. Yes, someone is there. Often it is a perception spoken by a part of

I did not wish to take a cabin passage, but rather to go before the mast and on the deck of the world, for there I could best see the moonlight amid the mountains. I do not wish to go below now.

HENRY DAVID THOREAU

ourselves that we have neglected and failed to attend. The punctilious part of ourselves may be correctly afraid that we *should* have written out the bass parts fully and not done the shorthand of "everything in treble clef, it's okay." It's *not* okay with the part of ourselves that believes, like the Boy Scouts, in being prepared. "I'm afraid I won't look professional enough," this fearful part insists. And it could be right. Fear asks that we check something for clarity. Fear requires action, not assurance.

As creative beings, we are intricate mechanisms. We have fine-tuned sensing mechanisms that extend beyond the ordinary realm of five senses. Sometimes we feel something large and good is about to happen. We wake up with a sense of anticipation and openness—spiritual attitudes we cultivate through Morning Pages and Artist's Dates. At other times, that very same openness brings to us a sense of foreboding. If we have bought into the currently popular spiritual position that fear is somehow "bad" or even "unspiritual," we will try to dismiss our fear without exploring its message.

"Don't feel that way," we will tell our fearful selves. "What's wrong with you?" By focusing on ourselves as the probable source of anything "wrong," we blind ourselves to the possibility that there might, in fact, be someone or something wrong in our environment.

Edward, a playwright, was committed to a large production of his newest and best play. The producer was all smiles and good vibes, all sunny promises and projections—yet Edward kept fighting a pit-of-the-stomach sense of apprehension in the man's presence.

"Stop it, Edward. What is this? Do you have some neurotic fear of success?" Edward's self-attacks were merciless as his fears continued to mount. "I am afraid this producer is too good to be true," Edward's instincts told him—in the form of bouts of insomnia and a few telling dreams about children's games in which the producer refused to play by the rules. As the dates for preproduction moved closer, Edward felt his fears rising further.

"It's all handled," the producer assured him, but Edward could not be assured. Beating himself up for "groundless fears," Edward finally picked up the phone and asked a few people a few questions. He learned that his producer wasn't producing anything. The venue was not locked down. Ads had not been placed. Deal memos for refreshments and concessions had not been finalized.

"I am so glad you called," a few people told Edward, "I need to be able to plan my schedule and, without a firm commitment on your side, I can't really do it."

Edward's producer was not productive. Edward's fears were not groundless, but well founded. The exploratory actions that Edward took—finally—on his own behalf taught him that he was traveling in company he could not afford. A few more phone calls and Edward learned that his producer's actions and attitudes had left a trail of burned bridges. Edward could not afford to have his name linked with a bad apple. He was involved with an opportunist, not an opportunity. Reluctantly but appropriately, Edward pulled the plug and disassociated himself from his troublemaking friend.

"I am so relieved you did that," a friend phoned to say.

"I didn't know how to tell you," another caller said.

"I hear you might be looking for a new producer and I would love to work with you," a third caller proposed.

Edward and his new producer worked rapidly and effectively. Edward experienced none of the mysterious fears and misgivings he had previously. His fear had truly been a messenger, and the message had been "Edward, you can do better and treat yourself better. You are right, here, to fear the worst."

When fear enters our lives, it is like a mouse scurrying across the floor of our creative consciousness. *Did I actually see something there, or was it a trick of the light?* we wonder. We get still and listen. Do we hear a faint rustling? Is that a tap of a twig on the window? A genuine problem of the arc of act two—or is it . . . there it is again. This time we turn on the overhead light. We

Every man feels instinctively that all the beautiful sentiments in the world weigh less than a single lovely action.

JAMES RUSSELL LOWELL

gently move the furniture away from the wall. Striving to still our hammering heart, we focus the flashlight of our consciousness into the dark and neglected corners, where we see, "Oh. I *do* have a mouse." Or "I have a dust ball the size of a healthy rat. I need to vacuum in here." In short, respected as a messenger, fear asks us to take a more accurate reading of our true perceptions to listen to *all* parts of our consciousness with care. As a rule of thumb, fear is *never* groundless. There is almost always some grounding action we can take in response to our fears.

How many cares one loses when one decides not to be something but to be someone.

COCO CHANEL

Often we are so quick to label our fears neurotic or ill based or paranoid that we do not ask what signal our fear is really sending.

When you feel afraid, tell yourself, "This is good, not bad. This is heightened energy available for productive use. This is *not* something to medicate—or meditate—away. This is something to accept and explore." Ask yourself:

1. What signal is my fear sending me?
2. What affectionate name can I give to this messenger part of myself?
3. What grounded action can I take to respond to this fear?

Many fears are based on a simple lack of accurate information. Rather than take a small exploratory action in a needed direction—say, finding a new voice teacher or signing up for a computer class—we allow our fears to be the bogeyman who keep us from entering the gates to our dreams. "I'm afraid my voice may not be strong enough" translates into "Strengthen your voice." Each of us has fears that are particular to our own needs. When we listen to our fears with tenderness and care, when we accept them as messengers rather than as terrorists, we can begin to understand and respond to the unmet need that sends them forward. When we employ humor and tenderness to our fearful selves, they will often stop shaking long enough to deliver a needed message.

TASK:
Admit Your Fears and Open the Door to Help

Very often the most damaging aspect of our fears is the sense of isolation and secrecy that they breed in us. We are afraid and we are afraid to admit we are afraid. Closeted alone with our fears, we forget that we are never alone, that we are accompanied at all times by a benevolent higher power who has sympathy and solutions for our problems.

Take pen in hand. The tool you are now asked to learn is extremely powerful and positive. It can be used in all times of emotional duress and it can be applied to any and all problems, personal or professional. This tool is affirmative prayer, and it works by singling out each negative situation and "claiming" divine attention and intervention upon our behalf. Let us say the problem is fear-born procrastination on entering a creative project. The prayer might go something like this:

"I am guided carefully and expertly exactly on how to begin work on my new project. I am shown carefully and clearly each step to take. I am supported fully and happily in taking each step into fruitful work on this new project. I intuitively and accurately know exactly how to begin and what to do to begin correctly."

In writing out affirmative prayers, it is important that we do not ask for help, we affirm that we are receiving it. Affirmative prayer is not a prayer of petition. It is a prayer of recognition and acceptance of the divine help that is at hand. Very often the action of writing an affirmative prayer clears away fear from our lens of perception. We suddenly see that we *are* guided, that divine mind is answering our request for help and support. We often intuitively know the right action to take and feel within ourselves the power to take that action. Fear becomes a cue for prayer and a deepened sense of our spiritual creative companionship.

Once you have written out your affirmative prayer, choose

Lord I disbelieve——help thou my unbelief.

E. M. FORSTER

the most personally powerful and resonant phrase in it to use as a mantra while you walk. Perhaps you wrote "My fearful self is clearly guided." You can distill that still further to "I am clearly guided," and you can walk with that reassuring thought until it begins to take on emotional weight.

Restlessness

Nothing is so perfectly amusing as a total change of ideas.

LAURENCE STERNE

For an artist, a bout with restlessness is best met with curiosity—not with the conclusion that your true cranky character is surging to the fore. Irritability is the flag waved by restlessness. Restlessness means you are on the march creatively. The problem is, you may not know where.

Restlessness is full of switchbacks, like a mountain trail. We feel one thing. Then another. We reverse ourselves. *I am full of energy and I have no energy,* we think. *I have no energy and I am full of energy,* we reverse the thought. We are a country of contradictions. North looks good and then south. Nothing feels right. Everything feels wrong. Nothing is right, but then, nothing is really wrong either. We are out of sorts. Under the weather—but the weather is fine except for our own emotional weather, which is stormy. We are volatile and changeable. Of course we are, we are restless. We cannot depend on ourselves to set a course—fortunately, we don't have to.

"Inspiration enters through the window of irrelevance," artist M. C. Richards has observed—many artists will tell you the same thing. It is as though the making of certain pieces of art on certain themes lie in our destiny, just below our conscious mind, where we feel that we are choosing. How our life and work will unfold. One clue at a time. A happenstance at a time, destiny and our destined work reveals itself to us. One day, often quite abruptly, clarity comes and we say, "Ah-hah! That's why . . ."

If you talk to enough artists, you will learn that lucky breaks and chance meetings are run-of-the-mill elements, stock characters that show up when our restlessness reaches unbearable levels. It is as though our restlessness calls to the very heavens for "something" to happen. And something—or many somethings—does. This is why, as uncomfortable as it is, as unpleasant, even unbearable—restlessness is a good omen. If you visit the reptile house at the zoo as a storm is coming on, you will see the creatures slithering in agitated anticipation. They know a change is on the way. Being alert to the possibility of change opens our ears and eyes to receive psychic signals more often and more quickly. Irritated, restless, ready for change, we snap, "Goddammit! What is it?" when destiny knocks. But destiny does knock, and it can be colorful and expansive if we will allow it to be. When we are restless and our lives feel colorless, it is a clue and a cue that they are about to become colorful—if we cooperate. Prayers, and especially creative prayers, are answered, but answered in ways we may not anticipate or appreciate. Again, this is why artists speak that spiritual-sounding word—inspiration. That is not some gauzy bromide, it is our actual experience. As artists, we *are* irrationally, intuitively, and insistently inspired. Sir Arthur Sullivan attended a traveling exhibition of Japanese art and returned home to write *The Mikado*.

About ten years ago I was living in Manhattan and I underwent an intense and nasty bout of cabin fever. I blamed it on the city. "This damn island," I groused, "it's like a giant cruise ship going through choppy seas with all of us shut up in our tiny cabins. I hate it. I want out. Out somewhere!" I started walking a lot.

Walking near the Morgan Library on Madison Avenue, I noticed a small corner bookshop with a neatly lettered sign, THE COMPLETE TRAVELLER. On "impulse," I opened the door. *This is stupid, Julia,* my rational side flicked on the voice-over. *Your commitments are going to keep you right here, so this is just an excursion in idiotic fantasy.* That's when I noticed the shelf full of old and battered books about explorers. I pulled one down. The thick,

Make friends with the angels, who though invisible are always with you. . . . Often invoke them, constantly praise them, and make good use of their help and assistance in all your temporal and spiritual affairs.

ST. FRANCIS DE SALES

creamy pages were dusty with age. They stuck together a little, even gave off a faint powder to the touch. Thinking, what the hell! I bought it—my father had loved boats and the sea.

Several months later, out on book tour, I was perched in Los Angeles on a cliff overlooking the Pacific, staring vaguely out the window toward—Australia? Hawaii? Somewhere. Suddenly, I remembered the book, tucked in my suitcase on another whim. Looking out the window at the vast flat sea, a few palm fronds dancing in and out of my sight line, I opened the book. That book opened an inner door. Suddenly, I heard music—a lot of music, wave on wave stepping ashore complete with lyrics. I grabbed a notebook and a pen, I grabbed my tiny toy keyboard, another traveling afterthought, and began notating what I heard.

My hotel, the old Art Deco "musicians" hotel, the Shangri-la, was a scant block or two from a mall where I found an electronics store and I bought a cheap tape recorder. The music was spilling through so fast, I needed to catch it on tape lest I miss some of it on the page. I heard soprano arias, booming bass parts, a large chorale—and I think I heard it all because in a fit of pique and irritability I went into a small travel store. That store was like Alice's doorway into Wonderland. An entire musical awaited my entry.

This story may not convince you that anything magic was afoot. You may not want to picture some invisible being giving me a quick shove—I don't blame you. And yet, it is my experience that when we are willing to be irrational and intuitive— even when we despise those words—we are rewarded by promptings, callings, that come to us from some mysterious and deft sources that guide and encourage us toward what might best be called destiny.

"I don't see why I should stick my head in this antiques store," we can catch ourselves grousing. And yet, opening an old photo album, some inner leaf turns within us and the notion for a novella rears its head.

When we insist on routine, when we insist on linearity, destiny will still knock, but it may have to work harder to get our attention. In my experience, destiny is willing to work very hard indeed—we are the ones who turn a blind eye, a deaf ear. We mire ourselves in a nasty mood and in our preconceptions about how change must come to us. We think, *It will have to be A or B or C.* In fact, when it does come, it is often, as my friend actress Julianna McCarthy ruefully notes, "H. Heliotrope."

Inner malcontent actually triggers outer change—if we are willing to listen to our malcontent with an open mind and listen to what will feel like a wave of irrational promptings. Those oddball, harebrained, nonlinear, and screwball itches, hunches, and urges are the path through the briar patch. Follow your strange creative cravings and you will be led into change a step at a time. I cannot prove this to you, nor would I. This is an experiment you must do for yourself and with yourself. You will never trust an unseen and benevolent partnering from higher realms unless you experience it for yourself and by yourself. As someone who is by nature exhaustingly skeptical—and equally exhaustingly open-minded and experimental—I am speaking from my idiosyncratic experience—and the experience of watching two decades of artists as they experimented and recorded the result.

"This is so stupid. What am I doing here?" we may ask ourselves when, on a whim, we have gone to an adult education class on the kooky subject of origami.

Yet, our lives are as intricately folded, as cleverly made, and as particular as that ancient pursuit. When we acknowledge the right of mystery to intercept and direct us, we acknowledge the larger issue that life is a spiritual dance and that our unseen partner has steps to teach us if we will allow ourselves to be led. The next time you are restless, remind yourself it is the universe asking "Shall we dance?"

We are never so ridiculous through what we are as through what we pretend to be.

FRANÇOIS, DUC DE LA
ROCHEFOUCAULD

TASK:
Find the "Rest" in Restlessness

These are only hints and guesses,
Hints followed by guesses,
and the rest
Is prayer, observance, discipline,
thought and action.

T. S. ELIOT

In writing out a piece of music, a composer uses a "rest" to indicate a tiny, nearly imperceptible pause that is sometimes necessary before plunging ahead into the sea of notes.

Sometimes, and particularly when we are restless, it is a good idea to take a rest and allow our inner leadings to bubble up to the surface unimpeded. Certain atmospheres can create a sense of rest in us and, while we are all individual, here are a few restful places to try a five-minute breather:

1. **The back of a church or synagogue:** There is often a calm humility that comes from just a few minutes tucked in a pew, even for the nonreligious. We breathe in "faith."
2. **A large plant store or greenhouse:** There is a sense of "other realms" that is palpable in visiting a green space. Plants do have a secret life and they will share it.
3. **A forest:** Even if you live in the city and your forest is in a park, you will sense a different rhythm if you allow it.
4. **A carpet store for fine Oriental rugs:** There is a sense of the sacred in the intricate patterns and handmade excellence. The very amount of time required to make a beautiful rug reminds us of the beauty of our own life's tapestry.
5. **A travel store:** The reminder that ours is a rich and various world filled with adventures can often, oddly, calm a restless heart. An imaginary junket down a jungle river, a trek through the Scottish Highlands, a bicycle trip through France—all of these are options for us, and knowing that we have such spirited options can be strangely calming.

Insecurity

I am trying to learn to play the piano. I have a friend who plays the piano as one who can leap across peaks in the thinnest atmosphere with no fear of falling. He is nimble and daring and may not even feel a need for nerve, he is so nervy. I would love to play like that.

Today I made the mistake of looking up the mountain and seeing that the peak was still far above me and wrapped in mysterious clouds. I saw that the way up to it was a treacherous climb of switchbacks and crevasses. I knew I would fall. I knew I would fall. I knew it was all danger, all failure. In short, I compared myself to my gifted friend.

At the root of comparison is something a little nastier: insecurity. Instead of saying "I wish I were better than *I* am," we say, "I wish I were as good as *he* is." In one fell swoop we negate our work and our originality. No two players play alike, and there is that word, play. As artists, we do better focused on the play of learning than on the work of getting ahead. Centered on our own creative trajectory, each small gain is an encouragement. Each slight increment of mastery holds the sweet promise that the days of awkward repetition and frustrating blunders do lead somewhere after all. When we compete and compare instead of strive to emulate and empathize with other artists, we greet their skills with hostility and our own lesser skills with dismay. When we embrace the idea that all artists at all levels are still learning, still struggling, still evolving, growing, and grappling with their craft simply at a different altitude, we are encouraged by another's mastery to know: "It can be done." We need such encouragement. Our talent may be large, but our struggles may be large as well.

This morning, trying to play "When the Saints Go Marching In," I started crying in anger and frustration. Why didn't I learn this in fourth grade like everyone else? Where was I then?

Every autobiography is concerned with two characters, a Don Quixote, the Ego, and a Sancho Panza, the Self.

W. H. AUDEN

As artists, most of us contain a highly evolved and sharp-clawed inner perfectionist. This perfectionist has nothing to do with having standards and everything to do with self-punishing, self-flagellating, and self-defeating premature judgments regarding our potential. The root word of "potential" is "potency," or "power." Just as the eagle's fledgling is less formidable than the eventual eagle, so, too, our embryonic steps in a new art form fail to accurately convey our later creative flight.

My music room is a geranium red and my piano is a small Chickoring upright. Gold gilt letters declare "Established in 1823." The piano may know far more than I. It has one sticky key, D above middle C, but with my lame and halting progress, that hardly matters. I type better than I play and I type with two fingers. And yet, I have written seventeen books and numerous plays and screenplays. So, too, my primitive piano skills have allowed me to pick out beautiful melodies. The trick is, *allowed* me.

Grace is available to us always, at any stage of the creative journey. As beginners, we need the grace to begin. As apprentice artists, we need the grace to continue. As accomplished artists, we need the grace to again accomplish what it is we can. At all levels of creative endeavor, the Great Creator is present and partnering us.

"We are brought along like fighters," remarks the estimable actress Julianna McCarthy. She means that the Great Creator always gives us strength enough and support enough and guidance enough to meet the precise creative challenges at hand. We may be overwhelmed, but God is not. If we fail at Plan A, God has an endless supply of Plan Bs. There is always not only a fallback position, but also a net. That net is having the faith to try again.

When we say that making art is an act of faith and that as we make art we pursue a spiritual path, we are not talking loosely. There is grace in our every artistic encounter. Miracles do happen. We do not plan them. We hope for them and then we are open to the creator's mentoring hand in improving our suggestions. What looks difficult or impossible to us does not appear

Authority poisons everybody who takes authority on himself.

Vladimir Ilyich Lenin

difficult or impossible to the Great Creator. As we set our egos aside and allow that creative power to work through us, miracles are routinely accomplished—seemingly by our own hand. Creative energy is like electricity. It will flow whether we allow it to or not. As we open our circuitry to conscious collaboration with higher forces, we are shaped by the energy that moves through us into the artists we dream we can become. The minute we relinquish the notion that our creative dreams are centered in the ego, the minute we begin to see them as spiritual adventures, we allow the Great Creator to shape us as only it can and will.

When I move a step at a time, I can edge up the mountain. If I go slowly and gently, playing "Twinkle, Twinkle, Little Star," I can even be proud to have edged up a ledge and I can say, "Wow, I am doing it." It takes vigilance to be gentle. It is easier to wail at myself, "Oh, my God, you will never learn."

We do not know how to ask ourselves for real growth. We do not know how to realistically dig in. We make our new art a mountain we cannot climb instead of trying our luck with a small incline and then a steeper one and then a slightly steeper one. Instead of being inspired by those creative climbers who hop crag to crag, we are discouraged.

I love the piano. How I play it can break my heart. That I play at all, at age fifty-four, when it is like going on a blind date and suffering through my insecurity, thrills me, and is a miracle.

There is certainly no absolute standard of beauty. That precisely is what makes its pursuit so interesting.

JOHN KENNETH GALBRAITH

TASK:
Exactly the Way I Am

At the root of most insecurity is the conviction that we must somehow be better—or other—than what we are in order to be acceptable. We want to play better than so-and-so—or at least as well as so-and-so. Lost in all of this improvement and striving for perfection is the idea that there is a great deal to like about ourselves exactly the way we already are.

*There are as many kinds of
beauty as there are habitual
ways of seeking happiness.*

CHARLES BAUDELAIRE

Take pen in hand. Number from 1 to 50. List 50 specific and positive things that you like and approve about yourself exactly the way you are. These likable traits can be physical, mental, spiritual, personal, or even professional. For a glimpse at their possible diversity, consider these examples:

1. My handsome hands
2. The shape of my nose
3. The general use of grammar
4. The shape of my feet
5. My Spanish accent
6. My knowledge of American history
7. My knowledge of twentieth-century art
8. My pie-baking ability
9. My choice in walking shoes
10. My consistencies of letters to friends

So often we are focused on what we would like to change—and change for the better—that we fail to celebrate what is wonderfully enjoyable exactly the way it is. We are often far closer to our own ideal—and ideals—than we dare recognize. Self-esteem is an active choice, not a sudden given. We can choose to actively esteem our many positive traits. By counting our blessings we can come to see that we are blessed and that we need not compare ourselves to anyone.

Self-Pity

Yesterday, wading through the rewrite of a play, I stepped into the black hole I call self-pity. I went down, sputtering, "But! This is silly! I have so much to be grateful for! Burble!"

The fact that I have been a writer for thirty years has done very little to armor me against a solid attack of self-pity. The fact that I have gotten through hard rewrites before, and will doubtless do so again, doesn't really matter. I am like any other artist—happy when I am working freely and unhappy when the work becomes too much like work. I write both because I love to write and because I have to write. I am called, and if I don't answer, the calling just gets louder until I do answer or I have a bout of self-pity because I "have" to answer.

At root, self-pity is a stalling device. It is a temper tantrum, a self-inflicted drama that has little to do, ever, with the facts. Self-pity isn't very interested in facts. What it likes is "stories." As Serah, the noted singer, likes to remark, "Facts are sober. Stories are emotion." Self-pity thrives on stories that go "Poor innocent me and terrible, mean them . . ." Self-pity likes to make us feel the world is an adversarial place and that the odds are stacked against us. Self-pity likes to point out the way we are never truly appreciated, valued, cherished. What self-pity really wants is a cheering section and a fan club. It wouldn't hurt, either, to have a few good designer suits to lounge around in, Camille-like, while our worried lovers hover and offer us sips of something cool. Self-pity is not interested in our getting over it. Self-pity is interested in our "getting over." Struck by a bout of self-pity, we want an appreciative audience for our suffering, not a bout of self-improvement.

Self-pity is not interested in our spiritual status. It turns a deaf ear to our peppy affirmations. For an artist, self-pity constitutes a chronic and formidable creative block. Self-pity has one job and one job only: It intends to stop us in our tracks. If self-pity can just keep us mired in what's-the-use, we will not have to do anything to find out. I am pretty sure that self-pity was a party guest in the Garden at Gethsemane. It was that satanic little voice that whispered "You can still wriggle out of this. They aren't going to appreciate you anyway."

"They aren't going to appreciate you" is often a trigger for self-pity. Please note that "they" (by which we often mean critics or even that more vague creature, "the public") has little or nothing to do with our own self-respect.

Any coward can fight a battle when he's sure of winning, but give me the man who has pluck to fight when he's sure of losing.

GEORGE ELIOT

Beauty is as relative as light and dark.

PAUL KLEE

Self-pity focuses our attention on how we are perceived rather than on what we are perceiving. It takes us out of our creative power and tells us that we are powerless, we will never "make it." Even if we already have, self-pity isn't interested in realistic self-assessment. It is interested in stalling us. For an artist, focusing on the odds "against making it" is like sipping a poisonous drink. It weakens us. When we focus on the impossibility of the outer world and its megalithic proportions, how small and weak and helpless and thwarted we all are, well then, we feel "what's the use," and the world doesn't get much better than that, does it?

Self-pity never asks "Well, what do you think of what you're doing, how you're living, what you are making?" That question might lead us to shake things up a little in some interesting directions. Self-pity doesn't want us to shake things up. It wants to shake us up, like one of those old-fashioned double-whammy martinis that puts you straight on the floor with its punch.

Self-pity wants you on the floor—and the floor feels like the floor even when it is the floor of a creative penthouse. All artists get attacks of self-pity, and we get them with our Oscars leering down from the mantel. We get them with our National Book Award glinting in the lovely golden light pouring through our study window. We get them—we get them—because if we don't watch out, we are about to do something big.

Self-pity is a scraggly red robin. It means that once we get over it, we are going to spring into action. Self-pity—as all of us know—is different from the vague gray numbness of garden-variety depression. Self-pity has an edge to it like a shard of glass. We can use that shard of glass to cut, not ourselves, but our sense of hopelessness, into ribbons. In other words, used properly, a good dose of self-pity is a jump start for creative action. "What's the use?" converts quickly into "What's next?"

If you don't medicate it with a walloping pitcher of martinis, an ill-considered love affair, a bout of overwork or overeating, a solid attack of self-pity is the signal that you are about to either make yourself sick or make yourself healthy. The healthy part of us cannot stomach self-pity and so it will be goaded into action. Oddly, that action may *not* be taken down the lash and laid across our creative back. The action may be something that starts with compassion: "Of course you are *hurt*. Your work was unfairly received. Cry a little."

Although self-pity *appears* to be grounded in the lack of appreciation from others, it is *actually* grounded in our *own* discounting of our self and our struggles. A few tears of sorrow over work ill used, a moment of surrender to our genuine fatigue and heartbreak—a little actual grief can very quickly take the claws out of self-pity's hold on us. When we say "Of course you feel bad," then we are on the brink of something a little interesting. We begin to raise the question "If this makes me feel so bad, what can I change?"

"I am tired of being talked down to by the academic poets," we wail, and then we start exploring master's programs. Someone points out publicly that we have a tendency toward something unforgivable in our painting—romantic blue washes, for example, and we think, *I'll show them romance! I'll show them shimmering light!* and we dig in, perfect our technique, and get even "more so" of the quality of question. We persist and persist and our fatal artistic "flaw" is often revealed to be our own strength. This was true of the hyperexpressivity of violinist Nadja Salerno-Sonnenberg. This was true of Hemingway's stripped and soldierly prose.

The answer to "What can I change?" often surprises us. We might get a stubborn "Nothing! I love that piece and I think I will play it more!" We might get "I am bored by this curriculum and I want to include a lot more." We might get "What I'd really like to get done is _____." In other words, the question "What can I change?" snaps us back onto our own creative spine. Now we are asking the questions that only we have the answers to: What do we respect? What do we like? What do we want to do more of? We spring into action on that.

Belief consists in accepting the affirmations of the soul; unbelief, in denying them.

Ralph Waldo Emerson

Of course, most of this self-pity springing into action is often accomplished after a nap. Have I said that self-pity is often born of fatigue? It lays us flat because we may need to be there for a while. There is something about being horizontal—without the benefit of drink or drug—that allows the imagination to do a little lucid daydreaming. We get up from our bed of pain thinking, *I could try that.* And we do.

TASK:
Take a Little Pity on Yourself

Most of the time when we are struck down by a bout of self-pity, it is because we feel underappreciated. The truth is, sometimes we *are* underappreciated. The efforts we make and the effort we expend seems to go unnoticed by everyone but us. It is as though we had a tiny, built-in resentment collector, an inner gauge that processes reality by tiny little clicks that say "You see? Not appreciated again."

We cannot make others appreciate us, but we can take the time, care, and attention to appreciate ourselves. "That was really nice of you," we can say. Or "How thoughtful!" One of the Toughlove spiritual laws advises, "Other people's opinions of me are none of my business." A more positive counterpoint might be phrased "My own opinion of me is all that matters."

Take pen in hand. Writing rapidly to avoid your inner censor, complete the following sentences valuing yourself:

1. It was generous of me to _____.
2. It was thoughtful of me to _____.
3. It was nice that I _____.
4. I was a good friend when I _____.
5. I was sensitive when I _____.
6. I did a good job when I _____.
7. I was very professional about _____.

8. I went beyond the call of duty when I _____.

9. I deserve a thank-you for _____.

10. I should get an Oscar for _____.

Self-appreciation takes practice, and it is the only reliable antidote to self-pity.

Doubt

Doubt is a signal of the creative process. It is a signal that you are doing something right—not that you are doing something wrong or crazy or stupid. The sickening chasm of fear that doubt triggers to yawn open beneath you is not a huge abyss into which you are going to tumble, spiraling downward like you are falling through the circles of hell. No, doubt is most often a signal you are doing something and doing it right.

Creativity is a spiritual issue, and although we seldom look at this squarely, the creative life features the same spiritual obstacles as any other spiritual path. The phrase "dark night of the soul" has gained common usage, and we think of it as it applies to the harrowing periods of doubt and drought that may come to someone on their spiritual quest.

Spiritual seekers of all stripe endure its painful ravages, whether they are Trappist monks like Thomas Merton or young Lord Buddha. What we don't talk about often is the fact that artists, too, are spiritual seekers, and we frequently suffer the dark night of the soul regarding our creative calling. Even worse, we often suffer it publicly.

To be an artist of depth, one cultivates a level of sensitivity that is acute. Performing artists, for example, listen with an ear cocked to the spiritual questions posed by a great piece of music or a great part onstage, and they open themselves to receive the energies required to manifest those questions creatively. Tackling these towering creative pinnacles, they are like tender

Beauty is one of the rare things that do not lead to doubt of God.

JEAN ANOUILH

birds who have learned to perch on skyscrapers as well as on trees. They still have all the acute sensitivity they have ever had, and they have also adapted enough to live in the fiercely competitive winds of high-altitude performance—but this does not mean it is easy. Artists facing an Olympian role *are* like athletes—highly trained, highly strung, and highly susceptible to injury, physical and psychic.

As I write, a gifted friend of mine is limping home after an extended tour. He is a musician of prodigious gifts, able to scale pieces whose heights and depths, whose creative cliffs, switchbacks, and drop-offs require the skills of a virtuoso. He has them. He uses them. And he doubts them. Doubt is a dangerous thing as you are leaping crag to crag above the artistic abyss. A well-placed doubt can send you tumbling—he recalls an entire Japanese tour bedeviled by troubling memory strain due to jet lag. He did not falter but feared he would, and carried that fear as a handicap, leaping ledge to ledge musically. This type of anxiety sends an artist to a place of darkness and terror that is difficult for most people to imagine.

In a sense, how we do as performers is none of our business. It is God's business how we do, and as we "suit up" and "show up," we are like monks doing matins—we fill a form and the form is larger than ourselves. Very often the beauty of a trained voice lifted in song can lift an untrained heart to a new altitude in connection to something or someone larger than our self. A great concert is an initiatory tribal experience. We touch the largeness of life through the largeness of the performer. Garland singing of yearning and love allows each of us to touch those feelings of yearning and love. The "somewhere over the rainbow" is a place located in the human heart, and art—and artists—allow us to access it.

Last night I had dinner with three young classical musicians, rising stars with phosphorescent talent. The dinner table should have floated like something from a hokey séance. There was that

It is not because angels are holier than men or devils that makes them angels, but because they do not expect holiness from one another, but from God only.

WILLIAM BLAKE

much creative power and light seated there, ordering pasta with pesto and arugula salad, fettuccine livornese and penne vodka.

"Do your teachers prepare you for doubt?" I asked them.

The young talents flickered like fireflies. The question alone created a certain shimmer of unease. One was headed to Japan on a tour with the Met, and was frightened by the prospect.

"Not really," one violinist said.

"We're told to just ignore it, I think," said a violist.

"Critics are often jealous," sniffed a second violinist defensively. She had not yet suffered a critical savaging, but she "had heard."

Under their cosmopolitan chic, these young artists were still novices hoping to get through on a wing and a prayer.

No, they were not prepared.

"Do not pick up the first doubt," creative elder Julianna Mc-Carthy warns me, the voice of six decades of experience on the stage, laying down the dictum.

For an artist, the first doubt is like the first drink for a sober alcoholic: We cannot afford to romance it. The first doubt leads to the second. The second leads to the third, and in no time you are staggering, hurting yourself on the sharp edges of the furniture.

One of the reasons artists need to talk to and hear from other artists is that the press is not a trustworthy mechanism for relaying information about the creative life. In the press, artists are either anguished or heroic, they are not what they must be—adroit, like spiritual samurai—to remain balanced amid turbulent doubts.

When a doubt moves at an artist, the artist must learn how to step aside and let the charge pass by. An artist cannot afford to be deeply pierced by doubt and finish the tour.

For an artist, doubt is both part of the territory and an ever-present danger. Doubt is the twister in Kansas. Doubt is the sickening temperature drop and unseasonable storm at twelve thousand feet. Doubt is the earthquake of the heart, the forest

Babies are necessary to grown-ups. A new baby is like the beginning of all things—wonder, hope, a dream of possibilities.

EDA J. LE SHAN

When it is not necessary to change, it is necessary not to change.

LUCIUS CARY,
LORD FALKLAND

fire of self-criticism that threatens to take down everything in its blistering path. In other words, doubt is both normal and deadly, like coral snakes in Florida. Doubt is not to be toyed with.

There is a difference between doubt and self-appraisal. Doubt likes to come to the door disguised in the worthy suit of self-appraisal, "Maybe you should work on your . . ." Like a suitor, you should consider, but under that respectable overcoat is the dagger of despair: "Maybe you really are rotten at this." Doubt should not be allowed to enter—and it *will* try, at three A.M., in a strange city, with a polite knock, like a serial killer asking to share coffee while you phone the police.

The annals of art are dark with the destruction wrought by this satanic saboteur. Symphonies have been tossed into the fire; novels, too, have been burned at the stake. Stradivarius routinely smashed violins far better than those of his rival makers. "Feel the feelings but don't act on them. This, too, shall pass," artists need other artists to tell them.

As the cool light of day reveals, doubt and self-appraisal are not the same thing. It takes practice, but an artist can learn the difference. Self-appraisal has a certain steadiness of character. It knocks in daylight and poses a simple question, and if you don't listen, it goes away. Then it comes back, knocks again gently, and poses the same question. Gently. As something for you to consider. To think about. To look at changing. "Maybe it's time to get a new bow." Self-appraisal has an opinion, a thought for your consideration. It has an idea to hand you, not an indictment. It doesn't whisper at midnight when you are alone and exhausted. Doubt is what does that.

Doubt is the one who likes to separate its victim from the herd, get the lamb off always and then call in its cronies. Doubt strikes you when *you* are alone, but doubt itself travels in packs. Along with doubt come its nasty friends: despair, self-loathing, feelings of foolishness and humiliation. When doubt attacks, it's always with the same lot of lower companions like the bad boys in an Italian gangster movie. An artist needs to learn to spot these characters and see them as lowlife bullies and not as Boy Scouts bravely bearing the truth.

Doubt comes to the door in darkness, pretending to be alone and in need of your compassionate ear. But if you let him in, he'll bring his friends, and doubt can be very persuasive getting in.

Doubt is a great seducer. "I just want you to think about this," it whispers. Out come the artist's ears. Out comes the dagger. "Maybe you didn't and don't have enough talent after all. . . ." Feel the sharp piercing? It might be your creative lung collapsing around the blade.

No, as artists, we need lucid self-appraisal, not shadowy and sinister doubt. Self-appraisal is best practiced in broad daylight in the comfort of your own home and among very trusted friends.

All artists suffer doubts. Great directors watch from the back of screening rooms and have to breathe their hyperventilated doubt into brown paper bags. Brilliant actresses suffer stage fright as painful as rickets. Doubt is a part of the territory as an artist. Surviving doubt, learning to discern what is emotional terrorism and what is a proper, suggested course adjustment, is something an artist becomes more skilled at over time—and often only with the help of his creative elders who have suffered doubt themselves.

In a convent or monastery, a suffering novice can speak to a spiritual director. "Doubt is normal," they are softly told. "Why, without doubt, why would we need faith?" When, as artists, we suffer doubt, we do well to seek compassionate counseling. "Doubt? It comes with the territory, kid," director John Newland used to growl at me tenderly.

Art is a spiritual practice. Doubt is normal. We need faith to survive it and we also need charity. When doubt attacks, we must be vigilantly self-loving. We must not open the door to the stranger who hands us the bottle of scotch, the pills, and the gun. Keep the chain on the door, politely or not so politely defer taking the doubt that is offered. Sleep with the light on if you need to. Call a friend in the middle of the night. Find an old

The changes in our life must come from the impossibility to live otherwise than according to the demands of our conscience.

LEO TOLSTOY

comedy on television. Travel with a beloved children's book like a Harry Potter volume or *The Little Engine That Could*. Your artist does not need to be scared by things that go bump in the night. The dark night of the soul comes to all artists. When it comes to you, know that it is simply a tricky part of the trail and that you will see better in the morning.

TASK:
Doubt Your Doubts

Imagination is more important than knowledge.

ALBERT EINSTEIN

All artists experience doubt. Experienced artists learn to weather doubt without succumbing to self-sabotage. When doubt darkens the heart, it is wise to think of this gloom not as "reality" but as passing weather, like a badly overcast few days. During bouts of doubt, our judgments will not be accurate and should not be acted upon. Like a nasty cold snap, doubt is something to be survived, and so we should aim for actions that are warm, loving, nondramatic, and non–self-destructive. Rather than working on self-improvement, focus instead on self-care. Try to be actively selfish on your own behalf.

TASK:
The Self in Self-Expression

Take pen in hand and list 10 small ways in which you could be *selfish,* that might make it easier for you later to be self*less.* For example:

1. I could let myself call my long-distance friend, Laura.
2. I could let myself subscribe to *Western Horseman.*
3. I could let myself buy a pair of parakeets for my studio.
4. I could let myself get a new easel.
5. I could let myself declare "me" off limits after seven, one night a week, and use that time and space to write.

6. I could let myself turn my phone off during my art hours.
7. I could let myself take a portrait seminar and get some expert tips.
8. I could let myself shoot a roll of black and white just because I'm crazy about it.
9. I could let myself make a weekly writing date to get me off the dime on my thesis.
10. I could let myself get that new recording I'm curious about.

Our personal journeys mark us.

DAVID HALBERSTAM

If you have difficulty thinking of 10 small ways to be creatively selfish, finish this sentence 10 times:

If I weren't so selfish, I'd _____.

CHECK-IN

1. **How many days this week did you do your Morning Pages?** If you skipped a day, why did you skip it? How was the experience of writing them for you? Are you experiencing more clarity? A wider range of emotions? A greater sense of detachment, purpose and calm? Did anything surprise you? Is there a "repeating" issue asking to be dealt with?
2. **Did you do your Artist's Date this week?** Did you note an improved sense of well-being? What did you do and how did you feel? Remember, Artist's Dates can be difficult and you may need to coax yourself into taking them.
3. **Did you get out on your Weekly Walk?** How did that feel? What emotions or insights surfaced for you? Were you able to walk more than once? What did your walk do for your optimism and sense of perspective?
4. **Were there any other issues this week that felt significant to you in your self-discovery?** Describe them.

Discovering a Sense of Camaraderie

Despite our Lone Ranger mythology,
the artist's life is not lived in isolation. This
week focuses your attention on the caliber of
your friendships and creative collaborations. Loyalty
and longevity, integrity and ingenuity, grace and
generosity—all of these attributes are necessary
traits for healthy creative exchange. The
readings and tasks of this week aim at
the difficult art of sorting our
personal relationships.

Keep the Drama on the Stage

Artists are dramatic.

Art is dramatic. When artists are not making artistic dramas, they tend to make personal ones. Feeling off center, they demand center stage. Feeling on tilt, they tilt at an imaginary windmill.

"This relationship is in trouble," they announce. "Why, it's got all sorts of problems."

Or "I'm sure it's nothing serious, but it's possible I'm going deaf. Did you hear what I said?"

All of us are creative, but those of us who are for a living had better learn to create with the same quotidian grace as our cousin who works at the bank, our father who administers his department at the university, or our neighbor who manages the hardware store. When we make our creative work and our creative lives too special and too dramatic, we uproot those lives from a sense of community and continuity—and that's exactly what we like to do whenever we get too nervous. Nervous, we create dramas to make ourselves more nervous.

We announce, "I've been thinking about *your* character, and I'm not so sure I should trust it. What do you think about that, wife?"

To the skilled ear, there is a predictively reactive tone to these sudden besetting dilemmas. Reality need not apply, the relationship is probably fine. Deafness would not drown out a compliment, and your character is less a question than the character you're dealing with: a nervous artist.

A friend of mine is a world-class musician who develops health problems on the cusp of every major concert tour. Health fears are his Achilles' heel. Mysterious maladies always arrive as his departure date nears. Another friend of mine, a fine writer, loses all humor and sense of personal perspective every time a writing deadline looms. His marriage is always "over" or, at least, on the rocks, until he settles down to write. People like these should furnish seat belts for those riding shotgun in their lives. You would think that *someone* would have the nerve to say "Oh, just stop it." As artists, we should say it ourselves, but drama gives us an excuse to not make art and so artistic anorexia is addictive. We get an adrenalized anxiety from not making art. We can binge on this chemical roller-coaster when work is due.

Artists love making art the way lovers love making love, and just as lovers become snappish when they need to go to bed and make love, artists become snappish when they need to make art. Artistic anorexia, the avoidance of the pleasure of the creative, is a pernicious addiction that strikes most artists sometimes and always takes us by surprise. Instead of making art, we make trouble—and we make it because we are bingeing emotionally on *not* making art. We need to get to the piano and practice. We need to do our vocal exercises. We need to show up at the easel or the page. We need to go full steam ahead, and when we don't,

Compassion is the antitoxin of the soul: where there is compassion even the most poisonous impulses remain relatively harmless.

ERIC HOFFER

we tend to blow off steam by venting inappropriately about any number of imaginary ills. Our aches and pains become the world's pain in the neck. Goddammit, art is a serious business, and you had better believe we will raise hell if anyone gets too festive in our vicinity.

"You just don't understand," we start snapping at people who do understand all too well. John Barrymore's performance as the imperious theatrical impresario in *Twentieth Century* should be required viewing for all artists prone to occasional bouts of self-importance. The *art* is what's important. We are intended to serve our art, not treat our friends and family as servants. The arrogant-artist archetype doubtless has its twisted roots somewhere in low self-esteem and posturing out of a need to disguise our vulnerabilities. If we have too much ego invested in our work and not enough ego strength coming from the rest of our lives, it's easy to act out the arrogant-artist archetype.

At root, we have lost our sense of humor and, as a result, our sense of scale. When we take ourselves too seriously and demand that others do the same, we inadvertently tighten our creative muscles and strain our own performance. Touring artists should probably carry a backpack of comedies. If we remember—or watch—*That's Entertainment,* we may loosen up, lighten up, and deliver the caliber of work we aspire to. There is a bumper sticker that reads "Angels fly because they take themselves lightly."

It is one of the paradoxes of a creative career that our careers take off once we loosen our fearful, ego-ridden grip. A sense of humor is attractive. It indicates a sense of scale. As an artist, a sense of scale is what gives our work proportion, perspective, and personality. As artists, we want to avoid being "over the top." The best way to do this is to avoid being top-heavy—that is, big-headed because we feel so small. As a rule of thumb, artists should repeat this mantra: Sudden problems in my life usually indicate a need to work on my art. Lest this sound like artist bashing, let me simply admit that I have bashed myself

Her great merit is finding out mine—there is nothing so amiable as discernment.

Lord Byron

against the rocks of my creative imagination countless times before arriving at this conclusion.

A book deadline is not a NASA launch. A concert date is not a countdown for nuclear testing. As one cellist jokes, "I could be getting hit by a bus right now. Instead, I'm walking onstage to play a Brahms sextet." High profile and high pressure do not need to be synonymous. But the temptation to make them that way is enormous, particularly if we are feeling slightly off our game.

Our dogs should bite when they sense this senselessness drama coming on. My dog, Tiger Lily, a gold-and-white cocker spaniel, has learned to roll her eyes and pout eloquently whenever my humor evaporates. Tiger Lily's Westie sidekick, Charlotte, smells a rat whenever the household mood darkens unnecessarily. She has a small purple toy, Ratty, suitable for such occasions. When too much drama sets in, she presents Ratty at the offender's feet, with the strong, yipped suggestion that a game of catch might get us a lot further than whatever the hell game *this* is.

It is probably not an accident that the verbs *exorcise* and *exercise* are so similarly spelled. Most of the time when an artist is engaging in drama instead of art, he needs to move out of his head and into his body—if not into his body of work. A brisk walk up a steep hill, a few forced laps in the pool, and reality threatens to set in—the reality that the only drama in our very nice life is the one that we're creating ourselves. With our fine imaginations, artists can be drama addicts. We can also become physically addicted to our adrenalized anxiety in place of authentic creation. Too much drama is not fun, but it gives us something to do instead of making art. Until we break the code on this avoidance, we *believe* our dramatic scenarios.

"I know I should paint," we wail, "but does he love me?"

"All right, I should get to the piano, but I'm not certain I get enough respect from my peers."

"I'll get to the typewriter and work on the book as soon as I fire off a letter about my goddamn tennis shoes not holding up."

"I'll pick up the viola and practice *after* I know where my musical career is going."

As artists, we can be con artists—not that we con others, we usually don't. But we do con ourselves. We con ourselves into thinking that our dramatic dilemmas mean more than our art, and that indulging in drama will ever-satisfy our creative impulses.

If we can just convince ourselves to indulge in a little terrifying doubt—about our talent, about our lovability, about our competencies, creative and otherwise, then we can usually manage to stall ourselves in our creative tracks and *really* give ourselves something to worry about. If we can stage a nice, nasty drama, we can often subvert or sabotage our genuine creative growth.

What a relief! How much easier to worry about boy/girl dilemmas than whether or not our book has the proper art, our rehearsal has been sufficient to move the music into our hands and hearts, our mastery of our new photographic equipment has actually sharpened the focus of our work.

Artists are dramatic. Channeled into our work, drama is fine, but artists risk being addicted to emotional drama. We can display an alarming predilection standing at the edge of the cliff, looking straight down, while asking gullible friends, "Will I fall?" or "Shall I jump?" "Why would anyone want to do that?" you may ask. The answer is that it gives us something to do instead of making art.

Art is the itch we have to scratch, but we're the only ones who can scratch it. And if we refuse to scratch the surface of our own dramatic resistance, if we refuse to allow ourselves the dignity of genuine creative risk, then you will know us by how close to the cliff we are standing.

What annoyances are more painful than those of which we cannot complain?

MARQUIS DE CUSTINE

TASK:
Keeping a "Ta-dah!" List

Facts are the opposite of drama. If you have been working with Morning Pages, you have probably become more and more accurate at generating grounded to-do lists that spell out the priorities of the day as revealed in the pages. In order to have a firm sense of self-respect as artists, we need to employ a second daily list. That list is the "ta-dah!" list, as in the bow well taken after a successful recital. "Ta-dah!"

Rather than always focusing on what is left to do, we need to give ourselves a hand for what we've already done. Your ta-dah list is a nightly bow to personal applause for the many small creative actions taken in the course of a day. A ta-dah list might read:

1. Did my Morning Pages
2. Dropped Carolina a note
3. Put in 15 minutes at the piano
4. Repotted the geraniums
5. Read the essay in *The Atlantic* related to my thesis
6. Threw together a pot of soup
7. Inputted the bills to my computer home management program
8. Talked to Bruce—instant emotional restoration
9. Worked on actual writing of the thesis for one hour
10. Scheduled the dog at the groomer
11. Hemmed my droopy skirt
12. Ordered thesis-related book from amazon.com
13. Picked paint for kitchen windowsill
14. Tuned into the classical station for *Opera Hour*
15. Did the dark laundry

A ta-dah list can easily escalate to double this length. Often our days are far busier and more productive than we realize. Additionally, a ta-dah list may function as a subtle goad—"I'll love

---

In our era, the road to holiness necessarily passes through the world of action.

DAG HAMMARSKJÖLD

writing it down," we think as we tackle a creative something we've been avoiding. If to-do lists live out our priorities, ta-dah lists recognize our accomplishments. Ta-dah!—I did work on my art today. Creative lives are made of minutes—and minute amounts of work *do* add up.

The Good of Getting Better

As artists, we are not interested merely in expressing ourselves; that realm may belong to therapy. We are interested in expressing ourselves more and more accurately, more and more beautifully. This brings us squarely to the issue of craft, to our need for accurate assessment by others and ourselves.

Accurate and useful are most often found in the company of the grounded combination of personal experience and excellence. It is for this reason that artists have always apprenticed other artists. A great music teacher certainly shapes and colors the playing of her students—they become at once more fully themselves and somehow also recognizably "hers." It is, in part, a matter of shared technique, but it is also a matter of shared musical values. A great teacher both attracts and produces great students. It is a sort of spiritual lineage or, to cast it in the terms of the market, a "brand name." A great conservatory with great teachers puts a recognizable "stamp" onto its artists.

Sometimes, teachers and students seem to intersect by divine planning more than by set curriculum. This was the case for Emma and her teacher.

The great violin and viola teacher Joyce Robbins retired to southern California after a long teaching career in New York. A gifted viola player spending an unexpected year in California found Robbins and embarked on a course of study that changed her playing and perception of playing. She learned to hear.

"I just missed studying with this great teacher in the East. She had retired to California the year I enrolled. I never expected to

In the greatest confusion there is still an open channel to the soul. It may be difficult to find because by midlife it is overgrown, and some of the wildest thickets that surround it grow out of what we describe as our education. But the channel is always there, and it is our business to keep it open, to have access to the deepest part of ourselves.

SAUL BELLOW

go to California, but when I did I had to look her up. It was a three-and-a-half-hour round-trip commute to study with her, and I really got to know the California freeway system. On the other hand, I learned how actually to listen to myself as I played. I began to play more softly, with less stridency, and to listen to the actual sound I was making rather than just focusing on the technique of how I was making it. As a result, I began to sound much better. In the time since, whenever I hear a viola student with a particularly full and gentle sound, I wonder if he hasn't studied with my teacher and learned some of the same gift of hearing that she passed to me."

Yet, artists are everywhere and fine arts conservatories are not. A brilliant young painter in South Milwaukee may not have the familial or community support to study other than locally— and locally may offer some very fine teachers, or it may offer teachers whose own work is underschooled, underdeveloped, and unduly influenced by the supposed sophistication of a few powerful arts publications.

Try to discover your true, honest, untheoretical self.

BRENDA UELAND

Wanting to bloom where we are planted, we may seek out local teachers and either get lucky or experience an inner certainty that they are cramped in their creative calling and that they in turn can cramp us. Not wanting to be egotistical, many students stay too long at the fair, studying with teachers whom they have outgrown, often experiencing an uncomfortable creative constriction that manifests as teacher-student tension, even competition, that cannot often be directly addressed. How do we say "You see, I think I have outgrown you"? Often we say it best by simply thanking our mentor for time and talent given— then moving on.

Just as an excellent teacher can strengthen and clarify an artist, a bad teacher can damage, muffle, and muddy an artist. It is the impact of poor teachers that has blocked or battered many artists into at first healthy and later self-defeating hermeticism. Declaring themselves above, beyond, or outside the market, they court two possibilities, and usually encounter a mixture of both. Freed from outer influences, they may incubate and develop a strikingly original style. That's the good part. Freed from outer influences, they may also hit an artificially low ceiling, having taken their work as far as they can without further input.

Art, in some ways, is like any other skill—we enjoy doing it. Then we enjoy doing it well; then we enjoy doing it better. The refusal to allow ourselves the tools and techniques to move from "well" to "better," often calling it sort of faux purity, has nothing pure about it. We have allowed our pride and fear to taint our creative process. Yes, our inner creator may be childlike, but we have allowed ourselves to cross the line to *childish*. Defensive and defended, we have shied away from authentic growth.

A talented regional string player may struggle for years with self-perceived flaws, only to finally encounter an expert teacher who says, "You outgrew that instrument years ago, it's crippling you—get rid of it!" Not a perception likely to be jumped to by the artist alone.

Art, as remarked, is a form of the verb "to be" and, as artists, our spiritual and intellectual perceptions often lead and goad our need for increased technique. We can see it but we can't paint it. We can hear it but we can't play it. We need help. We can get help—or we can give up, discouraged by the gap between our inner standards and our own ability to meet them. Writer Tillie Olsen warns correctly of the danger of "the knife of perfectionism in art." If we keep its blade constantly at our creative throat, we fail to progress because we so stifle our learning process. A teacher is a guide through creative pitfalls such as these.

Each of us learns in our own way and at our own pace, and yet *someone's* excellent method will have something to offer us if we are willing to offer ourselves the opportunity to learn.

Authentic growth, however, is the goal, and that will not occur if we enroll ourselves in classes and curriculums that are themselves stagnant, stifling, or simply inadequate and ill advised. What we are after is excellence, and it can be found, but

I will tell you what I have learned myself. For me, a long five- or six-mile walk helps. And one must go alone and every day.

BRENDA UELAND

we must look for it, not only in ourselves, as we have been, but also in others. We must be neither blinded nor dazzled by brand-name credentials—blinded to the possibility that they might mean something valid or too dazzled by what they *might* mean to see that in this particular practitioner they mean very little. In other words, we must be open to finding our teachers and open to being teachable—while simultaneously holding an awareness of our equally valid, genuine perceptions and skills that must be protected.

It is an often repeated spiritual axiom that "when the student is ready, the teacher appears." Over the years, I have heard many stories of miraculous intersections and meetings. The divine mind knows no distance, and so a student's prayer in Omaha is heard as loudly and clearly as a student's prayer in Manhattan. When we ask to be led, we are led. When we ask to be guided, we are guided. When we ask to be taught, we are taught. A young sculptor working in a small midwestern industrial city prays for guidance and is led to a renowned sculptor working ten miles away in the very same off-the-beaten-path locale. A talented actor in a tiny New Mexico town intersects with a retired Hollywood director, who helps secure him a scholarship at a famed acting conservatory. Guidance and generosity are always closer at hand than we may think. It always falls to us to be open to receiving guidance and to pray for the willingness and openness to know it when it arrives.

It is spiritual law that the good of our projects and our growth as artists must rest in divine hands and not merely human ones. While we are led to and drawn from teacher to teacher, opportunity to opportunity, the Great Creator remains the ultimate source of all of our creative good. It is easy to forget this and make our agent or our manager or our current teacher the source of our "good." When we place our reliance on an undergirding of divine assistance, we are able to hear our cues clearly, thank those who step forward to aid us, release

The best career advice to give the young is, find out what you like doing best and get someone to pay you for doing it.

KATHERINE WHILEHAEN

those who seem to impede us, and keep unfolding as artists with the faith that the Great Artist knows precisely what is best for us and can help us find our path, no matter how lost, distanced, or removed we may sometimes feel from our dream. In the heart of God, all things are close at hand, and this means our creative help, support, and success. As we ask, believe, and are open to receive, we are gently led.

TASK:
Becoming Teachable

Take pen in hand. List 5 personal situations that are, for you, lingering resentments, sore spots, and sources of self-pity regarding a lack of effective mentoring. For example:

1. My parents both got sick and I never got to Stanford for my poetry master's.
2. My viola was so difficult to play that I damaged my technique by compensating and am still undoing my bad habits.
3. My family had no idea what to do with a writer in their midst. They wanted me to be a lawyer. I had *no* literary support.
4. My hometown had never heard of modern dance. By the time I realized what it was, I was already in my twenties and on a career path as a physical therapist.
5. My very talented older sister got all the creative encouragement as a musician. I had to do the dishes while she serenaded on guitar.

These grievances are real, and you can't change them. You can, however, ask some pointed questions and take some nurturing actions. For example:

I happen to feel that the degree of a person's intelligence is directly reflected by the number of conflicting attitudes she can bring to bear on the same topic.

LISA ALTHER

1. Would I still like a poetry master's? There are many fine nonresidential programs for older students.
2. As to that viola technique, if you're not in a music program, there are still often excellent teachers who make themselves available for private lessons. The right teacher can undo the wrong learning quite quickly.

Address each of your historic grievances, looking for a present-tense action that creatively soothes your injured artist. Take those actions. Even the smallest can lessen self-pity's sting.

Before, During, and After Friends

One of the trickiest issues in a creative life is the issue of private support and encouragement for our creative leaps—no matter how they are received. As artists, we do not need private adulation, but we do need before, during, and after friends, those people who love and accept us no matter what our current creative shape and size. We need friends who understand that a creative success may bring an onslaught of pressures nearly as devastating as a creative failure.

Friends must be found who understand how to cohabit with our varied creative needs. Sometimes, we are the lonely larva; sometimes, the beautiful butterfly. Our needs and necessities vary with where we are and how we are doing in our creative process.

It helps us to become conscious of our needs first of all for ourselves and then to share our insights with those we know we can trust. Too often, we try either to "go it alone" creatively or we do not ask for what it is we need in ways that can be acted on or understood. When our creative well is low from having worked a long time on a hard project, we need to be enough of a friend to ourselves to take a refreshing Artist's Date to fill the well back up with images and adventure. When a deadline looms and we are dead on our feet from overwork, it can be

We do not mind our not arriving anywhere nearly so much as our not having any company on the way.

FRANK MOORE COLBY

very hard to take such breaks. Instead, we tend to want to flog ourselves forward, and both the work and ourselves suffer. In such times, a call to a friend might say, "Pray that I can get out of the house to see *Harry Potter*."

In 12-Step programs, participants learn the "sandwich" call. When they are about to do something difficult, they call a friend, do the difficult thing, and then call the friend back and report "Mission accomplished." There are stages of creative work when we can get so painfully stymied that a "sandwich" call is great first aid. We can call and say, "I can't get into my studio and I have work stacking up. I am going to go in for one half hour and just clean my brushes." We can call and say, "I am going to do the fixes on two pages and then call you to say I have." We can say, "I am going to read the first twenty-five pages of the manuscript to see what I think." Or "I'm going to rough out the choreography for the first movement."

Most of us have friends who are willing and ready to help us if we will just tell them how. In my early sobriety, I sold a script to Paramount and I was so terrified of rewriting it that my friend Jupiter used to come to my house, sit in my rocker, and read for an hour a day while I took my quaking self to the typewriter. An hour a day is a lot more work than no hours a day, and, as friends learn that small donations of time and support are more useful to us than grand gestures, they begin to know the cue lines: "Hook for half an hour and call me back." Or "Try to read the first twenty pages and call me back." Very often, we need help only to get a toe in the water. Once we are in, we can swim. Our help can be a phone call, a writing date where we both show up at Starbucks and scribble for an hour, a faxed check-in, an e-mail saying "I did it." The electronic age has allowed us to make our creative community far-flung. We can also "tame" a coffee-shop owner and faithfully eat a grilled cheese and work an hour in a back booth every day. For years, Dori's Bakery in Taos was like a zoo, full of writers, each of us with our table, nodding to each other and Dori as we sat down to

All who joy would win
Must share it,—Happiness
was born a twin.

LORD BYRON

Transport of the mails, transport of the human voice, transport of flickering pictures—in this century as in others our highest accomplishments still have the single aim of bringing men together.

ANTOINE DE SAINT-EXUPÉRY

toil. Our friends will help us if we let them know how. Often, all we need is a little welcome company.

An artist in the midst of making a large creative jump—a concert tour, a book signing, a one-person show—is a vulnerable and sometimes volatile creature. And there are those who will attack and exploit that vulnerability and those who will protect and support it. An artist who is suddenly "hot" often gets burned. Without the solid anchoring of tried-and-true friends who stay the course, how is an artist to sort opportunity from opportunists, management from manipulation? Snipers are snipers, creatively as in life. They will hide and shoot. Some colleagues are snipers. Unfortunately, some friends are. Some families are. Often unconsciously jealous and resentful, they greet our good fortune with a chilly reception. A conversation with them can leave us feeling dismayed and dispirited.

Sometimes, it's sarcastic teasing: "So, how does it feel to be flavor of the week?" Sometimes, it's freelance spiritual advice: "Better watch out that you don't get too big for yourself." Sometimes, it's simple guilt: "I had a feeling this was coming, that you'd be too busy for me once you started on this project. It must be great to be so in demand." A friend of mine, a veteran actress, joked: "I don't know why we're so busy trying to get to the top; what's waiting at the top is envy and resentment." Yes, among other things, and it can be hard to find willing ears for some of our odd, success-driven adventures. I remember thinking, *Who can I call to say Sammy Davis, Jr., invited me to his house, and then told me I was a great dancer?* (I'm not sure my mother *was* the right choice.) The simple fact of your new life can sound like bragging and name dropping, even to yourself. We must find people who can see our vulnerability in such passages and neither encourage it to become terror nor discount it.

As artists, we need people who can see us for who we are— as big as we are and as small as we are, as competent and powerful as we are, and as terrified and as tiny as we sometimes feel. As artists, we need people who believe in us and are able to see our large selves, and people who are able to be gentle and compassionate with our smaller selves. I have a very small and cherished list of people whom I *could* call with a creative terror in the middle of the night. Ed, Jim, Bill, Bob, Julie, Emma, Bruce. I'm not saying I *do* call them to announce at two A.M., "I can't write. I've never been able to write. I've fooled the world and they're finding out at dawn," but if I had to call them, they would understand. Similarly, I hold a willing place on their midnight call sheet. None of us wants to be suicidally depressed at four A.M., but all of us sometimes are, and knowing that we *could* call often calls off the demons. Take a moment to make your midnight madness medical team. Sometimes, it is difficult to find people who can feel equally at home with both our largest and smallest selves.

For this reason, it is tremendously important to accurately distinguish who among our friends can accommodate each size. If you call a friend who loves "little" you with big news, you may meet an upsetting silence followed by a tepid "Gee, that's great!" that sounds like you've just said your exotic blood disease was now in remission. Call a friend who loves "big" you when you're feeling small, and you may feel as welcomed as a malaria-bearing mosquito. This is especially true if you are surrounded by people who are out of touch or shaky in their own creativity; they may never be able to see your need for validation and support as an artist. To them you're the lucky one, so what's the problem? This attitude may trigger you into your own caretaking, where you join them in neglecting your artist. A young novelist with a best seller gave all his earnings to his friends' worthy causes, "just to put everyone back in the same boat," struggling to keep their heads above water. A recording artist with a hit began frantically producing projects for needy newcomers. When people are judgmental or withholding around our success, we unconsciously try to buy them off—peace at any price, even if it's a piece of ourselves.

Consciously or not, the withholding of approval and appre-

Know that if you have a kind of cultured know-it-all in yourself who takes pleasure in pointing out what is not good, in discriminating, reasoning, and comparing, you are bound under a knave. I wish you could be delivered.

BRENDA UELAND

ciation is a powerful manipulation that moves us off our personal perspective and into pleasing others. This can be very expensive. When people are afraid of being artistically diminished themselves, they may never be able to do anything but diminish you. What we want to find are people who are able to be generous to us and to our artist.

We must learn to avoid those who blackmail us by pointing at our abandoning them when we are pulling our energies in and gathering them for a creative jump. We must find those who can both help ground us and help nurture us as we leap.

A public appearance as an artist is best handled with a very clear understanding of the wallop the spotlight packs. Friends who see the glory but not its gory cost are the friends we may not be able to afford. Just as caffeine or an alcoholic drink can hit us hard on an empty stomach, so, too, the glare of the spotlight can throw us off center unless we are well fed spiritually, both before and after. Friends who see our success but do not see its stressors can tend to actually ask us to care for them just at those moments when we ourselves need care. This is why we need before, during, and after friends. We need those who can help us leap and help us land, help us celebrate and help us mourn. Some friends can do only one. Some friends can do only the other. We must find those generous enough in temperament and emotional range to do both.

It might be your aunt Bernice. It may be your little sister. It may be the doorman at your building or your best friend from grade school. All of us need a private cheering section when we undergo a public creative jump. We need those selected family members and friends who can provide us with the nutrients of love and creative support. If people see you only as the swan, that publicly graceful creature, and do not know about the feet churning beneath the water, then they are not the friends you truly need.

And yet, just as a swan is supported by water, which is see-through and ephemeral but "there," so, too, are we supported by

If the book is good, is about something that you know, and is truly written, and reading it over you see that this is so, you can let the boys yip and the noise will have that pleasant sound coyotes make on a very cold night when they are out in the snow and you are in your own cabin that you have built or paid for with your work.

ERNEST HEMINGWAY

higher forces that are unseen and ephemeral but "there." Our sincere prayers are answered. Furthermore, if we are lonely and beg for a little more in the way of human support, that support does show up.

Living lately in Manhattan, far from my nest in New Mexico, I have been craving before, during, and after friends, the day-in and day-out kind that I knew in New Mexico. To my shock and relief, I have been contacted by exactly that kind of person. An actor friend of mine from twenty-five years ago has turned up. A beloved teacher from thirty-five years ago. Another from fifteen years ago and a horseback riding girlfriend from further back than that. These friends knew me as young and wild as wistful and a lot of the ways that I still am when I get a chance to be. Today my mail contained notes from two of these recently re-met friends. My voice-mail had a message from my grammar school best girlfriend. All of these "miracle" reunions happened directly following a rather desperate prayer on my part, "Dear God, send me my real friends. I am too lonely with just you and me and good intentions."

With thee conversing I forget all time.

JOHN MILTON

Most of us are too lonely with just God and good intentions and no one knows this better than God. Instead of feeling so piercingly lonely, you might want to try, as I did, to pick up the phone and do some detective work. It took me three phone calls to find Sr. Julia Clare Greene, my high school writing teacher, but when I did and we talked on the phone, she did what a writer was bound to do: She wrote me. Now I have her picture and note tacked above my writing table, and it reminds me that I may have as many friends as I am willing to be friend to.

TASK:
There's a Somebody I'm Longing to Meet

Take heart and some heart steps. There are those who will tell you we should be "too mature" to need a cheering section.

That's stingy advice, and it's not founded in artistic reality. We both need a cheering section and need to *be* a cheering section.

Invent an imaginary supporter. Take a sheet of paper and write a want ad that expresses exactly what you would really like in a creative colleague. You may already know such a person. If not, your "ad" will help you recognize a possible candidate when he appears:

WANTED

A creative colleague with genuine enthusiasm and generosity for me and my work. Someone to share my hopes, dreams, and disappointments with, who will spoil me a little, cheer for me a lot, and believe in me when I can't believe in myself. Someone who can say—and mean—"That's beautiful, and so are you."

Catcher's Mitt

A compliment is something like a kiss through a veil.

VICTOR HUGO

As artists, we need to focus on process, not on product, and yet, we also need a catcher's mitt—somewhere or someplace where the ball we're pitching is aimed. In order to keep our art moving successfully on its true course, we need the right catcher's mitt. That is how we learn to throw the ball across the plate. Ideally, we want someone with enough range to catch a pitch that goes a little wild, someone with enough enthusiasm to yelp out, "Put it here!"

We make art to communicate not only to ourselves but also to the world. Someone or something must represent that world, and it must be the *right* someone or something. We must become smart about this.

The great writer Italo Calvino phrased it "The ears call forth the story." This is another way of saying that proper receptivity to our art helps to catalyze that art. "Oh, that's beautiful!" or "I love your phrasing" can be water to our creative garden. An eager "Tell me more about that" or "Show me that again" can bring our artist into blossom just as chill inattention or indifference can nip its growth or stunt it. So, too, skewed and premature criticism can cause it to compensate like a pine in a prevailing wind, and twist in an unnatural direction.

Early work is most often called forward by warmth. "That's going to be great!" You may remember the fairy tale about the bet between the wind and the sun as to who could make a traveler drop his cloak. The wind blew. The traveler, our artist, clutched his cloak. The sun shone gently, warmly, and pleasantly. Our artist took his coat off in the sun.

As a writer, your best catcher's mitt might not be an editor—it might be an avid, word-loving personal friend. Some of the best writing has been aimed to a specific someone—Rilke's *Letters to a Young Poet* was not generic. He didn't write them to "young people everywhere" but to one young mind and heart of interest to him. We can call such a person a muse, but we don't have to. You might like words like fuse lighter, spark, catalyst. It's someone whose particular intelligence lights your own. It is because of this alchemical attraction between souls that artists have always nurtured and encouraged other artists, and often championed their work. Haydn was nicknamed "Papa" because he was a catcher's mitt for Mozart.

At the end of his middle period, frustrated by his growing deafness—and the deafness of others to the music only he could seem to hear—Beethoven, in despair, made God his catcher's mitt and went on to write some of his most glorious music. Still, the story is a lonely one.

God can be the catcher's mitt for us as well, just as Christianity probably caught on because many people needed God in a human form in the same way many of us as artists need our catcher's mitt in a human form.

It is romantic nonsense to believe that we can, or do, make art in a vacuum. It is only a half-truth to say we make it to please ourselves. Even there we are pleasing a certain receptive aspect in ourselves, a sort of internal embodiment of our ideal viewer,

It is not what we learn in conversation that enriches us. It is the elation that comes of swift contact with tingling currents of thought.

AGNES REPPLIER

War talk by men who have been in a war is always interesting; whereas moon talk by a poet who has not been in the moon is likely to be dull.

MARK TWAIN

reader, or listener. I wrote *The Dark Room* to read to my friend Ellen Longo in installments. She was an avid reader and accountant. I wrote *Popcorn: Hollywood Stories* to make my first husband laugh at my version of the world we both survived.

Great art lies not in the generic but in the specific. It lies not in "More or less"—as we lamely conclude a thought to a bored listener—but in "Exactly like this!" as we excitedly show or tell someone perceptive. A tepid ear, a hurried glance, a lack of real focus—these can chill and even destroy an early work and a fragile worker. Yes, artists are resilient, but we are also like tender shoots. Our thoughts and our ideas must be welcomed or, like shy suitors, they get discouraged and go away.

Does this mean we want constant adulation and approval? Oh, probably. Does this mean we hate criticism and have no rigor, no discipline, no need for improvement? Emphatically, no. What it does mean is that our catcher's mitt must be receptive to our efforts, to our warm-up pitches and our looping fouls as well as to our sizzling fast balls and snaking curves that catch just the tiniest corner of the plate. Our catcher's mitt fields our creative energies, is open to all of them, and has faith in our artist's arm—wild, tired, serviceable, blistering. In other words, our catcher's mitt must be generous—which does not mean nondiscerning.

One of my best catcher's mitts is my friend Ed. When I tell him the writing is a little ragged, he says, "I'm sure it is, but it will tighten up later. It's great you're getting something down." When I tell him I am having a writing day that feels like I am suffering from rheumatism of the writing faculty, he says, "Everybody gets stiff once in a while. It can take a while to warm up. I am sure it's not as bad as you think it is, and you'll probably be limber again pretty soon." When I tell him, "I have so much work to do, I cannot believe it," he says, "True, but you've gotten through long rewrites before, and if you just keep chipping at it, you'll do fine."

Perhaps Ed's gentle coaching comes from the fact that he,

too, writes. Perhaps it comes from his years as a senior partner in a law firm, coaching hot young lawyers through pretrial jitters. Maybe it is his long years as a slow long-distance runner that have taught him the value of just logging the miles and not trying to sprint all the time. Maybe I am just lucky and Ed is very compassionate. Whatever the case, I need him. He is like the friend who turns up at the twenty-two-mile marker and gently runs me across the marathon finish line. I know Ed is a superb catcher's mitt because I have also had the other kind.

I have made the mistake of giving a rough draft of a book to one of my most fastidious and hypercritical friends. I have been told: "This book lacks your usual ease and poise. These essays are really heavy lifting and not very personable."

What do you say to that? "It's a rough draft, you idiot! There's a reason we call them 'rough'!"

I have also given rough drafts of my books to friends who are too nondiscerning. "I don't see how you could change a thing in this book. It's just perfect. Nothing seemed too long or too unfocused to me. I could always figure out what you meant and I just love the way you write anything. I could probably read the phone book if you wrote it. . . ."

Reviews like that from personal friends leave me pretty terrified that I *have* written the phone book. If the praise feels too syrupy, I get the terrible feeling that I will be like the wasp who gets her legs stuck in the sugary jam at a picnic—a good wallow until you want and need some liftoff. No, too much sugar from a catcher's mitt is not what we are really after.

What we want in a great catcher is what you see with a great catcher. Someone avidly crouched near home plate. Somebody slapping his mitt a little eagerly and saying, "Put it here."

How many are silenced, because in order to get to their art they would have to scream?

Ann Clark

TASK:
Catch Yourself a Catcher's Mitt

The part of us that creates is youthful and vulnerable. It needs an atmosphere that is friendly and even playful, certainly compassionate, so that it can expand, experiment, and express itself. In many ways, a catcher's mitt is like a spiritual sidekick. Even the Lone Ranger wasn't really alone on all his great adventures. He had Tonto at his side.

Often, when we think about periods where we have been particularly happy, we will discover that we had an unacknowledged sidekick, a creative companion who cheered us on by taking a lively interest in our adventures.

Take pen in hand and do a little digging to discover some of your earlier companions and just what qualities they had that let you sparkle.

I believe . . . that every human mind feels pleasure in doing good to another.

THOMAS JEFFERSON

1. As a child, did you have a catcher's mitt for your creative efforts?
2. Who was your very best catcher's mitt? Mine was my friend Lynnie.
3. What did he bring to you that created joy and excitement in your artist?
4. Do you know such a person now?
5. Could that person be your catcher's mitt?
6. As a child, did you have a larger-than-life creative hero in your favored art? (Someone you just plain liked and identified with, not someone so intimidating, your artist would hide.)
7. What did your artist like in that artist?
8. What would that artist like in your artist?
9. Write a letter to your childhood catcher's mitt or your childhood creative hero.
10. Write a letter back to you.

CHECK-IN

1. **How many days this week did you do your Morning Pages?** If you skipped a day, why did you skip it? How was the experience of writing them for you? Are you experiencing more clarity? A wider range of emotions? A greater sense of detachment, purpose, and calm? Did anything surprise you? Is there a "repeating" issue asking to be dealt with?

2. **Did you do your Artist's Date this week?** Did you note an improved sense of well-being? What did you do and how did you feel? Remember, Artist's Dates can be difficult and you may need to coax yourself into taking them.

3. **Did you get out on your Weekly Walk?** How did that feel? What emotions or insights surfaced for you? Were you able to walk more than once? What did your walk do for your optimism and sense of perspective?

4. **Were there any other issues this week that felt significant to you in your self-discovery?** Describe them.

Action is character.

F. SCOTT FITZGERALD

Discovering a Sense of Authenticity

In the end, an artist's life is grounded
in integrity and the willingness to witness
our version of truth. There are no set markets
that assure us of safe passage. This week focuses
on personal responsibility for our creative caliber
and direction. Self-respect lies in the doing, not in
the done. For this reason, our personal resiliency is a
key to our creative longevity. Defeat is transformed
into experience by our willingness to start anew.
The readings and tasks of this week ask us to
practice a beginner's mind, opening ourselves
to renewed endeavors despite setbacks.

Encouragement

Artists are people whose "real" job, no matter what their paying job, is the pursuit of excellence by listening carefully and well to what is trying to be born through them.

Artists are not fragile, but we are delicate. We are subject to the weather conditions in our life. Just as a long gray winter spent indoors can cause depression, so, too, a period where our creative life is led without the sunshine of encouragement can cause a season of despair. We do not notice the darkening at first. We just "don't feel much" like working. If we do work, there will be forced and dreary drudgery to our time at the pi-

Why should we all use our creative power . . . ? Because there is nothing that makes people so generous, joyful, lively, bold and compassionate, so indifferent to fighting and the accumulation of objects and money.

BRENDA UELAND

ano, the easel, the page. We will feel like it's a long hill we are climbing and may even, mistakenly, glance up and say, "Oh, dear, so far to go. I'll never get there."

As artists, we routinely tap an inner well, and that well is fed by our spiritual condition. When we have kept our spirit carefully nurtured, the creative water seems to flow easily. When our spirit is dried out with unacknowledged discouragement, our inner well runs dry.

The antidote to depression is laughter, and this is where we are blessed if some of our friends have a good, bleak sense of humor. Sometimes, we can make a phone call that says "I am torn between suicide and doing my fingernails." Or "I am torn between making a gratitude list and leaping off my tenth-story window ledge."

The uncomfortable fact remains that there is always one positive thing we could do—and, damnably, there *is* always some positive something—even though we may still not have the heart to do it. We have to admit that our discouragement is, as one wag puts it, "a dirty job, but one that we have volunteered for, dammit."

There are some impeccably tried-and-true cheer-er-uppers that most of us are loath to try. It is, for example, very difficult to bake a pie and remain suicidal. It is very difficult to send out postcards without admiring ourselves, just a little, for our pluck and valor, even if our card says "Dear God, I am having a terrible time and wish you were here to do it with me." It is very hard to be depressed and watch a vintage comedy. It is hard to be depressed and make vegetable soup. Making almost anything can keep us from making trouble and, since most of us intuitively know this, we may take to our bed, giving our discouragement full rein to mug us. If we are in a 12-Step program, the dire complaints of a newcomer can lighten most despair. There is something very edifying about hearing someone share a truly catastrophic story when what we are worried about is something as elusive as "inspiration." Reading the hard knocks story of a literary great can cheer up most writers. Knowing that Rodgers and Hammerstein went penthouse to penthouse playing the piano and singing—to no good avail—to raise money for *Oklahoma!* can make the doldrums of "I don't feel like writing a song" seem laughably self-indulgent. Then, too, there is something wonderful to be said about just giving in to the full five-hanky storm of life that has a certain cheery effect. Finally, and this can work wonders, there is the possibility of calling someone truly boring. As they launch into breathtaking detail on something you could not care less about, the idea of going back to doing a little creative work can actually seem attractive. That and repeating the following:

All artists get discouraged. All artists have deep inner wells of self-pity into which we periodically dive. All artists are doing better than someone else and worse than someone else. All artists are doing better today than they have in the past and worse than they will in the future. All artists specialize in self-doubt. It is how we hone the creative imagination. . . .

We cannot control everything and everybody in our creative environment. We cannot leap across the dinner table and muzzle the fellow guest who casually observes, "At your age, you must be facing the fact that many of your dreams won't come true." We cannot—or, at least, we do not—hire hit men to take him out for murdering our hope, but that is what an offhand remark can do, especially if we are not alert to flag it as it passes. And we seldom are. "Let it go," we may say, only to have it go underground. When it does, it's poison.

As artists, we don't want to be petty, but the truth is, we *need* to be. If we try to "let go of" a creative slight, we very often simply bury it. There, tucked neatly into our subconscious, it can do its slow and poisonous work. Too embarrassed to repeat to a friend the "tiny" comment that hurt you on your way out the door from an audition, it becomes harder to audition next time. Why? Because we have been discouraged.

"Courage" comes from the root *coeur*, heart. It is easy to tell

We will discover the nature of our particular genius when we stop trying to conform to our own or to other people's models, learn to be ourselves, and allow our natural channel to open.

SHAKTI GAWAIN

Artistic by
+ Constant

Discontent and disorder [are]
signs of energy and hope,
not of despair.

if you have been discouraged if you check the emotional tim-
bre of your heart. If you feel vaguely blue, a little cross, a bit
grumpy, odds are you are "disheartened," meaning discouraged.

It is well worth it to sleuth a bit, to assume there is a cause for
your discomfort instead of saying "I'm crazy. What's the matter
with me?" Very often, "What's the matter?" is an ignored injury,
however slight.

A friend asks to look at your video—and then doesn't. Weeks
tick past and your filmmaker thinks, *Oh, what's the use?* You
write an essay and send it to a colleague and no sound comes
back to let you know that the penny dropped in the well has
landed. You record a CD and out it goes to your family, where
it falls, evidently, on deaf ears. You have "dragged home the invisible bone," the trophy of all your hard work lies on the floor
unnoticed and unapplauded.

"No big deal," says your adult self. But your artist? Your artist
has the character traits of a terrier puppy. It was proud to have
made that bone and dragged it home, defending it against other
dogs and managing to lay it at master's feet. So, how about a pat
on the head? Like it or not, whether we hate the Disney description or not, artists *do* need pats on the head. We *do* need encouragement. We *do* need praise and we *do* need comfort. It
does not matter how accomplished we are; it is a daunting and
damaging thing to have our work ignored.

"I meant to" and "whoops" add up to discouragement. We
"should be" more mature—but we really shouldn't. What we
should be is alert to the damage of discouragement and clever
about addressing it directly. If no one else is cheering us on, we
must cheer ourselves on with tokens of our esteem for work
well done. We must care for our manuscripts well, not leave
them in shabby stacks where we spill coffee over them. We must
set Artist's Dates and celebrate our finishing a new story or finally laying to rest the portrait for the grumpy client from hell
who could not be pleased, although the portrait was pleasing to

everyone else who saw it. We must actively seek out friends who do not shame us around our discouragement and friends who can celebrate with us any small victory. In short, discouragement comes from an experience of stinginess—on the part of a critic, a colleague, a friend, our family. Encouragement just as clearly comes from an experience of generosity. Ideally, from others and ourselves.

At its root, discouragement is a decision in favor of stinginess. We are voting that the universe has done its last nice thing for us and that we have come to the bottom of Santa's bag of toys. No one will ever be spontaneously nice to us again—and we certainly aren't going to point the way by mustering any authentic and healing compassion for ourselves either.

We know how to stay discouraged when we are discouraged. We know how to choose our best negative friend to call. Most of us have a secret number emblazoned in our consciousness under the heading "Dial this number for pain and rejection." Most of us know how, if we are really feeling bad, we can feel just a little worse by calling it.

Jennifer has an excellent candidate for the worst person you could possibly call. He is a romantic ex. Someone who still owes her a great deal of money and who manages to ask for one whopping favor every time they speak. Superb at reporting the health and longevity of his stellar romantic involvements, where he is truly appreciated, this ex is skilled at remarks like "I heard you were in a terrible relationship—is that true?" Jennifer experiences the temptation to call this ex as a sign that the devil is alive and well and knows exactly where she lives. And yet, and still, Jennifer can fight calling this man the way a newly sober alcoholic can fight taking the first drink. It just doesn't seem possible to stay away from the pain and rejection that such a call can inevitably bring. Not when it's a clear-cut choice between encouraging herself and reaching for Mr. Poison.

All of us have some version of Jennifer's dilemma. We face

My business is not to remake myself,
But make the absolute best of what God made.

ROBERT BROWNING

the choice of thinking, *Actually, I'm doing pretty well and should really respect myself for my progress,* or, as we so often choose to think, *I am a spineless wonder, incapable of mustering the integrity, resolve, and inspiration necessary to address a postcard.* We all have people who think we are rather nice and doing pretty well and we all have other people who think—as we do often—that we could do better and be better if we would just listen to them. . . .

For most of us, the idea that we can listen to ourselves, trust ourselves, and value ourselves is a radical leap of faith. The idea that we can tell ourselves "Hey, you are doing pretty well and so much better than you did last year" amounts to a revolution. The possibility that we can trust ourselves, our decisions, and our painstaking progress, that this trust might be enough, even admirable, requires that we muster a soupçon of optimism. Optimism about ourselves and our chances is an elected attitude. We can choose to believe the best and not the worst, but to do that we must become conscious of our own negative voice-over and decide to change our mental sound track.

Optimism is critical to our spiritual health. Is our creative glass half full or half empty? Have we wasted a decade or two not getting where we would like, or are we strong and seasoned and facing another couple of decades where our age and maturity and sheer experience may allow us to actualize areas beyond our grasp when we were younger? It's a matter of perception—and faith.

The good news and the bad news is that artists are like plants that can thrive or wither with only a few simple variables. It is hard to kill an artist, but it is very easy to discourage one. All that it requires is a certain withholding quality, and that can cast a spell over a very fine piece of work.

We all know people who tell us our dreams are foolish, pie in the sky, whimsy, and that we should be grateful for what recognition we have won and settle for a lower creative ceiling than

Just trust yourself, then you will know how to live.

JOHANN WOLFGANG
VON GOETHE

our high-flying dreams require. (Those people have settled themselves and are uncomfortable with anyone willing to continue with substantial risks.) Fortunately, we also know people who do not bother to think about the odds or age or anything but the work at hand. Those people are the ones we must consciously choose to listen to. It is to those people that we must take our creative cuts and bruises for poulticing.

If we are to "take heart" and go on with our work, then we must take our heart seriously. We must listen to its pains and we must bring to it its joys. A heart does not need to be told "Oh, toughen up." It needs you to plan a tiny cheering ceremony and execute it. That done, you will find "the heart"—the courage—to work again and well.

Perhaps loving something is the only starting place there is for making your life your own.

ALICE KOLLER

TASK:
Taking Heart

If we are to "take heart" and encourage ourselves, we must first find our heart. Our truth lies in what we love, and as we remind ourselves that we have loved and do love, we find our way unerringly back to the place from which accomplishment is possible.

In horseback riding circles, fine riders will talk of "throwing my heart over a fence" and then "jumping after it." What they are talking about is the courage to commit, to be full-hearted. When we are discouraged, we are literally divorced from our hearts. We forget how large our hearts are and how daring. When we trust our hearts, we trust ourselves. The following exercise, taught so beautifully by Oscar Hammerstein as *My Favorite Things,* is a lesson that all of us can teach ourselves whenever the going gets tough.

Take pen in hand, number from 1 to 50, and list 50 specific and particular things your heart loves. For example:

"I have no name:
"I am but two days old."
What shall I call thee?
"I happy am,
"Joy is my name."
Sweet joy befall thee!

WILLIAM BLAKE

1. Red-winged blackbirds
2. Raspberry pie
3. Lemon curd
4. Beatrix Potter drawings
5. My daughter Domenica's bangs and sooty eyelashes
6. West Highland terriers
7. Plaid ribbons
8. Homemade rice pudding
9. Lily oil
10. The tassels on field corn
11. William Hamilton cartoons
12. Making this list

It's almost impossible to make a list of heart loves without concluding we live in a rich, savory, and enjoyable world where—if we will just "take heart"—things are bound to work out well.

Sometimes, we meet with creative encouragement that we savor, cherish, and act upon. Sometimes, however, we meet with creative encouragement that we discount and disown. Take pen in hand. Number from 1 to 10. List 10 examples of creative encouragement that you acted on *or* ignored. Next to those you acted on, note the action taken. Next to those you discounted, note an action that *could* be taken.

Integrity

What if we experiment with the idea that creativity is a spiritual and not an intellectual transaction? Not so long ago, cathedrals were built for the honor and glory of God. Art and artistry were routinely put to the service of higher realms. Higher realms were routinely credited for the worldly successes of creators.

Brahms exclaimed, "Straightaway the ideas flow in upon me, directly from God!"

"The music of this opera *(Madame Butterfly)* was dictated to me by God; I was merely instrumental in putting it on paper and communicating it to the public," Puccini confided.

If these men, masters at their art, could bow to mystery rather than their own mastery, might there be something medicinal for us in what they say? What if creativity itself is, as our creative ancestors teach us, actually a *spiritual experience,* a way to touch the divine and allow it to touch us? What if we reclaim the making of art as our birthright? Not some frippery on the edge of our serious business of making money. What if we remember and insist that art is central and dignified and important to the human experience?

We are an expression of the Great Creator, and we in turn are intended to create. It is not mere ego but our divine birthright to create. We carry creativity within us as surely as we carry our blood, and, in expressing it, we express our full humanity, which is far more than material. When we fail to answer this calling, when we turn it aside and listen to voices that deflect us, we are not in alignment with our own nature, nor with what might be called our destiny.

When we are headed in the right direction creatively, we feel a sense of satisfaction in each day's journey. We might not be moving as fast as we wish, but we are moving in the right direction and we do know it. At day's end, we can tote up our ta-dah list and say, "I placed three important phone calls. I reached out to check information that I needed. I jotted notes and got a few good paragraphs down."

Conversely, when we are not moving in the right direction, we experience a sense of unease. We have a growing sense of being off the beam. Something isn't sitting right with us. We feel stagnant or else stalemated. Sometimes, when we are moving in a wrong direction and events pick up velocity, we experience an alarming sense of being out of control. Something is "off," we know it and it is getting more and more "off." This is the time to step on the brakes. When we skid to a halt and the

Where there is great love there are always miracles.

WILLA CATHER

spinning stops, we can say, "I was headed straight for the cliff and I didn't have to go over."

Most of us experience the presence of what I often call "my beeper." I will get a "flash" that something is not quite right. If I ignore it, I will get another flash. My beeper will beep until I pay attention to it, checking in on the ominous feeling I am trying to ignore. Recently, my beeper went off that something I had written was not quite right. "Oh, it's bound to be fine," I tried to reassure myself. "How bad can it be? I wrote it. Everybody—three editors—read it. What's my problem?" When my beeper persisted and no amount of "It's fine" felt fine, I finally called back the questionable text right as the presses were ready to roll. Was it fine? Absolutely not. An immediate, thorough, page one, start-it-all-over rewrite was what was called for. I gladly rewrote the offending piece and felt I had had a very close call indeed.

And so, a sense of rightness will most usually mean all's well. A sense of wrongness will also usually mean something is wrong. Listening to such gut feelings is always worth the time and trouble it takes. When we let God be God and work through us, we experience both a sense of serenity and excitement. We experience integrity—which comes from the root word "integer," meaning "whole," unfragmented by doubt or discomfort. When we experience a sense of oneness with God, ourselves, and our fellows, we can safely know we are in our integrity.

If this language sounds "serious" and "spiritual," so is the matter at hand. "Know thyself," the Greeks inscribed above their temple door. As artists, we must take this to heart, working to express our inner imperatives and not just filling the form provided by the marketplace. Settling for convention over authentic self-expression, we are falling, in the biblical phrase, for false gods. In the long run, this works out no better for us as artists than it did for those worshiping the golden calf. The

Two things make a story. The net and the air that falls through the net.

PABLO NERUDA

"market" is the golden calf. When we worship it, we deaden our souls, risking, over time, our attunement to the work that would move through us. Commerce has its place, but that place is not first.

You will often hear an artist say, "Ah, they had only a shoe-string, so I didn't get my going rate, but it was really enjoyable to work on that film." Or "I *love* helping a new composer get something properly recorded, so I brought in a few of my friends and we really did a nice job." Or "They needed some publicity shots for their dance company, and I just loved helping them out. I mean, what's much more fun than shooting a batch of little ballerinas? And that troupe is first rate."

As artists, we have a different kind of accountability than many people. What pays us and pays off in the long run is really the caliber of our work.

As artists, we have an inner Geiger counter and it ticks loud and clear when we are near pay dirt—first-rate, high-caliber ore that means we are working at the top of our form. Because this device is an inner one, it isn't easily fooled by the prestige of a certain venue or the lack of prestige of another. What it detects is quality. It knows the real thing when it is near it. This is what "accountability" is for an artist, the blunt assessment: Is it any good? Fame, money, prestige—none of them can fool this inner meter of excellence. It boils down to the simple fact that artists respect good art—and we respect ourselves when we make it.

The great musician Stephane Grappelli remarked: "A great improviser is like a priest, talking only to his God." In a sense, all artists are like priests as they listen for the voice of inspiration, aspire to excellence, and hold themselves accountable to that high ideal more than to any boss or paycheck. When we violate our creative ideals, we violate our artistic conscience—and we become very uncomfortable.

Whenever we indulge in what might be called "paint by numbers" art, we are engaging in cynicism and skepticism. We

If you don't tell the truth about yourself, you cannot tell it about other people.

VIRGINIA WOOLF

I honestly think in order to be a writer, you have to learn to be reverent.

ANNE LAMOTT

are on a subtle level out to "fool" people. We are looking down at our audience and saying "If I just feed them what they are used to getting, I can fool them." Does this mean that we must always and willfully break the mold? No, a first act that is twice the normal length is too long for an audience to sit through comfortably—or perhaps at all. On the other hand, a first act that breaks arbitrarily because "it has to" is not an act that is listening to "where it wants to break" and finding the shape that is authentic for it as a piece of art.

As artists, we are always engaged in a delicate balancing act. We both know how things "are done" and we must strive to listen accurately to see if that's how our particular piece of art wants to be done. If we ignore all convention, then our rebellion is probably just as destructive and willful as if we blindly follow all rules, cynically calculating that if we "do it right," we can get away with something less than good because it's "done the way they always do it."

This is how skeptics are born. It also promotes a nasty hybrid of blade-runner artist—adapted to such a poisonous environment and promoting an ill-considered, self-aggrandizing myth that *their* adaptation is "normal," and that any "real" artist should be able to survive anything. Nonsense. Artists such as these like to appear on late-night talk shows, telling war stories and focusing as much on their corporate derring-do, the *Star Wars* of the studios and super-agents, than their art. Promoted in the press, and self-promoting, these artificially inflated *artistes* may intimidate genuine artists of a quieter stripe.

In cultures where creativity is embedded in the warp and woof of daily life, shyer souls may practice their creativity with more impunity. In this country, the artist is an endangered species. Grants are diminishing. Public appreciation is also more difficult to find. Too much power has gone into the hands of too few—reviewers stand in for viewers.

Fearing this process, fearing their capacity to survive it, many

gifted artists allow discouragement to darken their creative landscape. Of course they do. They may lurk too long in the shadows because they lack support—the before, during, and after
friends—to help them tolerate their turns center stage. Many
public art situations are toxic to artists themselves. We learn to
deal with them, but we do not do it easily. Just as the body must
develop antibodies, so in our current culture must the artist's
soul. Not everyone can do this. Many excellent artists cannot.

In my twenty-five years of teaching, working to unblock
damaged artists, it is my experience that it is not that artists lack
quality but that, as a culture, we lack sufficient quality of *character* to nurture and appreciate the artists among us. Until we
fiercely advocate and nurture ourselves, we feel stifled. Until
more of our reticent artists make more art, we risk continuing
to believe the assessments of those who critique but do not
create. The quality of our artists is not the true issue. The quality of our critical climate is. We do not have genuine receptivity to the arts.

In light of these facts, many superb artists are not stamped
with sufficient critical approval and so they may doubt the very
caliber of their art. Making art takes courage—and, although
our Lone Ranger, artist-as-loner mythology would tell us otherwise, it requires support.

The people who snort about there being a lack of quality in
amateur art have not seen enough diamonds in the rough. They
like to buy their art at Tiffany's stamped with a brand name and
someone else's approval. They haven't had the courage to walk
through church and hear a beautiful, if untutored, soprano, and
commit cash on the barrel for her education. They have not
been in a school hallway or on a sidewalk and seen a student
sketch that caught them by the throat with its unexpected vir-
tuosity—and inquired enough to know how they could help
and support that young artist. It takes courage and heart to make
art, and it takes courage and heart to support art makers. A cel-

*If you don't risk anything,
you risk even more.*

ERICA JONG

ebrated pianist who hails from a small midwestern town always
cites the generosity of an older couple from his home city who
staked him a no-strings-attached year's rent in New York when
he was trying to make his way. This couple had the wisdom to
serve the art in the artist, to see the unpolished stone and help it
find its setting. In our culture, their discernment and commitment are unusual.

Our culture diminishes both art and artists. Art is secular
now, mere ornament, where once it was central to civilized life.
Artists are seen as dispensable or, at best, marginal types, gifted
perhaps, but mere filigree.

Artists are everywhere, and if we do not see them—or see
ourselves as perhaps being them—it is because as a culture we
have bunkered our artistic soul in the safe citadel of cynicism.
We co-sign the assessment of critics who are chic and "critical"
but creatively impotent. Quality is not the issue, care is. When I
teach that we are all creative and I say that we should all use that
creativity to express ourselves, I am sometimes greeted by deri-
sive skeptics who snort, "Don't you think you might be unblocking an awful lot of bad art?"

Let's be real: There is already a lot of art in the world that
isn't exhilarating in its excellence. In fact, those who hang back
from "inflicting their art" on the world seem to often be those
who create more beautifully.

As an artist who teaches, I have far more often been humbled
by the superior quality of someone's unblocked work than
shamed by the quality of newly unblocked work. It is often ego
strength and not the strength of the art itself that determines
how far forward an artist is willing to put himself. We have made
such a spotlight-riddled, harrowing public spectacle of the arts
in this country that many people with enormous talent quite
sensibly choose to live outside the limelight.

In our current cultural climate, we have too much acid in the
soil of our creative garden. The limelight is acting like lime itself—poisoning the communal root system and support so nec-

*Good art is a form of prayer.
It's a way to say what is
not sayable.*

FREDERICK BUSCH

essary for arts and artists to flourish. Our critics are likely overly aggressive gardeners, busily weeding and heaping on the acid chemicals, unskilled in encouraging the tender green shoots that hold promise to bloom.

In our culture, we must consciously build safe hatcheries for our art. We must find people and establish places that allow us to flourish. We must become creative about being creative.

As creatives, we must learn to carefully and consciously put our money where our mouth is. We must learn to take the authentic risk of bettering ourselves. Setting aside a genuine hour a day to work on the play will get us further in the long run than telling ourselves we will write the play after we redecorate the apartment—which is why we are taking one more time-consuming freelance job so we can have the right computer table so then we can "really" write. Dreams become reality when we start to treat them as if they are real. When we stop postponing and evading them, and when we can answer "Today, I worked on my dream" with a grounded specific.

Creativity isn't something vague that we are going to do. It is something real that we actually *do* do. It is the refusal to sell ourselves short by shortchanging our artists with empty talk—or empty paychecks. We may have to work at a day job and that day job may give us structure and support, but it is a dangerous lie to tell ourselves that our paycheck from our advertising agency will ever give us the same satisfaction as writing the play we have dreamed about since grammar school.

Often, when we are afraid to try to make what we really want to make, we will say, "I can't make that." The truth is, we could, but we are frightened to try: Not trying, we do not really know whether we could or couldn't make our heart's desire. Very often when we say "I couldn't do that," we are again embracing an ideal of false independence, eschewing spiritual help. We are embracing an idea of God as a withholding God whose intentions for us are counter to our own dreams. Believing, even unconsciously, in such a toxic God, we do not see the Great

The imagination has resources and intimations we don't even know about.

CYNTHIA OZICK

Creator as a cocreator, a partner, in our dreams. Rather, we see God as a barrier, a withholding parent who denies our dreams. Most often, we are who denies them.

It is at this point that we must muster our integrity and be honest about what it is we really want. We must take the leap—or even the small hop—of faith that moves us slightly toward our true dream. This honest motion on our part is what triggers support for our authenticity—instead of support for a false self we can no longer comfortably inhabit.

"But what about the odds?" You may catch yourself grasping at straws. Odds are a favored guise of false gods. Odds are the denial of miracles. Odds are faith in being faithless, faith in being hopeless, faith in being stuck where we are, isolated from any power that might overcome the odds.

As we commit to our real dreams, we commit to ourselves. As we commit to ourselves, we also commit to trusting the power that created us. We are then aligning ourselves not with false gods but with the true power of the universe, the Great Creator through whose power all dreams are possible.

Surprise is where creativity comes in.

RAY BRADBURY

TASK:
Pat Yourself on the Back

You have already accomplished many worthy things. It is a good idea to have ready at hand a list of 25 things you are proud of. This list is where you value your own character and put down in black and white some of the things you have done right. It is important in writing this list to place on it what you are actually proud of, not what you "should" be proud of. There should be at least one entry that makes you grin at the memory, perhaps an episode where you stood up to a bully or managed to think of the exact right comeback at the actual moment of attack.

Take pen in hand and list 25 specific things you are proud of.

Do not be surprised by a positive leading to more positives, for example:

1. I am proud I taught Domenica how to ride a horse.
2. I am proud I took her to Sunday pony rides when she was a toddler.
3. I am proud I let her ride double with me to get her balance.
4. I am proud I signed her up for lessons and stood on the sidelines, watching.
5. I am proud I stuck up for Carolina in religion class.
6. I am proud I told the nun that Christian Scientists were as good as Catholics.
7. I am proud I brought my mother wagon loads of wild violets for her garden.
8. I am proud I tried to save the tomato worm by taping it back together.
9. I am proud I picked Tiger Lily from all the puppies at the pound.
10. I am proud I still write Morning Pages even when I am not teaching.

A list such as this one goes a long way toward establishing a beachhead of integrity.

Style begins when you seek and discover your strengths, then bank on them for all they're worth.

SARAH BAN BREATHNACH

Getting Back on the Horse

We are intended to make something of ourselves. When we feel supported by others, this is a festive feeling. There is a sense of community and a sense of shared purpose and humor—like we're the creative equivalent of a quilting bee or a barn raising. The collective group energy feels firm and exhilarating and fine. We don't wobble because there are helping hands to steady our ladder as we try to climb. Surrounded by support, making something—and something of ourselves—is easy. This is why the great summer music camps like Tanglewood and Aspen and Marlboro matter. This is why painting institutes and writing retreats are so valued. All of us need such support. We don't always have this luxury.

Sometimes, support fails us. Instead of help, we meet hindrance.

Sometimes, we suffer a horrifying creative injury. Our bones may not be broken, but our confidence is. An actress is emotionally disemboweled by a director who makes Hannibal Lecter look like an amateur. A pianist is reviewed by a critic who thinks "beat" is a musical term meaning "to club."

Creative cataclysms like these are common. They are the dangers of the trail. Artists are sensitive animals, and we do get spooked. Certainly, the sensitive horse of our talent gets spooked, and we may get pitched right off it. "I am never trying *that* again!" we vow—meaning the novel; the finger-twisting, heart-shredding concerto; that torture rack, the stage. And the longer we don't try "it" again, the more we convince ourselves we could *never* try "it" again. We say, "It hurt me once, and . . ."

There is one and only one cure for a creative injury, and that cure is to make something. If we do not make some small something, our injured yet active imagination will make an even bigger deal out of what happened to us. Sometimes, the only comfort we can find is naming ourselves. If no one else will pronounce us "artist," then we must say our name to ourselves— and the only way to say it is through art. The bandage must fit the wound. If your musical has been trounced, write some music. If your painting has been pounced on, paint something, even a kitchen chair. If your poetry has had its feet broken, walk to an open mic and read something. A famous director I know well, always conscious that critical reception might curtail his chances to do large-budget works, would remind himself on sleepless nights, "If I can't shoot 35, I can shoot 16, if I can't

Try again. Fail again.
Fail better.

SAMUEL BECKETT

shoot 16, I can shoot Super 8. If I can't shoot Super 8, I can draw, I can sketch. . . ." In other words, he knew his medicine for his creative losses, however huge and catastrophic, lay in the phrase "I can—and will—create."

We *are* intended to make something of ourselves, and sometimes that "making" has to be done without palpable support. We feel defeated and deflated by our interpersonal relationships. We feel like people have let us down, and often they truly have. Even more discouraging, we feel we have let ourselves down— we feel we "haven't been smart enough." And sometimes, we've done that too. As artists, we have off nights and off years. It is part of the territory. It is arguably a *necessary* part of the territory.

During my twenties, it seemed that everything I touched turned to gold. I was an award-winning journalist first—scooping *The Washington Post* and getting written up in *Time*. Next, I married a great love, Martin Scorsese, and worked side by side with him, contributing writing to his films. I became a popular newspaper columnist and had a winning streak as a screenwriter, selling a trio of films to Paramount and writing a successful television movie starring Don Johnson as Elvis. These were heady times.

Enter my thirties. First, a terrible divorce. Then I made a feature film but had my sound track stolen. I dubbed the film and released it in Europe to good reviews, but there was no American release, no "payoff" for three years of work. I wrote novels but didn't get them published. I wrote plays that won prizes but not productions.

Enter my forties. *The Artist's Way* was published. A dozen more books followed throughout the decade. The novels I had written finally saw print. My plays were produced. Instead of the pangs of failure and anonymity, I now learned the dangers of success. The best word for my forties might be "rigorous."

Throughout all of this time, I steadily, on a daily basis, kept writing. I kept working with the tools of creative recovery and even survival for myself and others. I knew from experience that

The way to find your true self is by recklessness and freedom.

BRENDA UELAND

a creative career took faith. In short, no loss of "time" when I was out of favor, no up or down when I was in vogue, ever went without later providing its usefulness. Everything—and I do mean everything—is fuel for the creative fire.

As a teacher and as an artist, I experience creative growth as characterized by periods where creative syntax and confidence shatters. We write "badly" because we are no longer writing as we were and not yet writing as we will. In our culture, there is little understanding of the growth process of an artist—which is often conducted in a very public arena. For the very public artists, for filmmakers and novelists in particular, there is little room for the work made during necessary periods of creative flux. Concert musicians report the same dilemma—a style matures idiosyncratically and spasmodically, moving not from beauty straight to beauty but from beauty through something different to more beauty. Few reviewers value the "something different" stage.

Art is made from talent and character. Adversity strengthens our character and can strengthen our art as well. It creates empathy and compassion for the adversity of others. This deepens our heart and our art. Adversity is educational, and like many educations, it is terribly hard to recover from without help. That help, in human or nonhuman form, as coincidence, as timely call, as "impulse" to do something off your beaten path, is a guidance and support we can rely on—but act on it we must. We are not so much rescued as joined.

When I first met veteran director John Newland, we were both living in a tiny mountain town. He was there in official retirement from a long and illustrious career—a retirement that lasted about four minutes before he was directing high school plays, community theater, college acting classes, anything that let his skills and experience have some play, however restricted. For myself, I was in what might best be called a "battered" period. I had taken a few creative tumbles—most notably around

You aim for what you want and if you don't get it, you don't get it, but if you don't aim, you don't get anything.

FRANCINE PROSE

discouragement on my musical work—and I was reluctant to get back on the horse. After all, falls hurt, and wasn't I getting a little old for them?

Feeling more than a little sorry for myself, I met up with Newland. I had gone to see an evening of high school monologues he had directed—my daughter was in his cast. I watched from a rickety seat in the tiny auditorium as student after student presented tough and edgy work, daring for our little town, daring for anywhere. I was used to community theater being more tame.

Who the hell did this? I wondered. Someone was putting up some great work. At evening's end, I was pointed to a tall, handsome man with a face like a ravaged cathedral and a shock of snow-white hair to top his alpine height.

"John Newland," he said, shaking my hand. "You've got a talented kid. I hear you're talented yourself, so let's eat some lunch and talk about things."

I met Newland for lunch and found his optimism to be the best thing on the menu. My age? "You're just a kid. I've got forty years on you and I'm still working." My discouragement? "Let me read that musical of yours. I'll bet it's good. We'll put it on." My worry about my career? "You've got another forty years to go, so buck up and let's do something."

We did do something. We put up my musical *Avalon,* and into that small auditorium three thousand miles from New York walked the woman who would become my musical collaborator. She "happened" to be playing chamber music in the same auditorium. A classical violist, she brought a small herd of her classical friends to hear *Avalon* on Newland's and my opening night.

What a good composer, she was thinking even as I sat curled up in the back row, wondering if I would live through the experience of hearing my music performed for the first time. She introduced herself that evening and she reintroduced herself when I moved in next door to her in New York, by "chance," four months later. Within months we were happily collaborat-

Art is our chief means of breaking bread with the dead.

W. H. AUDEN

ing—not, I believe, because I was smart enough to figure out my career but because I was willing to get back on the horse and know it when John Newland rescued me and then she did. It is my observation, after many years of teaching, that such "timely" rescues are par for the course. When an artist sends up a despairing prayer, the Great Creator does hear and answer it.

As artists, when human powers fail us, we must turn to the Great Creator for help. We must "surrender" our sense of isolation and despair and open ourselves to the spiritual help we frequently experience as an unexpected inner strength. Let me be clear about one thing: Artists at all levels experience adversity—some of us quite publicly, some of us in painful privacy. One way or another—bad colleagues, bad reviews—we fall off the horse.

It is a spiritual law that no loss is without meaning in all of creation. And so, the bitter defection of our creative colleagues who say "Thanks" and then try to shove us off the ladder (failing to mention our contributions at press conferences, claiming credit for our ideas in staff meetings) is actually, somehow, a boon to us. Yes, the shove hurts—and the treachery and the disillusionment. But we more often than not land in a pile of straw. We find our fall mysteriously cushioned. "Angels" appear. Sometimes, we sense them internally, as inspiration, the minute we ask "What's next?" and not "Why me?"

Because creativity is a spiritual issue, injuries to that creativity are spiritual wounds. In my experience, an artist's anguished prayers are *always* answered by the Great Creator. Even as we sob to the fates, and rightly, "I cannot go on," we are going on, and we are going on with spiritual assistance. Something is stirring that means we are already going on. We are gaining ground, first as awareness, and next as action. Creativity is a spiritual practice, and like all spiritual practices, it contains the tool of self-inventory.

We want colleagues of both talent and character. To find them, we must forge brighter our own talent and character. Very

Creative minds have always been known to survive any kind of bad training.

ANNA FREUD

often, the people who do betray us and our values are those whom we have felt a vague stirring of unease about and then dismissed that as paranoia. Our gift is that in the future we will hear our forebodings as spiritual telegrams and not as neurosis.

Sometimes, remarkably often, creative angels show up externally. (In the theater world, the term "angel" is actually used.) As our villains slink from the scene of the crime, our heroes and stagehands step forward to try to put up a new and better show. "What if you try this?" a friend asks. Instantly, we see a path— or, at least, a next right step—if only we will take it.

As artists, when we are sold down the river, we must look to see in what ways we are selling ourselves short. Yes, the others have been bastards—that is real and irrefutable and painful. What is often more painful is seeing our participation; usually the spot where we shrank back from trusting ourselves is the very point that turned the tide against us. This does not make other people's foul play our fault. It does not mean they shouldn't have acted differently and better—what it does mean is that we will act differently and better in the future. That is the part we can change.

But the way to change this is not through berating ourselves for our stupidity. It is not by trying to make their flaws our fault. It is not by claiming we "drove them to it" somehow. It is by treating ourselves kindly, listening to ourselves gently. It is by telling compassionate people and forces exactly how hurt we are and admitting we need help that we heal. Call your aunt Bernice and tell her that a critic broke your heart. Write a letter to Oscar Hammerstein II, who endured a decade of failures after the success of *Showboat,* and tell him you're on a losing streak, does he have any thoughts. Call the college teacher who thinks you're a huge success no matter how you feel right now. Call yourself home to that part of you that *is* strong enough to continue. That is when the help comes—it bubbles up within us and it enters as lightly as wind stirring a curtain. There will always be help.

I have a sense of these buried lives striving to come out through me to express themselves.

MARGE PIERCY

What we are charged with in "making something of ourselves" is making ourselves willing to listen for that help and to accept it in forms we don't expect. Then act we must.

As artists, we are engaged *always* in a collaborative process with the Great Creator. Stakes that seem impossibly high to us, casting that feels all wrong—these, when we ask for spiritual guidance, may be revealed to be necessary to the plot, important to the growth and maturation of our own creative process. As artists, it is important to remember that all breaks are lucky because bones are often strongest at the broken places. Art is healing, and artists heal.

As artists, the Great Creator *will* help us if we help ourselves. How do we find this creative help? We find the creator by creating.

As artists, we do not control our creative world, but we control a lot more of it than we care to admit. We evade knowing how much we do control because it is more comfortable and comforting to coast on the spit of our career resentments than to experience the terrifying vulnerability of trying yet again to bring our work into the world.

Most artists feel and respond like spurned lovers to the thought of really committing to their work. Like a broken-hearted bachelor or shy spinster whose tender dreams were abused, we refuse to be vulnerable again. We "know" how it's worked out before. We "fear" how it may work out again, and so we do not even make a coffee date with our creative dreams to see if this time might be different.

Turned down by a callow agent, we say, "Oh, they're all like that." But are they? Blasted by a cynical gallery owner or a bitter dramaturge, we conclude, "I'll never get into a gallery" or "My work will never be accepted." All too often we don't try again—fearing more damage to our broken creative hearts. We know too well that in our heart of hearts, our creative dreams do not die any more than our romantic ones, and we are frightened by the whispers of these dreams—the undead plays, novels, and paintings that we have shoved into our creative closets, where they live with the muttering ghosts of our broken dreams.

As artists, we are dreamers, and what we fear is the nightmare of our work being shunned, mishandled, or ill perceived. Fearing this, we allow our discouragement to globalize from one person to "they," from a single tough review to "always," from a stinging rejection to "they'll never." We elect a defensive cerebral cynicism.

We begin talking about how "they" will never appreciate our work. We feel alone and abandoned, and we are—not because "they" have abandoned us but because we have. We have given up not only on ourselves but also on God. We have said, "What's the use?" instead of "What's next?" Rather than risk the vulnerability of moving out again on faith, we have hidden our dreams and our hopes under what we call "realism about the market." We have said, "Oh, they're all like that" rather than allow ourselves the terror of discovering they might not be.

Artists, like gifted horses injured at the fence, may shy away from trying the fence again. And yet, a gifted horse can and must be rehabilitated. As artists, we are both the horse and rider of our talent. When we are thrown, we cannot let that throw us. It's part of the territory.

Get back on the horse.

"Healing,"
Papa would tell me,
"is not a science,
but the intuitive art
of wooing Nature."
W. H. AUDEN

TASK:
Ouch! Let Me Make It Better

Creative injuries tend to be secret injuries. "It shouldn't bother me so much," we say. Or "I just seemed to lose interest after that." We deny to others and to ourselves the devastating impact a creative upset can have on us. We fall down from the horse, and rather than get back on, we tell ourselves we have lost interest in riding.

Unmourned creative injuries create scar tissue. We "toughen

up," but the wound festers underneath. "I'm just not interested," we say, when we are *very* interested indeed—just injured.

The following exercise is one in compassion and forgiveness. We deserve compassion for the pain we suffered due to our creative injury. We deserve forgiveness because we have allowed ourselves to be stopped, stalled, or stymied and we usually judge ourselves harshly for that.

Take pen in hand and again number from 1 to 10. List 10 creative injuries or disappointments you have not allowed yourself to grieve, get through, or get over. Be very careful to be gentle with yourself. This is an extremely vulnerable and volatile process.

As you review your injury list, look for a very small and very gentle step you can take to move your artist back toward the arena where the injury occurred. But the steps must be very small and very gentle. Let us say, for example, that you wrote a novel and received some encouraging and some discouraging agents' letters in response to your manuscript. A first step might be rereading the positive letters and the first twenty-five pages of your manuscript. Allow yourself to go slowly and carefully. If you put up a play and received some savage reviews, you might be avoiding theater entirely. Get yourself a set of theater tickets. In other words, coax your artist out to play, then put your artist straight back to work.

Rationality squeezes out much that is rich and juicy and fascinating.

ANNE LAMOTT

CHECK-IN

1. **How many days this week did you do your Morning Pages?** If you skipped a day, why did you skip it? How was the experience of writing them for you? Are you experiencing more clarity? A wider range of emotions? A greater sense of detachment, purpose, and calm? Did anything surprise you? Is there a "repeating" issue asking to be dealt with?

2. **Did you do your Artist's Date this week?** Did you note an improved sense of well-being? What did you do and how did you feel? Remember, Artist's Dates can be difficult and you may need to coax yourself into taking them.

3. **Did you get out on your Weekly Walk?** How did that feel? What emotions or insights surfaced for you? Were you able to walk more than once? What did your walk do for your optimism and sense of perspective?

4. **Were there any other issues this week that felt significant to you in your self-discovery?** Describe them.

Always be a first-rate version of yourself, instead of a second-rate version of somebody else.

Judy Garland

Discovering a Sense of Dignity

The key to a successful creative life is the
commitment to make things and in so doing
make something better of ourselves and our world.
Creativity is an act of faith. As artists, we are sourced in
the Great Creator, meaning that our funding of strength
and power is limitless. This week focuses on the survival
of those difficulties encountered at the highest creative
peaks. Our graceful ability to encompass difficulty
rests in our ability to be faithful. The reading and
tasks of this week aim at acquainting the
creative practitioner with the survival
tools necessary for the successful
accomplishment of a sustained
creative life.

The Glass Mountain

Today, with charming Currier and Ives snowmen lurching to
life under tiny hands in Riverside Park below, I grapple with the
icy slopes of depression. *My* mood is the glass mountain of fairy
tale lore: I slither down every time I try to clamber up.

"It's the holidays," a friend of mine called to advise gravely—
secure that her depression, her heightened sense of nasty odds,
held common ground with mine.

I don't think so.

Today's depression and doubt is par for the course at the stage

There is only one journey.
Going inside yourself.

RAINER MARIA RILKE

I am in on a new project, this one a musical. I've got the jigsaw puzzle laid out on the floor and I can see a corner here, a corner there, but the big hole in the middle is exactly replicated by my own anxiety: Will I ever find the real substance of this piece? Trying to land a project—a book, a play, a song cycle—is like trying to land a big fish; as in Hemingway's *Old Man and the Sea,* the world boils down to that fish and me, and I am worried it will get away. As artists, we are often laboring to land big fish against big odds. What's worse, our fish are often invisible fish to the eyes of others, who see us as Daddy, as Mommy, as professor, as girlfriend or boyfriend, and not as someone engaged in a heroic struggle to drag something huge from the archetypal creative sea.

We want to pass for regular citizens. We do not want to turn our phones off or hide in the darkest corners of libraries, writing longhand. And yet, painting, writing, sculpting, and composing does take yards of quiet, uninterrupted time. How to manage this without seeming arrogant or standoffish? People come up with different solutions. My phone is off, but my voice-mail explains my writing hours and when a caller can expect a call back. Novelist John Nichols writes midnight to dawn, an eccentric practice, but it keeps him from snapping people's heads off—"I'm writing!"—when they call him during the day.

So reluctant are we to make a big deal of our work that we may make too small a deal of it. We do not communicate clearly the swaths of silence and solitude we sometimes crave. We fit our work into the crannies of life, and that's good a lot of the time. It lets us have a life, and that life enriches our art. But we do not talk often about sneaking out of our marital bed and stealing down the hall to write, to paint two to four in the night. We do not talk about running away to write our crime novel, holing up in a fleabag motel, on a stolen weekend from our marriage and law practice.

A pianist preparing for a concert tour may be teaching—and

teaching well—but he's preparing for a concert tour, wrestling down huge reams of music with his bare hands, even if he continues to teach his conservatory class load. A novelist listening to a book tell its tale may be listening to his children as well, but that book is always talking too, sometimes in whispers, and he *must* keep an inner ear cocked. A playwright cantilevering a new play from page to stage is worried about that brainchild finding its legs, and so listens like a new mother with ears in the night while "real" children, miffed and pouting, complain to their friends, "Mommy's writing."

Sometimes, mommies and daddies—no matter how we love our children—do need to write. Unexpressed art rises inside an artist until it reaches a level of restlessness and longing that must be addressed by making art—nothing else will scratch the itch. Nothing else is "wrong," although it may seem to be.

"What's wrong, Mommy?" our children wonder, sensing our distance and distraction. We have to fight not to snap their heads off if we are mulling a plot line.

"Nothing, Mommy needs to write."

"What's wrong, darling?" asks our significant other.

"Nothing, I just need to paint."

The year I taught film at Northwestern University and at Chicago Filmmakers while also teaching the Artist's Way privately and some classes of the Right to Write, I really needed to write. Teaching was taking too much of my time and focus and my family was taking the rest. I arranged for a brief getaway to Taos, and as I was waiting to board the plane a man's voice began speaking in my head. I grabbed for pen and notebook and began taking dictation. The writing was so welled up in me that it was the fast-paced flood, imperious and imperative: I must get it down. I wrote on the plane ride from Chicago to Albuquerque. I wrote on the bus ride from Albuquerque to Taos. I settled into my motel, still writing, and woke up to days of writing breakfast until dinner, ensconced at the outdoor table at

Your hand concentrates for you. I don't know why it should be so.

DAME REBECCA WEST

*Freedom means choosing
your burden.*

HEPHZIBAH MENUHIN

Dori's Café, where they were used to writers. Every night I would get a plaintive call from my family, "When are you coming home?"

"Not yet," I would answer. "I have to ride this out." I stayed in Taos for most of the month and most of a first draft of the novel. I reluctantly went home and began retreating to a corner coffee shop, where I hid in a back booth and wrote the rest. It was several months before I was back to my family in the role they preferred me in: "Mommy" and "wife." I had simply built up too large a debt to my writer not to give it absolute first place for a while. This experience taught me to be careful, to always honor my writer a little more fully. It is easier for a family to adjust to a daily writing schedule than it is for them to adjust to a season of abandonment. It is also easier for them to learn to batten down the hatches and make do during the glass-mountain phase of finishing a book than it is for them to live through that phase being conducted a thousand miles away with only phone calls of reassurance. Every project has a glass-mountain phase, a period when nothing is going well enough because the work is simply so hard. Families and friends learn to know and weather this. They do if we give them an explanation and a chance.

We work so hard at "normal" because we've heard so much about artists being crazy. We have heard too many stories of Jackson or Anne Sexton, too many of Sylvia, and Zelda, and fragile Scott. Our reluctance to be *that* kind of person has made us practiced liars—some lies are necessary and self-protective. Women know this. As an experienced artist, I carry my work like a secret pregnancy. I am *always* aware of inner life and the need to protect it. My apology if this metaphor seems gender linked. The creative men I have known and lived with often cast their creative projects as secret military campaigns, an equally gender-linked phrase, calling for secrecy, strategy, and protection.

Trained as we are to be mommies and daddies, and teachers and bankers, lawyers and judges, and so many responsible things, sickened as we are by the woeful tales of artists as irresponsible monsters, we may have difficulty mustering sufficient responsibility to our art and our artists, to protect them during the occasional, necessary times of hard climbing as a large project finally lurches into form—or does not. This delicate and treacherous stage, the glass mountain of creative doubt, is a slippery slope we face alone. It is on its icy flank that we must find small footholds, edging our way upward from concept to actual conception—a difficult birth, as pivotal as conquering our creative Everest—or nearly. "I hear it! I hear it! But I can't get it into my hands," a pianist friend once wailed to me. "I hear it, I hear it! But I haven't got it all on the pages," I have wailed back when a large wave of music knocked me sideways and I struggled to write notes fast enough as I went under.

As artists, we don't talk a lot about the quotidian anxiety of creation, at its worst during the glass-mountain phase, but difficult enough all the time. By and large, for most of us, the need to make art, the cost of making that art, and the higher cost of not making it is not something we lightly air. Our glass mountain is *our* glass mountain, and, like most fairy tales, it is invisible to others but very real to us. Art is a vocation, a calling, and if no one hears the call as loudly as we do, that doesn't mean it isn't there, that doesn't mean we don't hear it, and that doesn't mean we don't need to answer when it calls.

Over time, family and friends become more and more adroit at recognizing the symptoms of our creative calling. "Do you need to write?" or "Do you need to get to the piano?" they may begin to ask us. Most of us have drawn to ourselves partners who do love our artist—especially once they are assured that our artist has no desire to leave them. A novelist's wife knows that no meal will ever be as satisfying as a good round at the page. Sandwiches and slices of pie have a way of appearing at the edge of our writing table, where they are gratefully devoured. There is doubtless a special niche in heaven for those who have helped us to birth our creative children. Mere book dedications seem inadequate thanks compared to the gratitude we feel when we are

It's only when we truly know and understand that we have a limited time on earth—and that we have no way of knowing when our time is up—that we will begin to live each day to the fullest, as if it was the only one we had.

ELISABETH KÜBLER-ROSS

well understood, a gratitude matched only by the terror we may feel when we are misunderstood, as artists sometimes are by those who mistake our need to make things for a need to make something special—and elite—out of ourselves.

When I was young, I had a very good friend, Nick Cariello, who was very political. He invited me to visit his other good friends, who were even more political than he was. I remember a long, winey evening of talk, angry talk, about how artists were just like everyone else. They should not be considered special. They should take out the trash just like the rest of society.

"Yes, we can do our turn at that," I said. "But if you make an artist carry trash eighteen hours a day, an artist will still have to make art. It's our calling." And it is our calling. And so, we do carry the trash. But we carry, also, our stories, our symphonies, our dance, and our dreams. We carry them in daily life, and, every so often, up the glass mountain that is our Everest.

We are the hero of our own story.

MARY MCCARTHY

TASK:
Scaling the Glass Mountain

Take pen in hand and answer the following questions as rapidly as possible:

1. Do you have a project edging into the glass-mountain phase?
2. Can you protect your work schedule a little more rigorously than usual?
3. How can you steal extra solitude, even a half hour a day?
4. Can you manage an escape from family, friends, and telephones?
5. Have you made friends with Starbucks, the back room at the library, a back booth at Wendy's, writing in your car?

You may have in your vicinity a spiritual center where you can take a personal creative retreat and share communal meals. Many nuns, priests, and monks are great support during periods of creative doubt. Many convents and monasteries offer hermitage space to gather steam so that projects can be finalized. The sisters at Wisdom House in Litchfield, Connecticut, artists themselves, have long taught Artist's Way courses, and when staying on their grounds I have often walked my way into the quiet necessary to find renewed faith to finish projects.

Perhaps too much of everything is as bad as too little.

Edna Ferber

Landing

In order to make our art, we expand and contract. Expand and contract: big ideas and the minute, painstaking work of getting them down in finer and finer detail. As we concentrate like this, we are first big and then single-pointed. In the heat of the creative moment, our thought—or flow—is hot, thick, dense, fast, and light, like good ink. We are skywriting for a path.

Our creative size has a tidal aspect—we ebb and we flow. Or, if you would, we expand and contract, altering sizes and shapes like one of those luminous mysteries of the sea, the jellyfish, which closely resembles a parachute. When we are at the height of a creative flight and trying to land, we, too, resemble a beautiful, full-bellied parachute trying to touch earth. Lovely? Yes. But safe? Not necessarily. Completing a draft of a novel may spark thoughts of suicide rather than celebration. Creative post partum can be unexpected and *deep*.

Parachutes often land with a lurch. Our creative flights may land the same way. Our chute collapses around us and we stumble around blindly. Or the chute stays somewhat open and we tumble across the field, dragged along by our leftover velocity. In other words, a creative landing may leave us a little bruised, battered, and suddenly claustrophobic as our creative chute collapses and our normal life threatens to smother us.

When we are making things, we sometimes get very, very big. Or simply very, very free. In the height of the creative moment, we are not constricted and downsized by our daily rigamarole—our age, our family tensions, our feelings of being a cog in the wheel. It is hard to come back to our normal size after such a heady expansion—and often, we don't, at first.

Creative flight is exactly that—flight. We get a higher than bird's-eye view of our life and our dreams and often many other things as well. We "see" the big picture, and such a vision can leave our ordinary perception shattered. We are staggered by the magnitude of what we have seen, and our own size feels foreign.

As we try to land back in our own life, we may shoot past our real size and feel like someone very small. This is why astronauts undergo debriefing, and why veteran artists, over time, learn specific skills to help themselves reacclimate to their lives and families. Finishing a long project is also a little like driving cross-country—when you get home, you may need to hide out and sleep for a couple of days before seeing your friends—otherwise, reentry can be bumpy. This is normal, just scary. It is hallucinogenic, like *Alice's Adventures in Wonderland:* I was so big and now I am so small. Or our life may feel like Mother Hubbard's—we feel pinched and can't quite wedge ourselves back into the shoe we normally walk in. It's not so much that our head is too big but that it's still full of very big ideas.

The creative world is full of cherished and hoary stories of what artists act like and look like when they visit the ethers in creative flight. In the pitch of taking down the music for my first musical, I put a silk smock dress on and wore it backward—perhaps for days—without noticing. Seized by an idea that we fight to land, who has time to think about clothes, to worry about looking normal? A famous novelist I know often forgets to put in his teeth.

Comfort is the key during creative flight. Everything else

O world invisible,
  we view thee,
O world intangible,
  we touch thee,
O world unknowable,
  we know thee.

FRANCIS THOMPSON

goes by the board. And then the flight ends, and you think, *Oh, I should wash my hair, call my brother, sweep the kitchen, or clean and pitch from drawers.* Intuitively, we try to ground ourselves by a sudden binge of cleaning, scrubbing, cooking, calling friends. Reentry is a volatile process. We become seasoned only after time, learning to send up flares to show our progress: I am still in the chute and hope to emerge next week.

As a sober alcoholic, I am wary of anything too high and too fast. Euphoric is more of a memory than a sought-after state. And yet, when I do get a sudden rush of voltage, I find it a little thrilling as well as daunting. I know it is dangerous and I must remember that I will need to land carefully.

We do not land with grace, perhaps, but we can learn to land more and more safely. We can learn to let the intense energy of our fever-pitched work ebb from us more gently as we practice. Does a bath work? Cleaning? Calling a certain very old friend—that can be truly grounding.

Above all, we can remind ourselves: The ground does exist, and we find our feet again.

"I try not to talk with anybody for a couple of days," a seasoned novelist explains. "I know that when I have finished a big piece of work I am a little weird and so I try to give myself enough space to be weird in private." I might make a pot of soup. I might read a bad detective novel. I might take my dog out for some really long walks. Eventually, I start to feel normal again. I notice I need to scrub the floor or vacuum the car. I realize my running shoes are getting worn out and I think maybe I can handle going to town and getting a new pair. I might even put that off a day until I can't stand not going. The point is that a big piece of writing is a little like a big storm. It leaves you shaken and disoriented and things need time to settle down. You don't want to talk with your friends and sound like you just went through an alien abduction. You want to wait until you can ask how their kids are and if the movie at the art house is worth getting over to see. In other words, you don't want to

Learn the craft of knowing how to open your heart and to turn on your creativity. There's a light inside of you.

JUDITH JAMISON

reenter the world until the world has more in it than you and your capital-A Art. For me, that's a few days' transition, and when I try to skip it, I act pretty strange and people do notice. I like to let the dust settle now.

TASK:
What Makes You Feel Grounded?

Take pen in hand and list 10 activities that always make you feel more grounded, for example:

A little of what you fancy does you good.

MARIE LLOYD

1. Making soup
2. Vacuuming
3. Changing my sheets
4. Doing the laundry
5. Baking a pie
6. Watching those horse-training videos
7. Waxing the car
8. Cleaning the refrigerator
9. Calling my best friend from grade school
10. Cleaning my office and paying bills

The regular use of this tool is one of the most confirming rituals possible in a creative life. Like the daily ta-dah list, this tool helps to put a sense of grounded celebration into our creative life. It does this because it emphasizes life itself. While we may "live for our work," our life is, and must be, larger than our work. By allowing the dailiness of life to step forward again, we become, in a sense, our own parents, saying "Welcome home" after each of our creative flights. A student-turned-colleague adds the writing of congratulatory postcards to herself as a regular part of this routine. "Good work!" the postcard exclaims. She has postcards on successfully completing arranging assignments, recording assignments, and musical workshops. As her jumps get larger and more public, her private practice of self-congratulations grows even more important. Our work feels not only good, but better, when we place it within the comforting confines of our ongoing routines and relationships.

What you are after is a grounded sense of connection to your life and relationships before, during, and after creative flight.

Age and Time

There is a remarkable book of flower photographs by Irving Penn, who made his initial mark as the signature photographer of *Vogue,* photographing models at the height of their youthful bloom. His lens captured Suzy Parker, as glorious as a hothouse orchid, a woman as trained to a forced and topiary beauty as a single perfect bloom forced to perfection. Perhaps, as a reaction to this hybrid, highly bred haute couture, Penn turned his camera to the world of flowers in bud, in bloom, and past prime in ripening and glorious decay.

Penn's shots are remarkable. We admire the buds in all their nascent glory. We admire the vibrancy and potency of blooms at their perfect prime. But the revelation of the book is the beauty of the flowers as they pass from ripeness to gentle decay, falling from perfection to what Penn reveals as a different perfection. There is a poignancy and power to beauty nearly spent. It holds the remnant of what it was, and its fading grandeur reminds us that we die to bloom again. We are "gone to seed, according to plan."

Oh, if only we took our sense of aging from the natural world. If only we watched the mentoring and grave care and leadership and wit of older animals mentoring the young.

I worked with director John Newland during his seventies and eighties. A tall, snowy-haired man with a gloriously ravaged face and a hawk eye for cant and shenanigans, he was far more daring than the younger directors who have supplanted him in

And the day came when the risk [it took] to remain tight in the bud was more painful than the risk it took to blossom.

ANAÏS NIN

his field. Like Miles Davis, he had learned "Do not fear mistakes. There are none." He cut shabby scenes with a merciless glee. He allowed a full range of rage and daring—in fact, he demanded it. He knew the full range of the human keyboard. He expected all octaves to be accounted for and wasn't satisfied when they were not.

Yes, youth passes behind us, but we are blind so often to what we are gaining and to the beauty of what we become as artists. There is not a note of silvery sound or a hair turned silver that isn't perfect and beautiful. It is difficult not to rage at the passing of physical beauty and strength, the exquisite daring and dexterity we once possessed, the turn of a phrase or a haunch as perfect as a ripe peach, as gleaming and golden as the hard-won golden apple—of course we miss these things.

But we gain in beauty. We gain in tenderness. We gain in longing and desire and in satiation if we get the chance—not merely or only exquisitely in our sexual and our physical selves but our creative selves as well.

At fifty-four, I am still willing to learn. I am willing to entertain the idea that everyone who is learning something they care about—whether it is the piano, as with me, or the emotional weather of someone they are newly involved with—anyone who is learning will feel this treacherous mix of vulnerability and frustration, of hope and discouragement. There is an exciting element of self-respect: You are trying.

I think that one of the benefits of doing something "at my age" is that I have lived long enough not to think that "hard" means wrong or even un-do-able. It may just mean hard. And, too, I no longer think my hard is worse than someone else's hard. I think all beginners have high hopes and dash themselves against their own expectations and dreams like waves against a cliff until they get it: over and over, like a wave, yes, but perhaps, a gentler one. Water *does* wear away rock. Practice *will* make if not "perfect," then "better." Take me and the piano.

Clearly, it is mind and muscle and heart that must be trained.

*I wish that life should not be cheap, but sacred,
I wish the days to be as centuries, loaded, fragrant.*

RALPH WALDO EMERSON

All of them must learn patience, the virtue I hate, and repetition, the idea God had the sense to use daily. Ah, yes, the sun rises and the piano waits. I simply need to tell myself, make a routine, not a special occasion, out of this. Appreciate the players leaping up on the craggy heights, but don't be discouraged by them. They show you what players can do and what a piano can do. And even that word "piano" means "softly."

I also worked, during his seventies and eighties, with veteran actor Max Showalter. At eighty-two, he traveled to Taos to teach at a creativity camp that I was leading. He commandeered the piano and held a hundred of us spellbound for several hours as he replayed his seven decades in show business and his eight decades of life. "You have to be positive. They have to know life is good—every scrap of it," Max told me. He lived every scrap of his life fully—he husbanded a great and glorious half-acre of garden when I first knew him in Hollywood in the 1970s and thirty years later he had another glorious half-acre transplanted to Connecticut. In both gardens, we took pictures of each other and of our visions of life. Max caught a photo of me as a budding young woman and, in our last photo together, my hair has glints of silver in the gold. We talked on that visit of the garden of talent he was also husbanding, working with his good friends at the Goodspeed Theatre and in community projects to shepherd young talent into his old trooper's version of the theater: "A place of promise where we all can get bigger than life. *NO!* As big as life allows us and that's plenty."

It is the soul's duty to be loyal to its own desires. It must abandon itself to its master passion.

REBECCA WEST

TASK:
The Communion of All Saints

Have you considered asking your creative saints, those artists you admire who have passed over, for help? This personal practice, far from being heretical, honors the fact that art making is a spiritual lineage. Our artistic ancestors *are* sources of inspiration, not

Consider this: what if "original sin" is denying instead of celebrating your originality? Each of us possesses an exquisite, extraordinary gift: the opportunity to give expression to Divinity on earth through our everyday lives. When we choose to honor this priceless gift, we participate in the re-creation of the world.

SARAH BAN BREATHNACH

only in the survival of their work but in the survival of their creative spirit. By involving them directly, we correctly honor their contributions to our lives, and this practice often yields great creative fruit. Do you have any resistance to this process?

As a culture, we are quite primitive and arrogant in our refusal to honor and acknowledge the inflow and imprint of our ancestors.

Experiment: Select one creative elder who has passed on. Ask for help and input on a problem you are facing. Writing very rapidly, transcribe what you hear. Haydn may tell you to use proper files for your musical compositions and organize your workroom.

A young composer became accustomed to an extra sense of guidance in daily affairs—"Stop in this music shop," "Call your old professor," etc. As these leadings palpably paid off in creative terms, the notion of asking for inspiration from creative ancestors seemed, if not reasonable, interesting. Schooled rigorously in the classics, with at least a rudimentary notion of each composer's supposed temperament and life situation, our young composer began asking for specific help. Doing so, she reported that she found Haydn strict and very smart, she found Mozart goofy but inspirational, she found Beethoven kind, focused, and passionate, and that her own compositions were improving enormously. By asking to be inspired, she felt she was.

One day in her Morning Pages, she wondered if such inspiration was just her "imagination." Immediately, she heard, "There are a lot of souls over here who are very interested in what we did, and very interested in what you're doing. We like to help when we can."

Service

In centuries past, art was made for the honor and glory of God. Viewed in this light, a career in the arts was a career of service, not egotism. There is a cue there for us.

The dedication of our work to a higher cause than our own self-promotion frees the work from preciousness. It becomes not about how good we are but about how good we can be in self-less service to something larger than ourselves. Sometimes we can dedicate a book to a person whom we wish to reach. Rilke's classic letters to a young poet tapped his own inner reservoirs of wisdom and generosity.

As artists, we are the bearers of gifts, spiritual endowments that come to us gratis and ask only to be used. A gift for music asks that we give voice to it. A fine photographer's eye asks that we focus it. We are responsible to our gifts for the use of our gifts, and this is a form of accountability too.

But if you have nothing at all to create, then perhaps you create yourself.

CARL JUNG

Some of the best playwriting—Shakespeare's included—was done with an eye to making wonderful roles to serve the talents of friends. Anytime we elect to serve, we open the doors for higher inspiration. We may target a piece of work to someone or something that we feel is worthy; this elected humility removes the tightening that occurs when our work is all about us and our brilliant careers. We may be brilliant in passing but we will no longer be straining for brilliance. Asking to be of service, and to be open to the proper inspiration to serve through our work, we then become teachable, and when we are teachable, our work always improves.

When our work is made only in the service of our hope for fame or recognition, it is hampered by our self-consciousness as we wonder, *How am I doing?* When we are able to work without such self-consciousness, we are able to work more freely and more fully. Our ego steps aside and is no longer a constrictive valve narrowing our creative flows and focus. We think less about "us" and more about "it," the work itself.

I remember sitting under whispering trees at a music park, listening as a brilliant pianist lashed through a blistering performance as dramatic as the incoming storm. I was seated between two grown men who listened to the cascading notes as enraptured as small children, their faces lit with Christmas radiance. Magic was afoot, or, perhaps better, at hand. Later I learned that the musical magician we had so admired had played all evening uphill, against an inner critic that cited that missed chord, this muffled mordent. With a monk's devotion, he had played anyway—such nights are an artist's Gethsemane, a night to be endured only on faith.

"I have to remind myself there is something larger than me and my skill, something more important than my ego's perception," the pianist confided to me. That something is in art itself, the creative power that moves through us, healing and transforming those who encounter it.

"It was like watching Magic Johnson play," one of the men whispered to me on that bench. It was an accurate remark. That word "magic" again, and consummate skill. On Magic Johnson's off nights, he still "hits" more than others. His sailing long ball swooshes still have spooky ease. This is often true for artists. Our "best" nights to others may internally feel our worst. Our perceptions must not be allowed to capsize our professionalism. Novelists with long literary careers report ruefully the great reviews on the books they like least, and the tepid receptions to the works they most cherish. In a sense, the reception of our work by ourselves as well as others is none of our business. Our job is to do it. We work, and the work works through us.

Actors talk ruefully of having terrible nights with rapturous reception, and tepid response to the nights they felt themselves most connected. In a sense, a singer is merely the vehicle for a song, and the song is merely a vehicle for music itself. No matter how accomplished and acclaimed we may become as artists, there is always, at core, this essential anonymity: We are in service of something larger than ourselves.

We have very strange notions about art in our culture. We have made it a cult of the individual rather than what it has always been, a human aspiration aimed at communicating and community. We "commune" through art, both with the forces of inspiration when we work and with other humans who en-

We can't take any credit for our talents. It's how we use them that counts.

MADELEINE L'ENGLE

counter us and those forces through our work. To commune is to attune with an open heart, something impossible if we are thinking only of ourselves.

Manhattan abounds in musicians and music schools. Some of the very best of each are to be found in the vertical canyons of this tiny and overcrowded island. One of the finest music teachers in Manhattan teaches with the greatest amount of innovation—and out of a spirit of service.

"Beginning piano books are just terrible," he says. "Some of the very best students hate to use them. They just don't respond to the music in them and so they become bored." Boredom, of course, is the enemy of learning, and so this music teacher has composed a whole series of beginning music lessons with music he wrote himself and fairy tales to match. Who wouldn't want to learn the waltz that was danced when Sleeping Beauty was awakened with a kiss? Who wouldn't want to play the song a mighty organ played when it fell in love with a gifted young student? Piece by piece, lesson by lesson, seeking only to serve his gifted and disenchanted students, this master teacher has built a curriculum that is lively, innovative, and eminently playable.

"Here, let me write something out for you," he will say, and draw the lines of a staff and make handwritten music paper. "Wouldn't it be fun to learn this?" And the big black notes march across the page, crooked and enticing.

Setting aside all ego and snobbery, setting aside how music "should" be taught, this great teacher teaches from a spirit of love and service. Is it any wonder that his students develop a love of music that serves them very well?

As artists, we are intended to be conduits for inspiration. There are high thoughts and high intentions and higher realms that can speak to us and through us if we allow it. When our ego and our ego-driven fears are given a central place as regards our art, we have rolled a large boulder into our own way, and our career cannot unfold unimpeded because it must divide to make

Love is the spirit that motivates the artist's journey . . . it's a powerful motive in the artist's life.

ERIC MAISEL

To believe your own thought,
to believe that what is true for
you in your private heart is
true for all men—that
is genius.

RALPH WALDO EMERSON

its way with unnatural intensity and velocity around the boulder settled in the stream of our good. On rivers and in the rivers of creative flow, such rapids are treacherous. We are far better served by being of service.

Contemplating a piece of work, we do better to think *Whom is this work for? Whom will it serve?* rather than *How will it serve me?* Once we find a path for our work to be of service—even if that path is merely to create a wonderful role for a friend—then our work goes smoothly forward. It is not about "us" anymore. We have retired as self-conscious creator and aligned ourselves again with all of creation, a worker among workers, a friend among friends. When we do so, our work is less buffered by our own harsh fears. Our fears are set aside every time we simply ask again, "How can I make this work more serviceable?"

Director Steven Spielberg once remarked to an interviewer that he hoped at heaven's gate, God might say to him, "Steven, thanks for listening." This listening for inspiration, this willingness to align our creative will with a sense of higher guidance, is not contrary to a career but a better and more grounded way to establish one. A career solely grounded in the idea of self-advancement is not grounded enough in the advancement of ideas. For all their estimable craft, artists who fail to deepen their goals and their ideas find that their careers run into a certain shallow sameness over time.

Chekhov advised actors, "If you want to work on your career, work on yourself." It might equally be advised, if you want to work on yourself, work to make your career of service to something larger than yourself. Dedicate yourself to something or someone other than yourself. This expansion will make you larger both as a person and as an artist.

We used to routinely call God "the creator." We had a consciousness that our own creativity was a divine gift, an opening for God to work through us. When we enshrined ourselves and our individuality rather than our shared humanity at the center of our consciousness—a shift for which therapy may be thanked for a great deal of useless narcissism and also an unpleasant conviction that art was about compensating—we lost our proper understanding of art as service. We disenfranchised ourselves from our birthright as creators and we lost the understanding that art was an act of the soul and not of the ego. Whenever we take art back to the realm of the sacred, whenever we make it an act of service in any form, if only to such an idea as beauty or truth or humanity, but perhaps better when it is more personably serviceable, we again experience the ease of creative flow and the lessening of our creative doubts. When we ask to "listen," we create works worthy of being heard and we ourselves hear the heartbeat of our common humanity, which is grounded in divinity.

We may make a piece of art to promote planetary understanding. We may make beautiful music for the glory and service of music itself. We may write a play for alcoholic women to take heart. We might paint to express gratitude to our creator for the beauty of Queen Anne's lace. When we make our art in a spirit of service, it lightens the burden of our ego. It makes for clarity of focus, purity of intent, and follows a spiritual law that might be simply stated as "Form follows function." When the "form" of our work is open to higher consciousness, its function is raised as well.

Art moves through us. It is colored by our individuality, but we are not precisely its origin. Or, to put it differently, a piece of art may originate with us, but we originate somewhere larger ourselves. We are, each of us, more than we seem, more than the sum of our merely human components. There is a divine spark animating each of us, and that divine spark also animates our art. When we ask to be of service in our art, we fling open a window in our creative studio. Through that opening, the greater world of inspiration can enter us. A painter friend of mine talks about art needing a "hole for the imagination." I think I might phrase it as "When we dedicate a piece of art to something larger than our ego, that something larger becomes a

Whatever you can do or dream you can, begin it;
Boldness has genius, power and magic in it.

JOHANN WOLFGANG
VON GOETHE

The gift turned inward, unable to be given, becomes a heavy burden, even sometimes a kind of poison. It is as though the flow of life were backed up.

MAY SARTON

felt presence." A great painting, poem, or piece of music carries that indefinable something more. We sense it and, although we try to name it and define it, it eludes definition and containment. There is a breath of the divine that blows through us as artists and blows through our art as well. Walk into a cathedral and you will sense something larger than the artisans. Our hired hands, as artists, also hold a hand with a higher hand. Take Bach, hired to write music so that his church would have something to play once a week at service—that word again. What Bach wrote was more than merely serviceable. Inspired by a spirit of service, he wrote the cantatas, the "little songs," that we love and cherish centuries later.

Arguably, we are all in service to an artist greater than our own. Life itself works through us. We are the carriers of dreams and desires that may have originated generations earlier. Music runs in families. So does a gift for drama and for words. When we elect to make art from a spirit of service to a larger whole, we are really simply becoming truthful. We are all part of a larger whole and, in acknowledging that truthfully, we move a notch closer to humility, to a simple and sheer plainness that allows the beauty of the grand design to be seen through us. If beauty is truth and truth beauty—and I believe that this is so—then our acknowledgment of our place in a larger scheme of things strikes a first true note from which more beauty follows.

TASK:
Beauty Is Truth and Truth, Beauty

Each of us carries an inner capacity for awe. One of us will be wonderstruck by a musical sequence. Another of us is rendered humble and serene by the sight of a butterfly's wing. Each one of these gateways to the divine is there waiting for us to use it to make contact. There are some things that simply make us happy, some things that we plainly and for no apparent reason love. For this reason, we say, "God is in the details." Each of us experiences the touch of the Great Creator when we allow ourselves to touch upon something that we love.

Because the part of us that creates is youthful and innocent, an ideal place to collect "artist toys" is a good children's bookstore. Go to one now. If dinosaurs are your love, get a dinosaur book. If dogs make you happy, find a book of the dog. Make it a point that your bedside table contains at least one book on a topic that simply delights you. Delight opens the door for the Great Creator to touch us with a sense of well-being. You may love zebra finches or just plain zebras. Let yourself celebrate what you love and that you are the person who loves it. As you connect to the childlike part of you that loves and enjoys the material world, you are connecting to the sense Aristotle had when he remarked, "In all things of nature there is something of the marvelous."

Allow yourself to marvel.

Only the heart knows how to find what is precious.

FYODOR DOSTOYEVSKY

EPILOGUE

I WOULD LIKE TO END this book on a grace note: that is to say, I would like to acknowledge the place of grace in the making of art and artists. It is a great grace that we are born creative beings. It is a great grace that we access that creativity. Although you may language it differently, all creators feel the hand of the Great Creator touching them through their work. Art is a spiritual practice. We may not, and need not, do it perfectly. But we do need to do it. It is my belief that the making of art makes us more fully human. In becoming more fully human, we become more fully divine, touching in our finite way the infinite spark within each of us. Focused on our art, we connect to the artful heart of all life. The creative pulse that moves through us moves through all of creation. It could be argued that creativity is a form of prayer, a form of thankfulness and recognition of all we have to be thankful for, walking in this world.

SUGGESTED READING

My experience as a teacher tells me that those who read this book are better off doing something, rather than reading another book, but I have included many of my favorites just in case you feel compelled to research further. These books represent some of the very best in their fields. To keep it simple, try to finish Artist's Way work before adding this input.

Aftel, Mandy. *The Story of Your Live—Becoming the Author of Your Experience.* New York: Simon & Schuster, 1996. Persuasive and useful.

Ban Breathnach, Sarah. *Simple Abundance.* New York: Warner Books, 1995. Grounded in my own work and expanding on it, this is a profoundly touching book.

Berendt, Joachim-Ernst. *The World Is Sound: Nada Brahma.* Rochester, Vt.: Destiny Books, 1991. Eloquent and persuasive book on sound theory.

Bolles, Richard Nelson. *What Color Is Your Parachute?* Berkeley: Ten Speed Press, 1970. Whimsical and pragmatic guide to goal setting.

Bonny, Helen. *Music and Your Mind.* Barrytown, N.Y.: Helen A. Bonny and Louis M. Savary, 1973, 1970. An explicit guide to using music as an antidote for mental and emotional pain.

Bradley, Marion Zimmer. *The Mists of Avalon.* New York: Ballantine Books, 1982. A powerfully evocative novel of female spirituality in pre-Christian England. A mesmerizing novel of goddess worship in Arthurian times.

Brande, Dorothea. *Becoming a Writer.* 1934. Reprint. Los Angeles: Jeremy P. Tarcher, 1981. The best book on writing I've ever found.

Burnham, Sophy. *A Book of Angels.* New York: Ballantine Books, 1991. An elegant, deeply felt exploration of the spiritual powers and forces at play in our lives.

Bush, Carol A. *Healing Imagery and Music.* Portland, Oreg.: Rudra Press, 1995. A profoundly useful guide to listening for healing.

Came to Believe. New York: Alcoholics Anonymous World Services, 1973. Useful and touching book about embryonic faith.

Campbell, Don G. *The Roar of Silence.* Wheaton, Ill.: The Theosophical Publishing House, 1994. Seminal book on sound healing—clear, passionate and useful. All of Campbell's many books are important and persuasive, but this one remains a primer.

Cassou, Michelle, and Steward Cubley. *Life, Paint, and Passion: Reclaiming the Magic of Spontaneous Expression*. New York: Jeremy P. Tarcher/Putnam, 1996. Passionate and experienced into-the-water book for visual artists.

Chatwin, Bruce. *Songlines*. New York: Penguin Books, 1987. An exquisite, mysterious and powerful book.

Choquette, Sonia. *The Psychic Pathway*. New York: Random House. Crown Trade Paperbacks, 1994, 1995. Safe, grounded, practical guide to opening to spiritual gifts.

Choquette, Sonia. *Your Heart's Desire*. New York: Random House, Crown Trade Paperbacks, 1997. An extremely clear, step-by-step guide for manifesting dreams as working reality.

Eisler, Raine. *The Chalice and the Blade*. San Francisco: Harper & Row Publishers, 1987. Seminal book on the differences in masculine and feminine life approaches.

Fassel, Diane. *Working Ourselves to Death*. San Francisco: HarperCollins, 1990. A strong-minded intervention for workaholic personalities.

Fox, Matthew. *Original Blessing*. Santa Fe, N.M.: Bear & Company, 1983. An important corrective book on Christian tradition; brilliant, impassioned, compassionate.

Franck, Frederick. *Zen Seeing, Zen Drawing*. New York: Bantam Books, 1993. A fine treatise on the value of "attention" in the creative life.

Gawain, Shakti. *Creative Visualization*. Mill Valley, Cal.: Whatever Publishing, 1986. Helpful in learning to create and hold a vision.

Goldberg, Bonni. *Room to Write: Daily Invitations to a Writer's Life*. New York: Jeremy P. Tarcher/Putnam, 1996. A masterfully provocative and wise writer's tool.

Goldberg, Natalie. *Writing Down the Bones*. Boston, Mass.: Shambhala Publications, 1986. The best pen-to-paper writing book ever written.

Goldman, Jonathan. *Healing Sounds: The Power of Harmonics*. Rockport, Mass.: Element Books, Inc., 1992. Powerful and gentle teaching book on sound healing techniques.

Grof, Christina, and Stanislav Grof, *The Stormy Search for the Self*. Los Angeles: Jeremy P. Tarcher, 1990. A provocative book about the misunderstanding of spiritual experience in our culture.

Harmon, Willis, and Howard Rheingold. *Higher Creativity*. Los Angeles: Jeremy P. Tarcher, 1984. A valuable and often instructive book on creativity in frontline famous authors and others.

Hart, Mickey. *Drumming at the Edge of Magic*. San Francisco: HarperCollins, 1990. A great book on music as a spiritual experience.

Heywood, Rosalind. *ESP: A Personal Memoir*. New York: E. P. Dutton & Co., Inc., 1964. A delightful book of personal encounters with higher forces.

Holmes, Ernest. *Creative Ideas*. Los Angeles: Science of Mind Communications, 1973. A tiny, powerful and important book of spiritual law as applied to creative manifestation.

James, William. *The Varieties of Religious Experience*. Boston: Mentor Books, 1902. Seminal fountainhead describing different forms of spiritual awakening, much insight into creativity as a spiritual matter.

Jeffers, Susan. *Feel the Fear and Do It Anyway*. New York: Fawcett Columbine, 1987. An into-the-water book for getting past fear.

Leonard, Jim. *Your Fondest Dream*. Cincinnati: Vivation, 1989. Another into-the-water book; many brainstorming techniques.

Lewis, C. S. *Miracles*. New York: Macmillan, 1947. Inspirational, prickly, and provocative. A challenge in open-mindedness.

Lingerman, Hal A. *The Healing Energies of Music*. Wheaton, Ill.: The Theosophical Publishing House, 1983. Excellent book on music as medicine, learned yet friendly.

London, Peter. *No More Secondhand Art: Awakening the Artist Within*. Boston: Shambhala Publications, Inc., 1989. A manifesto for personal art as process, not product.

McClellan, Randall, Ph.D. *The Healing Sources of Music*. Rockport, Mass.: Element Books, Inc., 1994. A kindly yet wide-ranging source.

Maclean, Dorothy. *To Hear the Angels Sing*. Hudson, N.Y.: Lindisfarne Press, 1990. A lovely book, a fascinating spiritual autobiography by one of the founders of Findhorn.

Mathieu, W. A. *The Listening Book: Discovering Your Own Music*. Boston: Shambhala Publications, Inc., 1991. A companionable book that demystifies music as a life path.

Matthews, Caitlin. *Singing the Soul Back Home: Shamanism in Daily Life*. Rockport, Mass.: Element Books, Inc., 1995. A wonderfully rich book for grounded spiritual practice.

Miller, Alice. *The Drama of the Gifted Child*. New York: Basic Books, 1981. Seminal book on how toxic family dynamics dampen creativity.

Nachmanovitch, Stephen. *Free Play*. Los Angeles: Jeremy P. Tarcher, 1991. A wonderful book on creative freedom.

Noble, Vicki. *Motherpeace—A Way to the Goddess Through Myth, Art, and Tarot*. San Francisco: Harper & Row Publishers, 1983. Creativity through the lens of the goddess religion.

Norwood, Robin. *Women Who Love Too Much*. Los Angeles: Jeremy P. Tarcher, 1985. Seminal work on codependency.

Peck, M. Scott. *The Road Less Traveled*. New York: Simon & Schuster, 1978. A book for early spiritual skeptics.

Shaughnessy, Susan. *Walking on Alligators*. New York: HarperCollins, 1993. A companionable, savvy guide for anyone working to appreciate the worth of process as well as product.

Sher, Barbara, with Annie Gottlieb. *Wishcraft: How to Get What You Really Want*. New York: Ballantine Books, 1979. A potent, catalytic book for creative living, similar to my own work and my current thinking.

Starhawk. *The Fifth Sacred Thing*. New York: Bantam Books, 1994. Mesmerizing novel of spiritual ecology.

Starhawk. *The Spiritual Dance*. New York: Harper and Row, 1979. Brilliant on creativity and god/goddess within.

Tame, David. *The Secret Power of Music*. New York: Destiny Books, 1984. A lucid introductory overview of the healing powers of music.

Ueland, Brenda. *If You Want to Write.* 1938. St. Paul, Minn.: Schubert, 1983. The care and maintenance of the writer as a creative artist. Shrewd, personal and pragmatic.

W., Bill. *Alcoholics Anonymous: The Story of How More Than One Hundred Men Have Recovered from Alcoholism.* Akron, Ohio: Carry the Message, 1985.

Wegscheider-Cruse, Sharon. *Choicemaking: For Co-dependents, Adult Children and Spirituality Seekers.* Pompano Beach, Fla.: Health Communications, 1985. Recommended for dismantling co-dependent workaholism.

Woititz, Janet. *Home Away from Home: The Art of Self-Sabotage.* Pompano Beach, Fla.: Health Communications, 1987. Important for arresting the mechanism of aborting success.

Wright, Machaelle Small. *Behaving As If the God in All Life Mattered.* Jeffersonton, Va.: Perelandra. Ltd., 1987. A spiritual autobiography about work with "earth" and other energy forms.

SPECIAL INTEREST

These books are intended as special help on issues that frequently block creativity.

Alcoholics Anonymous. *The Big Book.* New York: Alcoholics Anonymous World Services. Care and maintenance of a sane and sober lifestyle for alcoholic and nonalcoholic alike. Inspirational guide.

Alcoholics Anonymous. *Came to Believe.* New York: Alcoholics Anonymous World Services, 1973. Useful and touching book about embryonic faith.

The Augustine Fellowship. *Sex and Love Addicts Anonymous.* Boston: The Augustine Fellowship, Sex and Love Addicts Anonymous Fellowship-Wide Services, 1986. One of the best books on addiction. The chapters on withdrawal and building partnership should be required reading.

Beattie, Melody. *Codependent No More.* San Francisco: Harper & Row, 1987. Excellent for breaking the virtue trap.

Cameron, Julia, and Mark Bryan. *Money Drunk, Money Sober.* New York: Ballantine Books, 1992. A hands-on toolkit for financial freedom. This book creates new language and a new lens for money management. It grew out of *The Artist's Way* because money is the most often cited block.

Hallowell, Edward M., M.D., and John J. Ratey, M.D. *Driven to Distraction.* New York: Touchstone Books/Simon & Schuster, 1994; first Touchstone edition, 1995. Invaluable book on attention deficit disorder.

Louden, Jennifer. *The Women's Comfort Book (A Self-Nurturing Guide for Restoring Balance in Your Life).* San Francisco: HarperSanFrancisco, 1992. Applicable to either sex as a practical guide to self-nurturing.

Orsborn, Carol. *Enough Is Enough: Exploding the Myth of Having It All.* New York: G. P. Putnam's Sons, 1986. Excellent for helping dismantle the heroic workaholic personality.

RESOURCES

Sounds True
413 South Arthur Avenue
Louisville, CO 80027
1-800-333-9135
A wellspring of spiritual sound and wisdom from all world traditions.

Transitions Bookplace
1000 West North Avenue
Chicago, IL 60622
1-312-951-7323
Largest American clearinghouse for titles like these.

Also, of course, www.barnesandnoble.com and www.amazon.com

INDEX

ABOUT THE AUTHOR

JULIA CAMERON has been an active artist for more than thirty years. She is the author of seventeen books, fiction and nonfiction, including *The Artist's Way, The Vein of Gold* and *The Right to Write,* her bestselling works on the creative process. A novelist, playwright, songwriter and poet, she has many credits in theater, film, and television. She divides her time between Manhattan and the high desert of New Mexico.

If you would like to order any of the following or to receive our catalogue please fill in the form below:

Wild Mind by Natalie Goldberg	£10.99
Living with Feeling by Lucia Capacchione	£10.99
Trusting the Tides by Anne Dickson	£9.99
Flow: The Psychology of Happiness by Mihaly Csikszentmihalyi	£10.99
Women Who Run With The Wolves by Clarissa Pinkola Estes	£9.99
Rituals for an Enchanted Life by Lynn Williams	£7.99
Secrets & Mysteries by Denise Linn	£9.99
Emotional Alchemy by Tara Bennett-Goleman	£12.99
The Little Book of Bliss by Patrick Whiteside	£2.50
The Little Book of Inner Space by Stafford Whiteaker	£2.50
The Little Book of Blue Thoughts by Rabbi Lionel Blue	£2.50

ALL RIDER BOOKS ARE AVAILABLE THROUGH MAIL ORDER OR FROM YOUR LOCAL BOOKSHOP.

PAYMENT MAY BE MADE USING ACCESS, VISA, MASTERCARD, DINERS CLUB, SWITCH AND AMEX, OR CHEQUE, EUROCHEQUE AND POSTAL ORDER (STERLING ONLY).

EXPIRY DATE .... SWITCH ISSUE NO.

SIGNATURE ....

PLEASE ALLOW £2.50 FOR POST AND PACKING FOR THE FIRST BOOK AND £1.00 PER BOOK THEREAFTER.

ORDER TOTAL: £.. (INCLUDING P&P)

ALL ORDERS TO:
RIDER BOOKS, BOOKS BY POST, TBS LIMITED, THE BOOK SERVICE, COLCHESTER ROAD, FRATING GREEN, COLCHESTER, ESSEX, CO7 7DW, UK.

TELEPHONE: (01206) 256 000
FAX: (01206) 255 914

NAME
....

ADDRESS
....

....

Please allow 28 days for delivery.
Please tick box if you do not wish to receive any additional information. ☐
Prices and availability subject to change without notice.